William A. DeMeester

A publication of the

CENTER FOR RESEARCH AND DEVELOPMENT IN HIGHER EDUCATION

University of California, Berkeley

LELAND L. MEDSKER, *Director*

Beyond High School

Beyond High School

A Psychosociological Study of
10,000 High School Graduates

James W. Trent
and
Leland L. Medsker

Foreword by
Edward Joseph Shoben, Jr.

 Jossey-Bass Inc., Publishers
615 Montgomery Street · San Francisco · 1968

BEYOND HIGH SCHOOL
A Psychosociological Study of 10,000 High School Graduates
  by James W. Trent and Leland L. Medsker

Jossey-Bass, Inc., Publishers
615 Montgomery Street
San Francisco, California 94111

Library of Congress Catalog Card Number 68-21318

Printed in the United States of America
by Hamilton Printing Company
Rensselaer, New York

FIRST EDITION

68055

THE JOSSEY-BASS SERIES IN HIGHER EDUCATION

General Editors

JOSEPH AXELROD *and* MERVIN B. FREEDMAN

San Francisco State College

Foreword

That college matters is hardly a thunderingly novel contention. Why else would enrollments be swelling to such unprecedented magnitudes? And yet, like many of our basic articles of faith, our adherence to the notion that college indeed matters has been under attack at the very time that attendance has been so dramatically rising. One line of criticism has suggested that a youngster's exposure to higher education is basically incidental to the background of experience he brings with him to the university; it is not college that determines either his worldly success or the lineaments of his adult character, but the same elements in his history and make-up that lead him initially to seek education beyond the secondary level. The effects of college are essentially epiphenomena. Another pattern of studies has raised doubts about the extent to which college has any modifying effect on the *values* of students, whatever may be its contribution to their marketable skills or general knowledge. Although higher education *may* make a difference in income earned and the range of information at one's command, it makes little impact on the way one votes, looks upon ethnic groups different from one's own, construes the moral world, or responds to nature and the arts.

In the light of these questionings of the significance of college attendance, it is reassuring for those of us who share the faith to have the documentation *Beyond High School* makes available. In a massive investigation of some 10,000 high school graduates in 16 different communities, Dr. James Trent and Dr. Leland Medsker have demonstrated that higher education matters in a variety of important ways. Four years after finishing high school, those young people who persist through college have not only more intellectual curiosity and more autonomous styles of thinking than their compeers who spent the same four years in the world of work; they also are more tolerant of ambiguity, less authoritarian, and more receptive and responsive to a wider environment than nonattenders. In personality as well as in cognitive performance, those who go to college and maintain their enrollment for the four-year period reveal advantageous gains relative to both those who do not enter some institution of higher learning and those who drop out within three years after their matriculation.

The detailed findings of this rigorously conceived, elegantly executed, and conservatively interpreted study are fascinating and merit close attention. They illuminate a variety of problems of fundamental importance and considerable complexity. One example is the nature of the interaction between the characteristics of the student—his predisposition to learn and, through learning, to change —and the characteristics of his particular college as a change-evoking environment. The data in *Beyond High School* make it quite clear that the potency of any given institution cannot be effectively assessed apart from the kinds of students in relation to whom its power is genuinely functional. A little ironically, few colleges (and proportionally fewer students) are very much aware of the nature of the complicated matching of youngster and institution that produces the significant and meaningful modifications that we properly call growth. The common pieties of the catalogue and the traditional rhetoric of our educational creed obscure the diversity in both undergraduates and colleges that must be dealt with if the college experience is to be most productive.

". . . if the college experience is to be most productive"—Ay! There's the rub. For how many of our youth is this educational opportunity, demonstrated here as, on the average, a clearly profitable enterprise, a "most productive" one? About 52 per cent of those graduated from high school in June presently enroll in some kind of college the following September. Of that group, only about half persist for four years, and only about half of those who persist take their first degrees on the conventional schedule. If college attendance is so favorable to growth, why is the rate of attrition so exorbitant?

Trent and Medsker deal with this question helpfully if neither exhaustively nor in a broad context. As they point out, persistence in college is basically a function of three factors: (1) the importance undergraduates themselves assign to the completion of a degree, (2) their having decided by the second year of high school or earlier that they would go to college, and (3) the fact that their parents had definitely wanted them to attend. Although other elements are correlated with the tendency to persist, these three seem to be most important; and what this triad most sharply implies is that success in college is rooted in parental encouragement and expectation, the acceptance by the child of his family's valuing either of traditional college attendance or of upward social mobility through such attendance, and the youngster's interiorization of the norms and aspirations of adults who look with favor—probably for a high diversity of reasons—on higher education. The harsh way to formulate this hypothesis is in these terms: The persisting student is one who conforms to an adult reference group which shares the modal values of the fundamentally middle-class college, and because his conforming tendencies are sufficiently well established relatively early in his life, he is able to conform to the demands that his college makes on him to change in directions along which he has already been pointed.

Such at least is a possibility—a possibility that helps to explain the puzzling, distressing rate of attrition among those who enroll as freshmen but drop out within the first three years. To the extent that this inference is worthy of further exploration, it calls for comment from at least three important angles of regard.

First, to say that the college—which does matter in a vital and meaningful sense—builds on conformity is not the same thing as to levy an indictment unalloyed by real appreciation or without an awareness of positive value. For all our contemporary liberal disdain for "conformity," we must remember that any viable society rests on the sharing of norms and interests by its members and on a willing and even enthusiastic acceptance of some central set of standards and aspirations. If the college experience promotes this kind of adherence to the broad traditions of civility and to a faith in human reason and inventiveness, it is hardly subject to carping. Similarly, the observation that the college's climate of change is most favorable to patterns of middle-class growth and development must be set against the historical fact that what is most humane, expansive, and generous in America has been constructed by the middle class. That segment of our society has not only been both most solid and most creative with respect to the structuring of our institutions and our mores, but it has been open and capacious, inviting ever increasing numbers of people into its advantaged ranks. Guilty not infrequently of boorishness in manner, of short-sightedness in its ebullient fouling of both the natural environment and the cities of its own elaboration, and of the inhumanity of racism and bigotry, the middle class in America has still represented consistently precisely those admirable traits that the college tends to foster—intellectual openness, personal autonomy, freedom from authoritarianism, independence of thought, and tolerance of ambiguity. If this state of affairs is paradoxical, paradox is inherent in big, dynamic, and complex societies, and there is little point of rejecting the positive pole because one is repelled by the negative. Contradictions of this kind are part of the imperfect human condition.

From our second angle of regard, however, the perspective *Beyond High School* permits us to draw on the problem of college attrition also provokes questions about the development of those graduates from secondary school who enter the world of work rather than the academy. On the attributes facilitated by college, these youngsters show little gain and even some regressive disposition. Trent and Medsker appropriately reflect on the somewhat ominous likelihood that in some occupational milieus, "independence, autonomy, and tolerance are not viewed as desirable traits." In many ways, this observation is not surprising. With some noteworthy exceptions, the realms of industry are not known for their prizing these characteristics except at certain special levels of the business enterprise. Like the military, the structures of commerce were not created to build character—not, at least, the same forms of character that shine most brightly in the distinctive light of academic halls. Although it is clearly legitimate to applaud the kinds of growth that college students enjoy, it may also be well, especially for those of us who are college bred and even donnish, to hold our tongues until we know more than we now do about the contributions to our overall culture of those who grow up in industry and whose personalities are shaped by the environment of trade and manufacture. Unless we do, we may be quicker than we intend to violate the value of pluralism, which most of us hold dear, and we may overlook the merits in such qualities as promptness and firmness in decision-making, the virtues of loyalty and followership, and the social advantages of specific varieties of dependence and uncritical commitment. There is much to worry us in the slow economic progress of the youngsters who do not go on to college, and there may be even more to evoke our concern about their rather widely shared sense of being unfulfilled and discontent with themselves. These sources of uneasiness, however, are not the same as the cognitive and affective traits that differentiate persistent college-goers from nonattenders. Meanwhile, we can take a bona fide pride in the evidence that college matters.

But, finally, for how long does it matter? Of all the questions brought into focus by *Beyond High School,* this one is perhaps most crucial. To what extent are the changes brought about by higher education durable and lifelong, and to what extent do they simply reflect accommodations to the press and demands of the academic environment? We don't know. On the basis of the argument from conformity to parental values, advanced earlier, it would seem to follow that the lines of development encouraged by college attendance should run well into a given undergraduate's future, and well they may. But two considerations must give us pause. One derives from the experience of a liberal women's college which showed a sharp impact on the political, social, and aesthetic values of girls from predominantly wealthy and conservative families. From the freshman to the senior year, the youngsters changed markedly in their behavior as well as their attitudes. Within five years after graduation, however, they had typically married boys from backgrounds similar to their own, begun to live according to variants on their parents' pattern, and retired into the political and social stances of their pre-college days; only their aesthetic commitments survived, mostly in the

form of patronage to art galleries, little theatres, and musical organizations. The other consideration that must be borne in mind
here is that the students studied by Trent and Medsker have not
yet been subjected themselves to the influences of business and
industry, perhaps similar to those that have already played over
their nonattending peers. Will they, as they develop their occupational commitments and settle into niches in the world beyond
the academy's precincts, show "regression" as they respond to the
milieu of commerce and the professions? We cannot guarantee
that they will not.

And we cannot guarantee that they will not because—in
part, at any rate—we are unsure what features of our college
programs are most effective in promoting growth and relatively
enduring change as against those that simply require temporary
patterns of adjustment, momentary participation in the fashions
of the academic community, and engagement in a distinctive style
of life that is subtly but definitely conceived by undergraduates as
a transient experience attached to the essentially instrumental purposes of a college education. Thus, we are brought back to issues
affecting the curricula of our institutions, the ways in which the
extraclassroom activities of students are thoughtfully related to
the more formal processes of learning and personal development,
and the nature and effects of instruction as a given college or university practices it. But when we return to these problems via Dr.
Trent's and Dr. Medsker's immensely competent and honest study,
we are sobered by their evidence that college matters and that it
matters most in the extent to which it shapes the character and
destiny of young people—or fails to provide that shaping influence. To deal responsibly with the restructuring of our apparatus
of higher education in an era when universal education beyond
the high school is a thoroughly tenable vision, we must learn a
good deal more about the sources and types of influence which
that apparatus contains within itself, and we must think more
deeply about the normative questions of whether those influences
are legitimate and desirable in today's somewhat harrowing world.
Simultaneously, we must also learn a good deal more about the
vicissitudes of college-induced growth in students *after* they have
taken their degrees and exposed themselves to other forms of
press and demand in the wider environment.

As background for considering these large and important matters, *Beyond High School* is and will for some time remain invaluable. Like a man's reach, which should exceed his grasp, a good book should invite and provoke more queries than it answers and should move the level of discussion to a more complex and significant plane than was possible before it was written. Dr. Trent and Dr. Medsker have put many of us in their abiding debt by having written just such a book.

EDWARD JOSEPH SHOBEN, JR., *Director*
Commission on Academic Affairs
American Council on Education
Washington, D.C.

Preface

A democracy's ability to maintain itself and to assume a position of leadership depends upon its utilization of resources, both material and human. Acutely conscious of the need to develop and utilize its resources, the United States has made spectacular progress in agricultural and industrial development and great strides in providing for the health, education, and welfare of its people. It has made perhaps more significant advances than any other country in recognizing the inherent dignity of the individual, yet along these lines much remains to be done.

No nation in modern society can rest on a status quo position. Thus, in the area of human resources, the demand for an educated citizenry is increasing and will become more severe as the social, civic, and economic life of the nation becomes even more complex. Assuming that a society is served best when every citizen develops his various capacities to the fullest, it follows that there must be a national commitment to creating the optimum conditions under which such development may be realized.

Admittedly, much of society's concern about its members has to be expressed on an en masse basis. In education, for example, while there has been increasing emphasis on better schools, for the most part this emphasis has been on schools in general or on students in general. Only in recent years have research workers begun to inquire more specifically into the types of students who tend to persist in school, to perform well while they are there, and to achieve an optimum personal development during their scholastic careers.

Various leaders have voiced concern about the great waste of human talent occasioned by the many qualified high school graduates who do not continue in college. In his 1962 State of the Union message to Congress, President John F. Kennedy said: "If this nation is to grow in wisdom and strength, then every able high school graduate should have the opportunity to develop his talents. Yet nearly half lack either the funds or the facilities to attend college." In another section of the same message the President declared: "A child miseducated is a child lost. The damage cannot be repaired. Civilization, ran an old saying, is a race between education and catastrophe." In an era of unparalleled social and technological advances, the importance of the maximum development of the individual for his own sake, as well as for the welfare of society in general, must be considered. Few people dare predict the changes that will be wrought in the American society within the next few years, but one point is clear: the average individual will face an occupational setting, as well as civic and personal problems, far more complex than those faced by any previous generation.

Reference to this increasing complexity of life may be found in the published statements pertaining to the effects of automation on American society. Many of them vividly set forth alarming implications of cybernation: unemployment on an unprecedented scale, more and more forced and meaningless leisure time, and the undermining of some of our most deeply ingrained beliefs and assumptions. The consensus of these views represents a plea for immediate overall national planning to meet the crises ahead and for concerted all-out efforts toward changing people's attitudes about occupations, use of leisure, and related matters. What then should be the education of a people more and more enveloped in cybernation and other complexities of a changing society?

If the nation's youth are to have optimum preparation for their role in society, the question of their education is important at all levels—kindergarten through college—but particularly at the time of graduation from high school. The distribution of high school graduates among the many pursuits open to them is, therefore, a matter for immediate and intense concern. It is common knowledge that many able students do not take advantage of any educational opportunities beyond high school. Many graduates go directly into employment, or military service; many of the girls, into homemaking. What are the characteristics of those who follow each of these various pursuits? What factors are related to their course of action? Of the graduates who enter college, what factors bear upon where they go and upon their performance there? Are some high school students inevitably "marginal" college students? Are others almost certain to succeed? Do the answers to such questions depend in part upon the types of colleges attended? If the changing social and technological scene suggests that an increasing percentage of America's high school graduates should continue their formal education beyond the high school, by what means may this be accomplished? What are the different effects of four years of college and four years of continuous employment on the personality development of young adults? Perhaps it is most important to ask what colleges can do to further the development of their students.

In the period ahead, those who teach and counsel high school and college students or who help plan the structure for education at the post high school level will surely need to know more than they now do both about the factors involved in meaningful educational planning and about the predictors of post high school behavior. Moreover, they must be aware of the extent to which the nature of the higher educational system is itself a determinant of what graduates do after high school.

As counselors, teachers, administrators, parents, and others concentrate on maximizing the number of young people who continue their education beyond high school and helping them to make the most of this experience, they must also recognize the evolutionary process of decision-making about college and the consequences of not entering college. Obviously, personal and career decisions do not suddenly begin at the point of high school graduation. The critical experiences and decisions that affect human development are part of a lifelong process. They are intricately dependent upon families, living conditions, peer groups, schools, and other individuals and institutions in society. Fortunately, within the last decade more data on these matters have become available. The accumulated evidence from these studies shows that the severest loss in the development of potential through a college experience comes from among those in low socioeconomic levels and that there is no single or easy remedy, such as scholarships, for this problem.

It is also evident that much of the development of youths' personalities and talents is attributable to different cultural factors and motivational patterns coincident with diverse backgrounds. This would suggest that the pursuits and development of young people after high school are dependent upon a multiplicity of psychological and situational factors, many of them interrelated. Thus, there is an obvious need for more information about the complex factors that affect decisions regarding college, careers, and ultimately, life satisfaction.

Despite the urgent need, information on the factors that determine students' post high school pursuits is scarce, particularly on those factors that may affect decisions about going to college and also college performance. Still less is known about the personality and vocational development of young adults who follow different post high school pursuits.

In an attempt to discover and analyze those forces that influence young people to choose different pursuits after high school and those that have bearing on their subsequent development, we undertook a four-year longitudinal study at the Center for Research and Development in Higher Education at Berkeley. By following the college and noncollege careers for some 10,000 high school graduates through patterns of work, college, and marriage, we were able to focus on our central concern: the different impacts of college and employment on values and attitudes.

Toward this end, we assessed the young people's personality characteristics, values, goals, academic aptitude, and social, economic, educational, and cultural backgrounds in their senior year in high school and at intervals during the next four years. The instruments used were psychometric measures, including ten attitudinal scales from the Omnibus Personality Inventory that measure anxiety and intellectual and social attitudes, a student questionnaire devised by the project staff, and interview schedules.

ACKNOWLEDGMENTS

The study reported here was made possible through funds from the Cooperative Research Program of the U. S. Office of Education. Such a large-scale and long-term study is dependent upon the contributions of many organizations and individuals. Primary contributors to the study were administrators and teachers in the school systems in the sixteen communities, the more than 700 colleges which enrolled the graduates in our sample who continued their education, and the students themselves who completed the numerous instruments before graduation and who responded to similar instruments during the four years following graduation. Without their generous cooperation no findings could have emanated from the research effort and the authors are thus deeply indebted to these thousands of individuals. Special appreciation is also due the several individuals, including members of the Center staff, who read the tentative manuscript and made suggestions for its improvement.

Those who helped with the incessant and tedious coding and clerical tasks are too numerous to be mentioned by name, but they are assured that their efforts are greatly appreciated. Certain individuals must be singled out, however, for their special contributions. Dr. Manford Ferris assisted with the statistical design of the analyses of change scores. Mrs. Julie Pesonen was instrumental in the final production of the report. Mrs. Joan Marsh, Mrs. Terry Berge, Mrs. Georgia Rosenberg, and Mrs. Marilyn Hillesland effectively assumed major responsibilities for the countless records, tabulations, and clerical operations involved over the four years of the study. Mrs. Judith Craise assisted with the processing of the interviews and provided bibliographical materials and helpful critical appraisals of various drafts of the report. William Raley and Dr. Irene Athey contributed to the construction of the interview schedule and the 1963 survey instrument used in the study, in addition to conducting many of the interviews.

Appreciation is extended, above all, to Mrs. Harriet Renaud and Mrs. Janet Ruyle. Mrs. Renaud, who put a great deal of sustained personal investment and diligence into her editing of the manuscript, patiently and efficiently dealt with the problems of communicating complex material, and the report is much enhanced through her efforts. Mrs. Ruyle supervised, coordinated, and implemented the far-ranging and multiple mechanical operations of the research as well as the data processing and analyses. Her unsurpassed creative, intelligent, and dedicated efforts represent an immeasurable contribution to this volume.

Berkeley   JAMES W. TRENT
April 1968   LELAND L. MEDSKER

Contents

Beyond High School

I

Education and
Human Development

Until quite recently, social and behavioral scientists have stressed that basic personality structure is laid down early in childhood. Now there is growing emphasis on the view that although the effect of early environment is critical, there is potential for change, growth, and personality development at all stages of life, and particularly in adolescence and early adulthood. The implications of such theorizing for higher education are evident. Increasingly, research on the phenomenon of change of values has turned to exploring the effect of the college experience on students' values (Sanford, 1962a). The present volume reports a study in this vein of research.

The study follows the personal and vocational development of a large sample of high school graduates during the first four years after graduation. It traces their employment and college attendance patterns between 1959 and 1963 and includes an investigation of factors associated with withdrawal from college. Its focus is on comparisons of two groups—those who became employed immediately after high school and those who entered college. The groups are compared on the basis of their values and attitudes as measured by psychometric instruments, and also ac-

1

cording to their reported evaluations of work and college experiences during the course of the study. Thus, employment and college attendance, regarded as primary intervening environmental factors, were studied for their possible influence on the development of young adults.

Existing theories have taken into account the importance of environment and opportunity in the development of personality and attainment of occupational status. Only now, however, are theories being evolved to account for the effect of higher education on human development. If efforts are to be made to improve the preparation of youths to live effectively, it is important to understand how young people develop after adolescence. What attitudes, values, and goals do high school graduates bring to jobs, college, and society, as they assume adult roles? What effect does their education have on them, and to what use do they put education in handling life experiences?

Interviewers of a representative sample of the group of high school graduates surveyed found that a large number had not been equipped by their education to meet the demands of the adult world. Three years after graduation, they already felt unsuccessful in their postgraduate lives, bewildered about the factors which had contributed to their difficulties, and powerless to effect any changes. They talked about needing to find directions which would eliminate their sense of discontent and insecurity. They talked also about the need for further training so that they could do a good job at something which would satisfy them. A number were on the way to fulfillment in their lives and careers, but a great many had already floundered in their educational and work experiences. Many had yet to feel any pride in their accomplishments.

Underlying the troubled comments they volunteered were unformulated questions; but their intent was clear. Essentially they wanted to know: What constitutes a really good preparation for adult life? What personal qualities make for the successful assumption of adult roles? The importance of the answers they find and use cannot be overestimated. For while it is imperative for young people to make major decisions about their lives with information and awareness, what they decide is increasingly important to a complex, changing society.

Consideration of the interrelatedness between the needs of youth and those of society, however, brings conflicts to light. The competitive pressures of a fast-changing world demand that young people make serious decisions about specialities and careers, yet society may outgrow its need for their skills almost as soon as they are mastered. Young people are being forced to make major decisions which will critically influence their lives, yet the increasing complexity of society has reduced assurances that their decisions will lead to viable goals. If today's youths are compelled to make accurate and precise decisions about matters which tax the powers of experienced adults, then the educational system must prepare them for nothing less than the task of decision-making. As early as 1950, the Educational Policies Commission stated that training for the young must develop talents appropriate to the "complexities and specializations of contemporary life" as well as "a sense of social responsibility and other qualities of character that will direct the use of their talents toward socially beneficial ends [p. 2]."

The educational opportunities our youths accept or reject, the use they make of their potential, is of vital national concern. Yet all indications have been that the ever-accelerating demand for more highly trained people has not been met with a sufficient increase in post high school education for those who could make use of it.

Berdie (1954) observed that in spite of increased needs for specialized manpower, a large proportion of able Minnesota high school graduates were neither attending college nor preparing themselves for specialized jobs. That same year, a survey of the national scene pointed up similar waste of human resources (Wolfle, 1954). A number of subsequent studies described the same tendencies in Wisconsin (Little, 1959) in Indiana (Wright and Jung, 1959), and in seven other states (Medsker and Trent, 1965). In Congressional testimony, Diebold (1962) estimated that about half of the students in the upper 25 per cent of their class do not enter college, and that about two-thirds of those best able to fill positions of scientific and technical leadership do not receive training commensurate with their abilities. This failure to educate and utilize talent is particularly striking in light of the Manpower Report of the President (U.S. Department of Labor, 1964), which stressed that our greatest manpower needs through the foreseeable future will be for personnel with extensive training, especially in the areas of science and mathematics.

Indications are that the proportion of able youths entering college after high school is now increasing (Flanagan and associates, 1964), but even more specialized training for more high school graduates will be insufficient unless qualities of flexible, adaptive thinking are also fostered. In a labor market where unskilled jobs are rapidly being replaced by specialized ones, many men with a single skill may not have job security. They may not only frequently be forced to take further training in order to keep pace with a continually narrowing specialty, they may also have to stand prepared to change to other vocational areas. Such a life orientation will call for a high degree of specially developed competence. To quote Browne-Mayers (1964):

> Continually keeping pace with technological change means that the student will have to become competent in relation to his job, himself, to the society about him, as well as to the variety of social forces that impinge on his daily life [p. 24].

Education for this kind of competence must be concerned with human development as much as with training for specialized skills. It must assert the values of self-direction, creativity, and flexibility as firmly as the importance of readiness for a particular job. Wrenn (1962) takes note of this need in his recommendations to counselors in a changing world:

> That primary emphasis in counseling students be placed on the developmental needs and decision points in the lives of the total range of the students rather than upon the remedial needs and the crisis points in the lives of a few students, with the major goal of counseling being that of increased self-responsibility and an increased maturity in decision-making upon the part of the student [p. 109].

What Wrenn conceives of as the function of counseling might well serve, in an era of continuous change, as a goal for the whole educational process. The development of self-responsibility and the ability to make informed decisions—traditionally considered among the major by-products of education—today must constitute education's primary focus. Although social critics' estimates of the effect of automation vary widely, their theories clearly imply that no system of training for the young can omit consideration of the possible effects of an increasingly technocratized society. Michael (1965) and Theobald (1964) believe that the effects will be far-reaching and possibly devastating; Bell (1965) asserts that economic and social forces already at work can absorb the effects of automation once the economy begins to match the national rate of productivity; Magnum (1964) doubts that the effects of automation will be rapid; Shils (1966) and Silberman (1966) agree that technology will eliminate existing jobs, but not work; and Hechinger (1964) feels that the problem will not be job displacement, but rather the task of changing attitudes toward jobs. Whatever the stand toward automation, most indications point to shifts in the economic and social structure which inevitably will have important bearing on the lives of young people, and it is not unlikely that certain social and economic phenomena are imminent, including the following:

1. New concepts and attitudes regarding work and the use of leisure. (Traditionally, man's sense of self-satisfaction and the respect accorded him by the members of his society have been gained largely through work for which he has been paid. In the future, opportunities for paid work may be severely limited.)

2. Activities designed to promote the fullest possible development of the individual's potential and personality, regardless of whether he is "gainfully" employed.

3. Specific training for the making and implementing of complex decisions based upon knowledge and wisdom rather than bias or partisan pressures. (If unlimited leisure is to lead to creative development and social productivity rather than to stagnation and waste, the age-old cry of general educationalists may come to be heeded and the value of liberal education for all finally recognized.)

4. The assumption, by the system of higher education, of responsibility for providing universal education of an exceptionally high quality, according to ability level.

6   BEYOND HIGH SCHOOL

5. Integrated social planning to motivate youths to take advantage of the education without which they will be unable to find adequate and satisfying places for themselves in tomorrow's society.

6. Widely expanded re-education in order to assist people to make major changes in their value systems and to adapt to changing industrial and social needs.

Projections such as these underline the necessity for more specialized training at higher levels for more young people, and for the kind of universal education which will train young people in the habits of learning and flexibility so that they can tolerate and utilize new experiences and information.

To meet these needs, educators must not only have a broad picture of the current patterns of college attendance but also information about students' backgrounds and characteristics and the motivational factors behind their college attendance, non-attendance, and withdrawal. More information is also needed about the nature of personal and vocational development during the transition to adulthood, and the effect of college on this development. Knowledge about the paths and life patterns of youths in and out of college is particularly relevant because of the apparent contradiction between greatly increased college enrollments and the simultaneous great loss of the talent of many able young people who either do not attend college or who enter and withdraw. Such information would provide educators with a basis for "re-tooling" educational enterprises and make available to young adults reliable facts with which to project what lies ahead.

THE PERSONAL AND VOCATIONAL DEVELOPMENT OF YOUNG ADULTS

The development of young people as they settle upon occupations and assume adult roles has been the concern of a number of social theorists. The theory that the basic themes of personality are formed early has been supplemented by the recognition that there is a sequence of decisions made at different critical periods, as for instance in puberty, late adolescence, and young adulthood. The function of higher education in the developmental process has also been of growing concern. In discussing the need for a new theoretical foundation, Fishman (1962) said that:

First of all, I believe that we suffer from a serious lack of a theory of personality factors that relates them to a theory of college behavior, generally, and to the academic learning processes more specifically. Of course, we also lack something even more fundamental, namely, a general theory of college prediction —analagous to the prediction of adjustment, of marital success, or of voting behavior. . . . At this point I merely want to emphasize my strong conviction that nonintellective predictors of intellective criteria will finally become both important and comprehensive variables only if we realize that they require alternative theoretical models and empirical designs depending on the specific nature of the individual and of the institutional differences that are known or assumed to obtain between the high school and college settings in a given study context [pp. 678–79].

Fishman indicates that high school graduates change after entering a new environment in college. He proposes that a deeper understanding of this process of change is to be gained by studying the "contingency factors" or intervening variables in the student's development between high school and the end of his college career. Fishman implies that personality theory about development during the college years is scant, but singles out Erikson as a source of ideas about the 18-to-28 age group.

Erikson (1963) has formulated the theory that the period immediately following high school might be regarded as a moratorium during which the adolescent seeks and learns his identity in preparation for adult maturity. In an attempt to integrate the developmental sequence of social roles, Erikson has posited an epigenetic diagram for important critical stages in the life development of an individual. Of adolescents, he says:

The adolescent mind is essentially a mind of the *moratorium,* a psychosocial stage between childhood and adulthood, and between the morality learned by the child, and the ethics to be developed by the adult [pp. 262–63].

The adolescent is, so to speak, in a no-man's land until, through experimentation and discovery of himself, apart from the image his parents have given him of himself, he discovers his

identity—who he is and where he is going. This involves in part
what White (1952) expressed as a "humanization of his values."
That is, he forms his values out of his own experiences and observation rather than passively accepting the morality and mores
handed down by his parents.

Maslow (1962) has offered an important adjunct to Erikson's theory. His theory of personality development emphasizes
aspects of the development of the healthy, mature individual.
Every child and every adult has certain "deficiency needs," such as
the need for basic love, respect, security, and prestige, which must
be fulfilled if the individual is not to become severely hampered
in exploring his own potentialities and those in his environment.
If these needs are fulfilled, he becomes a healthy, self-actualizing
adult, characterized, says Maslow, by: superior perception of
reality; acceptance of self, of others, and of nature; spontaneity
and richness of emotional reaction; the ability to identify with
people coupled with a desire for privacy; creativeness; openness
to change of certain values; and a democratic character structure.

Theories of vocational development appear compatible, if
not parallel, with personality theories such as those espoused by
Erikson and Maslow. In fact, vocational theory is in many ways a
form of personality theory. For example, Ginzberg and associates
(1951) theorize that the occupational choices of young adults
actually evolve out of a developmental process during which a
series of decisions are made over a number of years. Irretraceable
steps are taken which limit future decisions so that compromises
must be made: The youth who early rejects the idea of studying
chemistry cannot in the end choose to become a doctor. The
process operates during three distinct periods of a young person's
life. In the first period, a youth is free to make a fantasy choice
without committing himself and without reality considerations.
In the second period, he makes tentative choices which approach
reality situations, but still without commitment. In the third
stage, he is forced to make a realistic choice and to act upon it
in preparation for his work.

The young adults in the present study were just entering
that period when they had to make the inevitable compromise
between what they wanted to do and what opportunities were

available to them, between their choice and their ability to achieve it. Ideally, this period is characterized by awareness of reality considerations; fantasy gives way to practical goals, and a firm commitment is made to an occupational goal. The success of this transition and the appropriateness of the final choice depend on how well the operative factors in the tentative occupational choices are understood. It should be said here that this power of insight and the ability to manipulate the environment effectively call for a high degree of competence and maturity, and that these traits are largely fostered by the family and educational agencies.

Super (1957) and Ginzberg and associates (1951) both consider that the crystallization of the decision-making process is achieved only after a phase of exploration of reality. But Super emphasizes the importance of the reality process both before and after the commitment to work is made. Thus, it is actual work experience which is the best test of whether or not a young adult has successfully assumed a work role compatible with his needs and nature.

Super describes the early adult phase noted by Ginzberg as the floundering or trial process during which the individual attempts to implement his self-concept after his first initial commitment to a job. This period during which the commitment to a vocational role is "put on trial" is characterized by attempts to find one's place in the world of work, to adjust to work requirements, and to seek ways of life which will lead to final self-establishment. After this phase, the individual enters adulthood; he has presumably embarked upon a relatively permanent career which adequately meets his desires and the concept he has of himself.

IDENTITY AND AUTONOMY

Two elements essential to personal and vocational development, either explicit or implicit in the theories, are the concepts of autonomy and identity. In this context, identity may be conceptualized as a self-awareness which includes not only consciousness of needs, interests, and potential, but also perception of the environment and one's relationship to it. And autonomy, often more narrowly construed as the ability to think for oneself without reliance upon authority, here incorporates the ideas of flexible, objective thinking and an openness of attitude which facilitates awareness of and adaptability to the environment.

When the development of autonomy is limited, the development of identity and realization of potential are also generally limited. This has been observed in a wide range of clinical and empirical research, and the implications of this view for the role of education are, of course, great. Autonomy and a sense of identity are such important aspects of the disposition which a student brings to the educational setting that they greatly influence how he will develop. Since these personality factors are evidently basic to the learning experience and human development, it seems clear that if students deficient in these traits are to develop fully, the educational agency must be concerned with ways to encourage their growth.

In his studies of healthy persons, Maslow (1962) observes that, among other important characteristics, they all showed growth in autonomy, resistance to enculturation, and relative independence from their environment. In a similar vein, Rogers (1951) emphasizes that the main movement of growth in the healthy individual is "in the direction of an increasing self-government, self-regulation, and autonomy, and away from heteronomous control, or control by external forces [p. 488]." Jahoda (1959) also stressed the importance of autonomy in the mentally healthy individual.

Autonomy is also intimately related to the development of creative impulses in man. MacKinnon (1961), Barron (1961), Crutchfield (1963), Gough (1961), and Helson (1961) have shown that the more creative people in architecture, literature, mathematics, and engineering science are distinguished from less creative ones by, among other traits, their greater autonomy and independence of thinking. As Sanford (1966) points out, the general tendency to yield under group pressure correlates negatively and significantly with almost all of the numerous measures of originality and creativity that have been used.

Finally, the development of autonomy is intrinsically related to the development of intellectual awareness, just as the development of an authoritarian personality is related to nonintellectuality. The two patterns which evolve seem clear: The autonomous individual is capable of the objective, open, and flexible thinking which characterize intellectuality, and the authoritarian individual is distinguished by the highly opinionated, closed thinking which is the mark of nonintellectuality. Considerable research shows that the trait of authoritarianism "constitutes a particular failure of maturity," and is a manifestation of anti-intellectualism (Webster, Freedman, and Heist, 1962). More specifically, varying degrees of authoritarianism have been found to be related to different rates of progress in various educational programs (Dressel, 1958; Funkenstein, King, and Drolette, 1957; Stern, 1962; Webster, Freedman, and Heist, 1962).

Although they are central to self-understanding, the exploration of personal and vocational roles, and the realization of potential, autonomy is not easily developed and a sense of identity is not easily achieved. Questions about the extent to which adults within or outside the educational system can or do provide adequate guidance and models for this purpose were repeatedly raised by contributors to the American Academy of Arts and Sciences Conference which comprised the Daedalus issue entitled, *Youth: Change and Challenge* (1962). Eisenstadt, for example, argued that because the roles learned in the family are insufficient for "full identity or full social maturity," young people join groups in order to seek out, develop and crystallize their identity, attain personal autonomy, and make their transition to the adult world. Parsons also considered "concern with problems of 'identity'" a prominent preoccupation of youth. He added that young men and women must find their own way as they enter college because their elders do not have the knowledge to provide the necessary guidance and role models in a continually changing "medium," and because, as a result of continual change, there are so many uncertainties about the nature of opportunities in their chosen fields. Addressing himself to the same kind of problem, Eisenstadt wrote:

> In terms of personality development, this situation has created a great potential insecurity and the possible lack of a clear definition of personal identity. Yet it has also created the possibility of greater personal autonomy and flexibility in the choice of roles and the commitment to different values and symbols. In general, the individual, in his search for the meaning of his personal

transition, has been thrown much more on his own powers [p. 40].

Educational agencies could create an environment "within which youth can forge its identity and become linked to adult society," and in which there would be increased opportunity "to develop a reasonably autonomous personality" and "role models and symbols of identification." As Denny sees it, however, the educational agency as an environment for student development is troubled by "inequality of opportunity, premature specialization, and the glorification of the average [p. 128]." Overriding vocationalism exists in the college to the extent that the American college graduate is, on the average, "culturally illiterate."

It is during the critical period of early adulthood that young people make their sometimes irretrievable commitments toward a career and way of life. As they change from one role to another and make the transition from high school to college, from the end of adolescence to adulthood, what the educational agency expects of them integrally affects their personality development.

HIGHER EDUCATION AND ADULT DEVELOPMENT

Francois (1964) is firm in his conviction about the press which is being placed on education in an increasingly technocratic society:

> Prevention of an android society of human beings rests in the hands of our educators, who must balance the national need for technical competence against the equally vital need of man to grow intellectually in order that he may discern, comprehend, and control inventiveness so that it is no longer an instrument of his own destruction—either economically or militarily. But if education is to be the hope of the future and the guardian of that future is to be worthwhile, then action must be taken at once to strengthen and enlarge its mandate. This is necessary because a time-lag will prevent an immediate effect and during the hiatus, we shall be swept inexorably into the flux of the Age of Automation [pp. 156–57].

Francois reflects the growing awareness among educational theorists and social leaders of the increasing responsibility being given to the educational agency. Schools and colleges have assumed the educative functions once rendered by family, neighborhood, and church. Intrinsically related to the social order, schools and colleges are a major vehicle for integrating the individual with society. Education continues in its three primary and traditional roles: 1) to instill the society's culture; 2) to prepare youths for adult roles; and 3) to provide pre-work instruction and the allocation of individuals to the "occupational structure" (see Clark, 1964). But of late, theorists have also stressed the role of schools in developing all human potential, specifically the intellectuality, creativity, autonomy, and adaptiveness needed to cope with a changing, increasingly technocratized environment.

Sanford (1962b) and Dixon (1963) take the position that the college's aim should be to develop the individual potentialities of all students and to influence them and society to change in the directions of the highest ideals of our culture. The need for a collegiate environment conducive to the development of autonomy and freedom from authoritarian constriction has been emphasized. Bay (1962) goes further and assumes that, "individuals need to grow as much as they are capable of," free from conformity to social norms, which are characteristically anti-intellectual. He takes a stand against the "erosion of rationality in the processes of higher education" and the "conforming opinions" which "keep the individual from gaining a broader understanding of himself and of society, an understanding that could help him anticipate his own future needs and society's changing requirements." Bay is critical of the many colleges and their faculties which, he feels, stress "narrowly academic course requirements" instead of trying to develop in students "the frame of mind for embarking on a joint intellectual adventure [p. 992]."

Education's humanistic role in developing human potential, including intellectual and autonomous disposition, also has pragmatic value for vocational development. This value is considered by Clark (1964) in his discussion of "Education and Social Integration."

As unskilled work diminishes and semi-skilled work is made subject to rapid obsolescence, educators need not only train the mass of the population up to an ever-rising threshold of functional literacy, but must also, above that threshold, educate for ever-rising levels of versatility and retrainability. . . . In the modern era, the rapidity of social change in itself presents problems of unparalleled depth and intensity in the relation of the major training institution to social integration. . . . No one knows ahead of time . . . what will be the functional behavior patterns of the future. Rapidity of change, then, to the degree it is perceived and responded to, is likely to be a pressure on the schools to educate for "adaptability"; i.e., educating the young to be perceptive and understanding of the social environment and flexible and imaginative in dealing with it, with little control by the patterns of the past [pp. 748-49].

There are reasons for questioning just how much college should be involved in encouraging students to change in value and attitude, whether in the form of "adaptability," intellectual development, or otherwise (see Dressel, 1965). There is also argument that, even if that is its intent, the college experience generally seems to do little to liberalize and humanize student values (Jacob, 1957). The consensus seems to be, however, that the college can and should foster human development as described in the previous pages (see Bay, 1962; Fishman, 1962; Freedman, 1965; Heist, 1966; Sanford, 1967; and Stern, 1962).

Sanford's premise is that it is quite possible for personality development to continue to take place during the college years, and even beyond that point (Sanford, 1962c, 1967). He sees college as encouraging development in three ways: 1) it stimulates the imagination and encourages liberalization of values and perception; 2) it encourages awareness of the social purposes of values and of their meaning for human growth; and 3) it fosters ego development.

Fishman and Sanford agree that the college environment should be established deliberately to effect students' change of attitude, values, and perspectives. Sanford (1962c) points out, however, that even if the bureaucratic structure of the college were designed for this purpose, students may not be responsive. Before this stimulation can have effect, students must be at a state of readiness:

The personality does not just unfold or mature according to a plan of nature. Whatever the stage of readiness in the personality, further development will not occur until stimuli arrive to upset the existing equilibrium and require fresh adaptation. What the state of readiness means most essentially is that the individual is now open to new kinds of stimuli and prepared to deal with them in an adaptive way [p. 258].

This state of readiness is crucial to personality development in college. It is conceivable that the subsequent development of the entering college student rests more on his predisposition toward change than on any other factor. There is evidence that the orientation of parents toward higher education constitutes a key factor in determining whether a child's disposition toward learning will be positive or negative. His educational experiences, peer relations, and other early background or environmental factors are also likely to have enduring influence on what he is ready to gain from college. Indeed, these factors all bear on the initial decision to attend college.

If the student is ready enough, with enough proper facilitation from the college he can grow in autonomy and begin to realize his potential. But if the student enters college without sufficient readiness for personality development, it is not yet clear enough how colleges can create a disposition open to changes in values and attitudes which in turn lead to intellectual interests, autonomy, and self-understanding. There is some evidence that a very few selected experimental schools have effected marked changes in students' values (Jacob, 1957), and one role of a college might be to identify students not ready for change, and experiment with programs and environments designed to foster flexibility and growth.

The college environment is important, however, even if it does no more than facilitate growth for those ready for it. To that extent, it represents a moratorium not normally available in the routinized subprofessional work world. Even mediocre colleges afford some opportunity to explore self, society, and work through a few courses, books read, between-class "bull-sessions," and certain preprofessional curricula. However, young adults who go to work right after high school are confined to available jobs, without opportunity to explore, and usually without a chance to meet intellectually stimulating peers. Working on an assembly line, clerking and typing in an office, or operating a machine is not usually conducive to a high degree of human development.

Perhaps many who withdraw from college, especially those with ability, are not ready to assume the levels of autonomy and intellectual development expected of them. (This assessment omits from consideration withdrawals who are in effect "creative drop-outs," and who return to college after having re-grouped emotional, intellectual, or financial resources.) Many nonattenders may be even less open to development of this kind, less encouraged in this development by their environmental and work situations, and consequently least capable of coping effectively with the complexities of society.

The hypothesis of this study is that personality development—growth of autonomy, intellectual interests, and enlightened self-awareness—will be most evident among young adults who persisted in college for four years, and least evident among their peers who did not enter college. This is expected even with the factors of ability and socioeconomic background held constant. It is also hypothesized that the factors which will be found to be related to persistence in college will be the same ones which are associated with change in attitudes and values, and that this finding will corroborate the idea of the function of predisposition for change. Finally, it is posited that noncollege youth do not find, in their working environment, the options and opportunities for exploration necessary for adequate vocational and personal development.

II

The Preliminary Study
of Post High School Pursuits,
1959

The present inquiry into the postgraduate experiences of high school graduates was designed to explore further the ideas and issues discussed in Chapter I. A number of these issues were suggested by the findings of a preceding study (Medsker and Trent, 1965), to be discussed in this chapter.

The earlier research was undertaken in response to the growing concern and discussion about the various restraints on access to higher education. Generally referred to as the College Attendance Study (CAS), its original intention was to investigate the relationship between the rate of college attendance and the type of college available to young people in their community. Although this remained the primary focus of the one-year project, shortly after its inception it became clearly desirable also to explore a number of other variables—social, cultural, economic, and psychological—for their influence on the graduates' decisions to follow different pursuits after high school. The study finally, therefore, not only delineated the relationship between enrollment in college and institutional availability, but also identified additional factors associated with entrance into college.

A large sample of representative high school seniors was surveyed in 16 communities through the Midwest, California, and Pennsylvania. For purposes of comparison, the graduating classes of 37 high schools were chosen from communities which offered different kinds of institutions of higher education: Five had a junior college, four had a freshman-sophomore extension center, four had a state college, two had no colleges of any kind, and one had a diversity of types.

In other respects, the communities were considered "typical," or "average," and—with the intentional exception of the metropolitan area—were matched as closely as possible in population, ethnic background, level of income, proportion of white collar workers, proportion of workers employed in factories and trades, and number of industries. All multi-industrial cities, their populations ranged from approximately 35,000 to 100,000, except for one of the two noncollege communities, with 25,000, and the metropolitan city with a variety of colleges, with 800,000. The populations were principally Caucasian; the overall average proportion of Negro inhabitants in the communities was 4 per cent, and no city had more than 8 per cent Negroes.

The northeastern and southern United States were excluded from the survey. It was feared that the then atypical emphasis on private schools for higher education in the Northeast, and the racial and socioeconomic problems of the South, would so affect research findings as to distort the overall picture of the relationship between the availability of the various types of colleges and the rate of college attendance. Further details of the rationale for selecting the cities are in Appendix A.

The sample was composed of the entire public high school senior class in all the communities chosen, with the exception of the very large one. In the latter, seniors were surveyed in three high schools representing a demographic cross-section as determined by the superintendent of schools. Except in the metropolitan community, the senior classes of private and parochial schools were included if these schools enrolled an appreciable proportion of a community's high school students. The final sample consisted of approximately 10,000 high school graduates.

INSTRUMENTS AND THE SURVEY

The sample was first surveyed late in the spring of 1959, after the research instruments had been revised and refined on the basis of a pilot study conducted in one community. The high school seniors were asked to respond to the following instruments: Thorndike's 20-item CAVD verbal intelligence test described by Miner (1957); a comprehensive Student Questionnaire devised by the project staff; and five attitude scales from the Omnibus Personality Inventory (Center for the Study of Higher Education, 1962). High school ranks were obtained, and the academic aptitude scores in the students' permanent records were converted to School and College Ability Test (SCAT) score equivalents as described in Appendix B.

The Student Questionnaire elicited information about: academic interests and extracurricular activities; educational and occupational plans, values, and goals; occupational, cultural, political, and religious backgrounds of families; quality and kind of interest and encouragement received from parents; and post high school plans of peers. The five scales from the Omnibus Personality Inventory which measure manifest feelings of anxiety and scholarly and social attitudes are described in relevant chapters and in Appendix C.

In the September following their 1959 graduation, data were gathered about the educational, vocational, and marital status of 98 per cent of the original sample. Most of these subjects answered a postcard questionnaire; nonrespondents were telephoned by their respective high schools.

The next spring, the programs and academic standing of 93 per cent of the students in the sample who entered college were procured. Approximately 400 registrars cooperated by filling out a checklist on each student and supplying records in grade points earned.

Complete follow-up data were thus gathered on 9,778 of the some 10,000 graduates who formed the basic sample.

Ninety-one per cent of the sample was Caucasian and 4 per cent Negro (the same proportion found in the communities) —almost equally divided between men and women. The group was predominantly Protestant and Roman Catholic (64 per cent and 25 per cent, respectively).

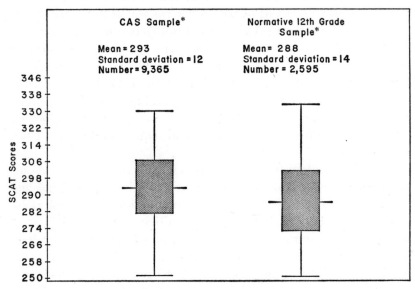

a The vertical line represents the ranges of scores for the samples; the midpoints of the shaded areas denote sample means; and the extremes of the shaded areas lie one standard deviation above and below the mean. The normative data were drawn from the Examiner's Manual, Cooperative School and Ability Tests: First Manual, 1955. Princeton, New Jersey; Cooperative Test Division, Educational Testing Service.

Figure 1. DISTRIBUTIONS OF SCAT SCORE EQUIVALENTS OF SENIORS
IN THE COLLEGE ATTENDANCE STUDY AND SCAT SCORES
OF A NORMATIVE SAMPLE OF HIGH SCHOOL SENIORS.

As determined by comparisons with the general population, the sample was fairly representative of high school seniors throughout the country with respect to ability, educational level of parents, and socioeconomic background. The seniors in the sample scored very slightly higher than a normative sample of 12th grade students on tests of academic ability. This may be seen in Figure 1, which shows the distributions of the SCAT score equivalents of the research sample and the SCAT scores of the national sample. Although the range of the two distributions are nearly identical, it is apparent from the mean scores and the shaded areas which indicate the standard deviation of the scores about the mean, that the research sample was more homogeneous and at a higher level of ability than the national sample. The graduates also came from families educated to somewhat higher levels than the men and women of a national sample (Table 1). For example, 16 per cent more of the seniors' fathers had attended high school than adults in the general population, and 5 per cent more of their fathers had at least some college education.

Table 1

EDUCATIONAL LEVELS OF SENIORS' PARENTS AND THOSE OF THE
NATIONAL SAMPLE OF MEN AND WOMEN, IN PERCENTAGES

	Men		*Women*	
	Fathers of seniors	*National sample 25 years and older* [a]	*Mothers of seniors*	*National sample 25 years and older* [a]
	(N = 9778)	*(N = 47,041,000)*	*(N = 9778)*	*(N = 50,437,000)*
Elementary school				
8th grade or less	21	37	15	34
High School				
12th grade or less	47	41	59	49
Some college	11	8	10	8
Finished college; some graduate study	12	10	9	6
No response	9	4	7	3
Total	100	100	100	100

[a] Source: Government Printing Office (1961, p. 107).

These minor deviations from national norms did not cast doubt on the general representativeness of the group studied, but were interesting in light of its socioeconomic background, commonly determined by father's occupation. Possibly because of the matching of the communities, it can be seen from Table 2 that the students' fathers were overrepresented in the managerial and proprietor category (7 per cent more than the national figure) and underrepresented in the sales and clerical occupations (9 per

cent less than the national sample). Despite these variations, however, it was clear that the distributions of occupations engaged in
by the seniors' fathers and by men throughout the country were
generally similar (Figure 2), and that the sample was reasonably
representative on this dimension.

Table 2

OCCUPATIONAL CLASSIFICATION OF SENIORS'
FATHERS, IN PERCENTAGES

Occupational classification	Students (N = 8784)[a]
Professional I	5
Professional II	3
Managerial	7
Semiprofessional	2
Proprietary—small business	11
Sales and clerical	12
Skilled	37
Semiskilled	13
Unskilled	10
Total	100

[a] Includes only the students whose responses were sufficiently precise to be
categorized with accuracy.

In 1959, the young people as a group showed little inclination towards intellectual pursuits, and although interest in "serious
reading," classical music, and discussions of current affairs was
positively correlated with socioeconomic background, the differences between the groups at different social levels were small at
best.

A large minority of the young people (including one-third
of the men) came out of high school with no vocational plans,
although 63 per cent had been enrolled in college preparatory or
general curricula, and one-third in various vocational programs.
Asked about preferred occupations, 37 per cent of the men and 34
per cent of the women chose professional and managerial occupations; over 7 per cent of the seniors chose semiprofessional
occupations; nearly one-third of the women chose a clerical occupation; 16 per cent of the men chose skilled occupations; and
very few of either sex chose a semiskilled or unskilled occupation.
Twenty-three per cent of the women wanted to become housewives

right after high school, and an almost equal proportion, irrespective of their decision regarding college, had no vocation in mind other than the possibility of homemaking.

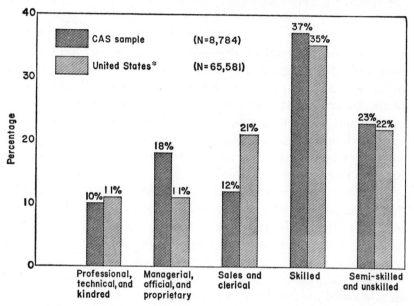

* Source: Statistical Abstract of the United States, 1960, Government Printing Office, Washington, D.C. [p. 216].

Figure 2. PROPORTIONS OF SENIORS' FATHERS IN VARIOUS OCCUPATIONAL CLASSIFICATIONS COMPARED WITH THE NATIONAL LABOR FORCE, 1959.

Many of those who did express plans and goals—whether for college or a specific occupational level—turned out to have made unrealistic appraisals of their ability, the requisite training for vocations to which they were attracted, and the availability of the kinds of jobs they had in mind. Nearly one-fourth of the men who did not enter any kind of post high school education chose a vocation which requires a minimum of a year of college training or its equivalent. Nearly one-third of the men who entered a special school of a subcollegiate level, as defined by the *Directory of Education*, chose vocations which require at least a baccalaureate degree.

Nearly two-thirds of the men thought that they would ultimately prefer to work in their own business or a large firm or corporation, and the women in a school, hospital, or small business (although it seemed clear that for many of the women these were simply the settings they preferred to work in before achieving the ultimate goal of marriage).

THE FIRST YEAR AFTER HIGH SCHOOL

By the September after graduation, 50 per cent of the men and 37 per cent of the women were in college, in contrast to the stated plans of 54 per cent of the former and 49 per cent of the latter. Thirty-four per cent of the total sample were employed, and the rest were in special schools, military service, unemployed, or housewives. The unemployment figures of 5 per cent for the men and 7 per cent for the women corresponded with the national unemployment figures for 1959.

Forty per cent of the sample entered college full time and 3 per cent part time the semester following graduation. Attendance varied by community from about 25 to 65 per cent. The highest entrance rate was found in communities with junior colleges, which drew more students from every ability and socioeconomic level than any other type of college; the lowest rates were found in the communities with extension centers and those with no college. Among the two-year colleges, extension centers showed a marked tendency to attract the more financially and academically able students, while the junior colleges characteristically drew a wide diversity of students.

The students' rate of persistence during the first year of college was high; over 80 per cent enrolled in 1959 remained through the spring semester. The persistence rate was lowest among students in extension centers (71 per cent) and highest among students in public and private universities (89 and 91 per cent, respectively). Ability was related to persistence the first year, but not as much as might be expected. Eighty-seven per cent of the students in the upper 40 per cent of the ability distribution remained in college the first year, but so did 73 per cent of the students in the lowest 40 per cent of the distribution.

THOSE WHO WENT TO COLLEGE

Both ability and socioeconomic status were found to be associated with college attendance. Approximately 60 per cent of the graduates in the upper two-fifths of the sample's ability distribution (as measured by School and College Ability Test scores) entered college in 1959, but less than 20 per cent of the students in the middle fifth and less than 10 per cent in the bottom two-fifths did so. It is noteworthy, however, that although high ability was seen to be related to college attendance, not only was a wide range of ability also apparent among college entrants, but confirming earlier research, it was found that a very large proportion of the sample's brightest students did not enter college (see Berdie, 1954; Wolfle, 1954; Wright and Jung, 1959).

Of the two salient factors positively related to college attendance, academic ability and socioeconomic status, social status was found to have more bearing. Three out of every four students from professional families entered college in 1959, compared with only one in four from homes of semiskilled and unskilled workers. Of the graduates at the high socioeconomic level (with fathers in professional or managerial positions), nearly 60 per cent in the lowest 40 per cent of the sample's ability distribution matriculated, but of the graduates at the low socioeconomic level (with fathers in semiskilled and unskilled occupations) only about 40 per cent in the upper 40 per cent of the ability distribution went on to college.

There was also a strong association between a senior's decision to go to college and his parents' educational level. Thirty-six per cent of the fathers and 32 per cent of the mothers of the college attenders had had some exposure to college; these figures were 11 per cent and 8 per cent, respectively, for the nonattenders. Analysis of the postgraduate pursuits of the sample according to mother's education showed that, as a factor related to college attendance, it held equal importance with father's occupation, and further, that regardless of father's occupation, men and women enrolled in equal proportions if their mothers were college graduates. Another finding which also held true at all occupational levels, although to a lesser degree, was that two indices of cultural background distinguished between college and noncollege populations: the amount of serious reading done by the parents and the frequency with which the young people discussed world affairs with family and friends.

From the outset of the study, marked differences in parental encouragement and academic motivation distinguished those in the sample who went to college from those who did not. While still seniors in high school, over 57 per cent of the college-bound reported that a college education was extremely important to them, compared with 12 per cent of those with no college plans; only 29 per cent of those who reported a great deal of interest in college failed to attend. A question about parental encouragement yielded an equally dramatic difference: More than twice as many college attenders as nonattenders reported having been encouraged to enroll.

A striking relationship also was apparent between plans of peers with respect to college and the personal decision to attend: 84 per cent of the future nonattenders reported having no friends with college plans, whereas more than twice as many of the future college attenders as nonattenders reported that two or three of their closest friends were planning to continue formal education. However, since young people generally have friends who belong to their own subculture, this finding may simply have reflected another aspect of socioeconomic status, and thus, of parental influence and environment in general.

Differences in attitudes measured by the Omnibus Personality Inventory also distinguished those who entered college from those who did not. As assessed by the Omnibus Personality Inventory scales, personality traits which particularly distinguished the college group from others in the sample were: greater liking for reflective thinking and abstract ideas (Thinking Introversion); greater flexibility, cultural sophistication, and intellectual curiosity (Social Maturity); and a greater degree of objectivity, tolerance, and independence of thought (Nonauthoritarianism and Social Maturity). However, although these differences between the groups were statistically significant, they were not very large; much more notable was the finding that at the point of graduation from high school, the scores of this large sample of young people very markedly overlapped.

THOSE WHO WENT TO THE DIFFERENT TYPES OF COLLEGES

The type of college available in the community made the most difference to young people of high ability from low socioeconomic backgrounds, and least difference to their bright peers with high socioeconomic status: Fifty-three per cent of the academically able young people whose fathers worked at semiskilled or unskilled jobs went to college if their home communities had a junior college, but only 22 per cent of them went if their communities offered no public colleges; 82 per cent of the bright graduates whose fathers worked at a high ocupational level went to college regardless of what their communities offered.

The proportions of high school graduates who entered college from the various communities with different types of public colleges were: junior college, 53 per cent; state college, 47 per cent; multiple colleges, 44 per cent; extension center, 34 per cent; and no college, 33 per cent.

The majority of the college group (56 per cent) enrolled in local community colleges and public four-year and five-year colleges, and 21 per cent entered private colleges. Public universities attracted 17 per cent and private universities, 4 per cent. Students of all levels of ability were distributed through all types of colleges, but more students of high ability were found in public and private universities, and more students of low ability in public and private junior colleges.

Both measured attitudes and motivational factors distinguished students who entered various types of colleges, as they had between the college-bound and those with no college plans. Although no group could be said to have shown evidence of exceptional intellectual disposition, autonomy, or flexibility, two-year college students generally scored the lowest on these characteristics measured by the Thinking Introversion, Social Maturity, and Nonauthoritarianism scales, and university students, particularly those in private universities, the highest. The junior college group also included the smallest proportion, and the university students the largest proportion of college attenders who, as high school seniors had considered college "very important" (43 per cent and 74 per cent, respectively) and had discussed college plans with parents "quite a lot" (63 per cent and 80 per cent, respectively). The percentages for state college students on these items fell between those of the other college groups.

Once again, however, the delineation of differences between the graduates, in this instance differences in the types of colleges they entered, showed the strong influence of socioeconomic background. The fathers of almost half of the students in private universities and one-third of the students in private four-year and five-year colleges were at professional and managerial occupational levels, whereas the fathers of the majority of junior college students were in sales, clerical, skilled, and semiskilled classifications.

The findings of the College Attendance Study made it clear that the factors associated with college attendance are multiple, complex, and interrelated, and that these results, interesting in themselves, had many implications for further research on the development of young people in the first few years after high school. The major study reported in this book was planned to investigate and elucidate a number of those implications.

III

The Longitudinal Study, 1959-1963

The longitudinal investigation which is the subject of this report was stimulated by the realization that inherent in the findings of the College Attendance Study discussed in Chapter II lay questions which could best be answered with additional information about the original sample. Consequently, a study was planned to follow the seniors for four years after graduation from high school and to focus on testing not only the basic theory—that high school graduates develop differently according to their differing post high school pursuits—but also the general hypotheses derived from that theory (see Chapter I).

The longitudinal data were therefore primarily addressed to the following major issues and related questions raised by the earlier research:

1. Although many of the high school seniors did not know what they wanted to do after graduation, almost none conceived of themselves as semiskilled or unskilled workers, and the vocational preferences of many of the noncollege group were clearly unrealistic inasmuch as they were unattainable without further education. Yet the sample experienced no disproportionate amount of unemployment immediately after high school.

Did the relatively nominal rate of unemployment remain constant throughout the four years the subjects were studied?

How realistic and successful were the high school graduates in finding satisfying jobs?

How did the young adults, in their first testing of reality, reconcile their stated goals with what was available to them?

2. Although both high ability and socioeconomic status distinguished students who entered college from those who did not, a large proportion of students with high ability did not attend college.

What variety of pursuits did the high school graduates engage in during the first four years after graduation, and with what success? What personal, familial, and experiential factors characterized them?

3. The less-than-half of the sample which entered college immediately after high school had a high rate of persistence the first year, regardless of the type of college attended.

What was the progress and rate of persistence over the next three years of students who entered college immediately after high school and persisted at least through their first year?

What proportion of the sample entered college after 1959?

What was the progress and rate of persistence of the students who had delayed entering college or had entered part time?

4. Although subjects who entered college were distinguished somewhat from those who did not by a higher degree of personal development in terms of academic attitudes, tolerance, flexibility, and objectivity, the scores of the two groups markedly overlapped on Omnibus Personality Inventory measures of these traits.

Did the sample of young adults who were exposed to college for four years undergo greater personal development and change their values more than those who spent the time in the world of work?

What kind of post high school experience seems to contribute most to the development of the kind of intellectual awareness and autonomy needed in a rapidly changing and complex society?

5. Many of the young people revealed themselves as being

vague, uninformed, or unrealistic about their plans for jobs and careers.

Four years later, how did they evaluate their preparation in high school and college for the jobs they took?

What factors had proved most and least helpful in high school and college?

What different choices would they make if they could retrace their high school experience and the four subsequent years?

What roles did they see their families as having played in the decisions about college, jobs, and careers?

THE DESIGN

The study was designed to investigate the intellectual and nonintellectual development of high school graduates and to provide information about their patterns of college attendance and employment. The sample was followed up several times between 1960 and 1964. Late in 1961, a brief questionnaire, pretested on over 200 California high school graduates who were not part of the sample, was sent to those subjects known to have withdrawn from college, and to those who had not originally attended. The questionnaires were accompanied by a cover letter from their high schools, urging cooperation. Graduates who did not respond were sent a second questionnaire. Those who did not respond a second time were telephoned by their high schools, whenever possible. The educational, occupational, and marital status was thereby obtained for 93 per cent of the original sample who had withdrawn from college, or who had not entered in 1959.

In 1962, and again in 1963, academic records and transcripts were obtained for 99 per cent of the students known to have attended college, including those who had transferred. By 1962, the students in the original high school graduate sample had entered some 600 colleges and universities; by 1963, over 700.

In the fall of 1962 and 1963, over 500 subjects were interviewed. Every twentieth graduate from a list of the basic sample was arbitrarily chosen to be an interviewee. Unavailable candidates were substituted for by the next student on the sample roster who could be matched for sex, post high school pursuit in 1959, and high school origin.

The average interview lasted two hours, and consisted of

a structured but open-ended questionnaire which had been refined on the basis of two pre-test sessions with students at the
University of California who were not part of the research sample.
The graduates were asked to express ideas and feelings about:
family background; the purpose of education; high school, work,
college, and marital experiences; values, goals, and activities. In
these face-to-face interviews, the young adults told their stories
more comprehensively than would have been possible through a
paper-and-pencil questionnaire. And what they said provided
much of the basis for the questionnaire which was administered to
the entire sample the following spring.

Four years after the graduates were originally surveyed as
high school seniors, they were again asked to respond to a questionnaire and a personality inventory, which together took approximately two hours to complete. The instruments had been
refined after having been administered to an independent sample
of over 100 California junior college students. The questionnaire,
composed of nearly 100 items, repeated a number of pertinent
questions asked in the high school senior survey, and included a
number of new items designed to assess, on a broader base, the
areas probed in the interview protocols. The personality inventory included the same five attitude scales from the Omnibus
Personality Inventory originally administered in 1959, and five
additional scales from the Inventory which assessed traits of autonomy, readiness to express impulses and imagination, and social,
esthetic, and religious attitudes and interests. Repetition of identical questionnaire items and personality scales made possible direct
assessment of opinion and attitude changes between 1959 and
1963. Inclusion of additional items and scales permitted these
changes to be considered within a broad context of the young
adults' personal experiences and perceptions.

Efforts were made to get maximum response from the
sample. Letters urging cooperation were sent both by the high
schools and by the Center for the Study of Higher Education. The
instruments were administered by school officials in the more than
50 colleges which enrolled 10 or more of the sample, and colleges
in the original 16 communities even tested nonattenders. Nonrespondents were mailed a second set of instruments. During in-

terview trips, project staff members urged the cooperation of nonresponders by telephone.

Complete longitudinal data were obtained from nearly 50 per cent of the original sample; over 70 per cent of those still in college responded. Although a considerable percentage of both college and noncollege subjects responded in 1963, the college group was overrepresented among the respondents (Table 3). While no claim can be made that the longitudinal sample was necessarily representative of the original high school senior sample, it is known that the respondents were similar in the important personality and background characteristics to be discussed subsequently. (See page 103 and Appendix D for a comparison of the longitudinal and original samples.) However, one exception to the general similarity of the two groups should be noted from the beginning. The respondents, even those who did not attend college, had manifested more measured academic aptitude as high school seniors than those who did not respond in 1963. In any event, the very many who responded did at the least represent themselves, and it can be assumed that their opinions and attitudes were representative of those of their peers.

Table 3

REPRESENTATION IN ORIGINAL AND 1963 LONGITUDINAL SAMPLES OF
COLLEGE AND NONCOLLEGE RESPONDENTS

| | *Original* | | *Longitudinal* | |
	(N)	*Per cent*	*(N)*	*Per cent*
College	(4760)	49	(2809)	60
Noncollege	(5018)	51	(1863)	40
Total	(9778)	100	(4672)	100

Late in 1963, a postcard follow-up questionnaire was sent to those in the sample who had attended college, mainly to estimate the rate of entrance into graduate school and to record the beginning occupations of the college graduates. Another follow-up study, to be reported in a future publication, was conducted in 1964. From the two final follow-ups, information was obtained on the post college pursuits of 3,555 students, or approximately 75 per cent of those in the sample who had attended college at any point, and of over 90 per cent of those who had graduated from college by 1964.

For the most part, the analyses in the present study were made of the longitudinal sample of 4,673 high school graduates who responded both to the 1959 and 1963 research instruments, excluding the final postcard questionnaire. However, occasional analyses were made of the large returns from the earlier postcard questionnaires, and of the almost complete college records. It was thus possible to examine the vocational, educational, and personal progress of a large number of young adults during the four years following their graduation from high school. The chart that follows shows how and when the various groups under consideration were surveyed (Table 4).

The study first describes the working and college terrain entered by the subjects in the sample. The types of jobs they held, their progress in employment, and their rate of college entrance, transfer, and attrition are examined in order to establish the functional limits within which the subjects developed as young adults. Factors which distinguish college persisters and withdrawals are discussed, and subsequently the study focuses on the differential changes of attitudes and values of those in the sample who persisted in college for four years, those who withdrew from college, and those who did not attend. The primary groups compared are composed of the subjects consistently employed for four years after high school and those consistently in college during that period. The employed might be considered the control group and the college persisters the experimental group inasmuch as the relationship of college experience and working experience to personality development can be observed through the design of the study. The data presentation concludes with the subjects' evaluations of their post high school experiences.

AN OVERVIEW OF THE FINDINGS

Some of the major findings were that:

1. A very large proportion of able youth either did not attend college or withdrew before graduation.

2. Although college attendance and performance appeared to be related to native ability, socioeconomic background, and community educational opportunities, other factors singly and

Table 4

Date	Sources of Data	Number Contacted	Responses Received
Spring, 1959	Comprehensive questionnaire, five scales from the OPI, CAVD intelligence test, rank in high school senior class, and high school intelligence test scores converted to equivalent SCAT scores	10,755	10,755
Fall, 1959	Postcard questionnaire about the high school graduates' fall activities, including education, occupation, and residence	10,755	9,778 [a]
Summer, 1960	Programs and academic standing of those in sample who entered college, September, 1959, reported on special forms by college registrars	4,206	3,892
Winter, 1961– Summer, 1962	Postcard questionnaire about pursuits and activities of high school graduates known to have withdrawn from college (from college registrar data in 1960) and those who had not originally entered college	6,550	6,390
Fall, 1962– Spring, 1963	Interviews of representative sampling of the original sample, inquiring into work and college experiences, marriage, family background, and personal values	524	524
Summer, 1962– Fall, 1963	Academic records and transcripts of those enrolled in college, 1959–1963, obtained from college registrars	4,808	4,778
Spring, 1963	Comprehensive questionnaire and 10 scales from the OPI mailed to original sample	9,778	4,673
Winter, 1963– Fall, 1964	Postcard questionnaire about current pursuits and activities of those who had attended college	4,778	3,555

[a] Postcard return was actually 9,858, but the sample was reduced to 9,778 because there were subjects in the original sample who returned incomplete sets of instruments or who did not actually graduate from high school in June 1959.

interdependently associated with college attendance were: students' perceptions of their parents as emotionally supportive, alert, and interested in their progress; a view of education as worthwhile in itself rather than as utilitarian vocational training; academic motivation; personal autonomy and nonauthoritarianism; intellectual disposition; and the decision to attend college before high school.

3. Academic interest and motivation, instilled early in life, were related to college entrance and persistence, together with and independent of ability and socioeconomic status. And academic motivation and educational attainment were related to the development of flexibility and intellectuality.

4. The degree of intellectual and personal development varied with the degree of motivation to enter and persist in college. The longer students attended college, the more they showed a gain in autonomous, intellectual disposition. Young people not in college showed little and sometimes no discernible personality development, as measured by the instruments used. The least flexible, tolerant, and intellectually disposed individuals were found among high school graduates who never attended college, followed by college withdrawals.

5. Although many young people who did not attend college expressed themselves as satisfied with their lives and livelihoods, many more did not. Four years after high school, a large proportion remained dissatisfied with their vocations, and many showed a continuing lack of realism about their vocational plans. Although unemployment was not high at any one time, it affected many of the noncollege young adults at some time during the four years of the study. A great many of the noncollege men expressed regret that they had not entered college.

These findings have particular relevance to one of our major theses—that society will need a greater number of flexible, creative people with highly developed human potential and intellectual power. It has been observed that the educational system will have to assume a primary responsibility for fostering this kind of human development. If the data just summarized are representative of the situation at large, however, educational opportunity is clearly not yet equalized in the form of community facilities and social environment. Large numbers of society's ablest youths place little or no value on higher education and demonstrate few signs of intellectual or innovative behavior. Still larger numbers forfeit the opportunity to continue education beyond high school, and even those who do graduate from college exhibit too little of the kind of intellectual development and flexibility required in an age marked by so much change. Many young people betray ineptness in making basic decisions and assuming adult roles.

The challenge has always been to educate so that each individual could realize his own best potential. The goal has not changed, but new paths to its attainment are needed. The added challenge now is to discover how to prepare young people to live effectively in a world which is changing in their own lifetime. It is hoped that the study will provide information and offer some insight into those correlates of the educational experience which are related to the development of effective people in a demanding society.

IV

Patterns of
Employment

The fact that at present nearly half of the nation's high school graduates do not go to college raises many questions about what occupations they will be able to pursue. The same questions also apply to the many youths who start college but do not continue. Such issues are serious because of the ever-increasing complexity of today's occupational structure, which tends to place a premium on education for both vocational and personal competence.

Yet little is known about the kinds of jobs these youths with little or no college education find, or with what difficulties. There is also little information about how much they know about jobs, or to what extent they have access to work that is satisfying to them. The data in the present study provided an opportunity to inquire into these matters. Consequently, this chapter will trace a four-year "work history" (from 1959 to 1963) of the youths in the sample who were available for employment during the four-year period of the study. Generally, the sample includes both those who did not persist in college (withdrawals) and those who never entered college (nonattenders). However, several groups have been singled out in a number of analyses for purposes of comparison with the group which had no college training at all or with the group that withdrew: those who had some special post high school training, but not in an accredited college; those who elected a terminal program in a junior college; and those who entered military service.

Since these groups undertook different degrees and types of vocational training, the expectations were that this would be reflected in different patterns of employment. It was assumed, for example, that by 1963, four years after graduation from high school, those in the sample with some form of post high school training—even uncompleted—would be at a higher occupational level, or in a position to achieve a higher level, than those who had had no training after high school.

A final analysis group drawn from the larger sample of workers was composed of those who remained consistently employed during the period of the study and also responded to questionnaires both in 1959 and 1963. Data obtained from this longitudinal sample of full-time workers provided a basis for an examination of changes in employment during the first four years after high school.

A major premise of this study is that young adults who do not attend college are more restricted than college students in opportunities for vocational choice and the development of personality and self-identity. Data to follow relate to this hypothesis. Aspects of the limits within which high school graduates were free to develop and found employment are described, and their job choices and occupational status are compared with the occupational status in 1963 of youths who had some college experience.

It should be noted that much of the data presented in this chapter will be unique in the literature in this field, and it is hoped the findings will stimulate badly needed and more comprehensive research of a similar kind. Related research in the past has concentrated primarily on brief polls of high school graduates' vocational aspirations (Bradley, 1943; Heath, Maier, and Remmers, 1957; Lipset, Bendix, and Malm, 1955). There have been few longitudinal studies of high school graduates that follow them during the period in which they begin to assume their vocational identities.

Apart from Ginzberg and Super, Roe (1956), Tiedeman and O'Hara (1963), and Tyler (1961) are among those who have made important contributions to the construction of theories of vocational choice and development. Super and associates (1963), in particular, have begun to undertake empirical investigation of the validity of the theories, but mostly among small samples of college or college-bound students. In the past, the steps of small samples of high school graduates have been traced as they entered the adult world of work (see Byrns, 1939; Christensen, 1942). But no recent research is known to the authors which sheds light on current trends in employment patterns and follows broadly based samples of high school graduates with varying degrees of post high school education for several years.

The present study terminated before the employment patterns of the college graduates could be examined. But several basic questions, following from the premises of the study, were addressed to the data available on those who withdrew from college and those who never entered:

1. How did the high school graduates of various levels of ability and socioeconomic status distribute themselves among jobs (classified by primary activity and level of activity)?

2. To what extent did the graduates' jobs and occupational levels, during the four years of the study, conform with their original occupational plans?

3. Did the occupational experiences of college nonattenders differ from those who had attended for a time but withdrew?

4. To what extent were college nonattenders and withdrawals affected by unemployment?

5. To what extent was geographical mobility related to change in occupational status?

6. What was the relationship between post high school noncollegiate training, including military service, and the graduates' occupational level four years after high school?

7. At what income level were graduates working four years after high school, and what effect did marriage have on their employment and income?

8. Did differences between communities affect the graduates' job patterns?

OCCUPATIONAL CHOICE AND ATTAINMENT

The high school graduate who immediately goes to work does not have the benefit of the specialized training he could get in college, nor does he ordinarily have the benefit of a placement office which will make special efforts to find employment suitable to his interests, talents, and background, except for the United States Employment Services, or a comparable state agency.

More than half of the high school graduates in the original sample did not major in an applied subject which could lead to some specific job area. Fifty-two per cent of the women in this group had taken a commercial or other vocational curiculum; only 30 per cent of the noncollege men had majored in any type of vocational curriculum. The rest of this group had been either in general or college preparatory programs.

Many in the sample who did not attend college apparently finished high school without a clear notion of what they wanted to do. Over 40 per cent of these students, particularly the women, were unable, just prior to their high school graduation, to state a vocational choice of any kind, and most of those who did state a choice were vague or indicated unrealistic goals. For example, although in some instances the responses may have been somewhat recklessly made, approximately 15 per cent of the graduates who did not enter college during the course of the study nevertheless expressed a desire for a career that ordinarily would demand at least four years of college training; over 5 per cent of these students chose occupations that would call for a minimum of three years of graduate or professional school.

Lipset and associates (1955) found that while in high school, 47 per cent of their subjects who completed high school but not college reported no job plans, whereas only 13 per cent of those who became college graduates reported no plans. Sixteen years previously, Byrns (1939) found that of his large sample of Wisconsin high school seniors, 24 per cent of the men and 14 per cent of the women were undecided about their vocational choice. However, Byrns' study was done before World War II, when choices may have been less complex than they are in the mid-1960s, and this may account for the discrepancy between Byrns' finding and the 40 per cent and 47 per cent with no stated plans found in this study and Lipset and associates' research, respectively. Both Byrns and Bradley (1943) also found that unrealistic vocational choices were prevalent among the students in their samples. Students chose occupations apparently beyond their reach from the standpoint of their tested intelligence and job availability, and there was a great difference between stated vocational aspiration and attainment.

If jobs were not clearly anticipated by the youths in the present sample, neither were they reported as being easily obtainable, and this was true for college withdrawals as well as for those who never entered. Over 40 per cent of the men and 20 per cent of the women who did not enter or persist in college stated they had difficulties in finding a job they wanted; 13 per cent of them reported they had difficulty finding any job at all. Apparently this situation is not unique to the very young adults. Palmer (1954) found in his study of adults 25 years old or over in six cities that 23 per cent of the men and 37 per cent of the women held their jobs largely through "accidental circumstances." Nevertheless, all but 6 per cent of the men and 7 per cent of the women in the present sample who either did not enter college or entered and did not persist, were employed, in the military service, or in college by the September following their graduation from high school. Approximately 10 per cent of those who never entered college were unemployed at this time. Of those who remained unemployed, half had not been able to list a vocational choice three months before.

The general types of occupations held by the subjects both one year after their graduation from high school and four years after graduation are noted in Table 5, which compares the occupations of the subjects who had some college experience with the occupations of those who had none. Subjects referred to as having had "some college education" withdrew from college without obtaining a baccalaureate degree during the period of the study and were working by 1963.

Jobs were classified according to the systems devised by the U.S. Department of Labor (1965) and Roe, in her book *The Psychology of Occupations* (1956). Roe's classification system, which divides occupations into groups and levels within them, is emphasized here because it indicates not only the kind of activity and interest involved in an occupation, but also the degree of responsibility and skill required—factors left more vague in the grosser classification systems used by the Department of Labor and the Bureau of the Census.

Table 5

COLLEGE WITHDRAWALS AND NONATTENDERS BY OCCUPATIONAL
GROUP IN 1960 AND 1963, IN PERCENTAGES

Occupational group and college experience	*Men*		*Women*	
	1960	*1963*	*1960*	*1963*
Some college [a]	N = 173	N = 264	N = 241	N = 355
No college [a]	N = 284	N = 350	N = 824	N = 632
Service				
Some college	13	6	12	8
No college	7	5	14	12
Business sales				
Some college	12	12	8	4
No college	8	5	4	3
Organization				
Some college	20	28	66	59
No college	21	22	72	69
Technology				
Some college	49	48	4	2
No college	59	63	6	5
Outdoor				
Some college	5	1	0	0
No college	3	2	0	0
Science				
Some college	0	2	6	13
No college	0	1	3	10
General culture				
Some college	1	3	2	12
No college	1	2	1	1
Arts, entertainment				
Some college	0	0	2	2
No college	1	0	0	0

[a] Numbers vary according to the number of respondents employed full time at each time period.

Roe's book should be referred to directly for detailed examination of the rationale for her classification system. Following is a brief summary of her classification of occupational groups by primary focus on activity:

Occupation	Primary focus	Examples
1. Service	Serving, attending to personal needs and welfare of others	Guidance, social work, domestic and protection aid
2. Business contact	Face-to-face sale of commodities	Sales of products, real estate, or stocks
3. Organization	Organization and functioning of commercial and government activities	Managerial and white collar jobs, including clerical
4. Technology	Production, maintenance, transportation of commodities	Engineering, machine tooling, and transportation
5. Outdoor	Cultivation and preservation of crops, animals, natural resources	Agriculture, fishing, forestry, and mining
6. Science	Scientific theory and application other than technology	Medicine, pharmacology, laboratory assistance
7. General cultural	Preservation and transmission of the general cultural heritage	Education, journalism, jurisprudence
8. Arts and entertainment	Using special skills in creative arts and entertainment	Visual and performing arts

Table 5 includes all those in the responding sample who were employed either in 1960 or 1963, and shows the jobs held by the subjects grouped only according to Roe's classification, by primary focus of activity. Therefore, the numbers of individuals accounted for are different in the two time periods, reflecting the fact that many young people shifted to work from military service, unemployment, or college, or from work to marriage or some other activity.

The great majority of the men were in sales, business organization (most often as automotive parts men and stock clerks), and particularly low level technological jobs (usually related to factory manufacturing and production). Both in 1959 and 1963, half of the men with some college experience and a majority of the men who never attended college held technological jobs. These jobs, as described in the Census classification, frequently included operative occupations such as apprentice electricians and machine operators. Few subjects were in any kind of occupation related to conservation or artistic, general cultural, or scientific fields, even at semi- or unskilled levels. Even though the Service category is quite comprehensive in Roe's classification, and includes not only the more professional therapeutic, guidance, social work, and protective occupations, but also those of domestic, attendant, and food service, relatively few of the men held jobs in this category during the period covered by the study. Moreover, proportionately fewer working men held such jobs in 1963 than in 1960.

Proportionately more men with some college experience held a business-oriented job, and fewer were in the industrial trades compared with the men without any college experience. This was more the case by 1963 and does suggest that even a minimum of college education can affect an individual employment pattern. Otherwise, differences between the two groups of men appeared nominal. Indications are, therefore, that most jobs were in the industrial trades and business, in that order.

Proportionately more women than men held jobs in the general cultural and science areas. Again, this was more evident in 1963 than in 1960, and was almost exclusively true only of women who had had some college training. It can be assumed that most of the women who held jobs in the "General culture" area were those who had been given provisional credentials and teaching positions before obtaining a baccalaureate degree. Jobs within the field of Science presumably consisted mostly of laboratory and medical assistants. According to Roe's classification, the majority of all women held business Organization jobs, which are classified as Clerical or Kindred Work by the *Index of Occupations* used in the Census (U. S. Department of Commerce and Bureau of Census, 1960).

The "holding power" of the various occupational groups between 1959 and 1963 was indicated by data not shown here in table form. Of those who were employed full time in September, 1959, and remained consistently employed throughout the four years of the study, the majority of men worked in some area concerned with lower level Technology (to some extent, perhaps, because of the great availability of jobs in this field), and a greater proportion of men (83 per cent) remained in this occupational group than in any other. Three-fourths of the few men who entered Outdoor occupations also remained in this area, but the majority of men in all other groups had shifted to another occupational group by 1963, particularly the relatively few men who began with sales jobs (Business Contact). However, a large proportion (44 per cent) of the men who entered business Organization were still there in 1963.

The vast majority of women took a business organizational job, and only 8 per cent of them had shifted from this occupational group to another by 1963. Women in general changed their type of occupation less than the men, and only in the case of those few women who first took sales jobs, did a majority change to another occupational group.

The occupations listed by each subject during his first four-year work period were classified according to level of training, skill, and responsibility, as suggested by Roe.* Roe distinguishes six levels of occupations within each occupational group, from the highly professional, independent, and responsible (Level 1), through the semiprofessional and skilled (Levels 3 and 4, respectively), to the unskilled (Level 6). The classification system, summarized below, is based on "degree of responsibility, capacity, and skill."

1. *Professional and Managerial I.* Independent responsibility. Innovators, creators, high level administrators. Criteria: important, independent and varied responsibilities; policy making; education at the doctoral level or equivalent in talent and training.

2. *Professional and Managerial II.* Responsibility and independence required, but to a lesser degree than Professional I. Criteria: medium responsibility to self and others; policy interpretation; minimum education at the baccalaureate level or equivalent.

3. *Semiprofessional and Small Business.* Criteria: low level

---

* Assignment to each subject of an occupational level, using Roe's criteria, was made independently by five judges. The intraclass correlation between judges' assignments was .75.

responsibility for others; application of policy or determination for self only; high school education plus some post high school technical education or equivalent.

4. *Skilled.* Criteria: apprenticeship or other special training or experience.

5. *Semiskilled.* Criteria: some training required but less than for skilled occupation and with less demand for autonomy and initiative.

6. *Unskilled.* Criteria: little ability and no special training or initiative required.

Table 6 shows the occupational levels at which the non-college subjects worked, as reported in 1959 and 1963. Only those respondents who had no college experience and were in the labor force in 1959 are included in the table at both time periods. In this way, the patterns of progress over three years could be observed for the same individuals.

Among the men, the greatest shifts between 1959 and 1963 occurred at the semiprofessional and unskilled levels. The proportion of men employed at semiprofessional or equivalent levels increased from 6 per cent to 18 per cent; the proportion of unskilled men decreased from 19 per cent to 8 per cent. The proportions of men at the skilled and semiskilled levels were almost identical in 1959 and 1963. The increase of men in the semiprofessional group was particularly interesting since many of them, in order to qualify for jobs in this group, needed and evidently received some kind of special training. Forty per cent of the men and 5 per cent of the women who did not attend or persist in college reported obtaining their training "on the job." And a number of subjects who attended vocational schools could also have received on-the-job training for a semiprofessional job while working full time at a lower level.

The decrease in the number holding unskilled jobs is open to more than one explanation. It is known that many of the men consistently employed full time over the period of four years were promoted to another occupational level. But the explanation for the decrease in employment in unskilled jobs may also hinge on the fact that, as is commonly believed, such jobs are being displaced by automation. Further corroboration of this possibility was gained from data not shown in Table 6.

Table 6

OCCUPATIONAL LEVEL IN 1959 AND 1963 OF THOSE
CONSISTENTLY EMPLOYED, IN PERCENTAGES

| | Men (N = 193) | | Women (N = 294) | |
Occupational level	1959	1963	1959	1963
1 Highly professional and managerial	0	0	0	0
2 Professional and managerial	1	2	1	1
3 Semiprofessional	6	18	2	5
4 Skilled	35	34	41	50
5 Semiskilled	39	38	53	42
6 Unskilled	19	8	3	2

According to the Census system of occupational classification, less than 15 per cent of all working men in the sample were common laborers in 1960. By 1963, this proportion was reduced to approximately 7 per cent, even though the proportion of working men had increased by over one-third. This drop could be partially attributed to the young men who had entered the work force after 1960 with some training received in the military service or in college, and therefore did not start at an unskilled level of work. Nevertheless, in light of the evidence that preferred jobs were not readily available (Chapter IX), it is remarkable that the proportion with unskilled jobs was this much reduced by 1963. Few women reported holding unskilled jobs either in 1959 or 1963, and in 1959 very few men or women were engaged in Service, as classified by the Census system. Fewer still were Service workers by 1963: less than 3 per cent of the men and 7 per cent of the women. This situation was already observed on the basis of Roe's classification system, but perhaps is pointed up more specifically by the Census Service category which, for the most part, includes those lower level service occupations that are thought to absorb workers displaced by automation. The data did not demonstrate this trend in the present study. Evidently, young adults leaving unskilled occupations were not absorbed in Service occupations.

Apparently, the proportion of men moving upward from the unskilled level was almost paralleled by the proportion of men moving from the lower occupational levels to the semiprofessional. This might account for the similar proportions of workers at skilled and semiskilled levels between 1959 and 1963. Also, the few men (and women) who reported occupations coded at a professional or managerial level may have magnified the nature of their work. Such occupations usually demand a minimum of a bachelor's degree or the equivalent in training, and it is difficult to see how many of those who did not attend college could have received such on-the-job training.

The greatest shift in proportion of women workers occurred at those levels where the least shift took place among the men—the skilled and semiskilled levels. In 1963, fifty per cent of the women were at the skilled level compared with 41 per cent in 1959; the proportion of women at the semiskilled level declined from 53 to 42 per cent over this period of time.

The differences in distribution of workers at different levels of occupations between 1959 and 1963 were statistically significant for both sexes. Despite this statistical difference, most of the employed in the sample failed to raise their occupational level, and a substantial proportion were at a lower level in 1963 than in 1959. Thirty-nine per cent of the men and 26 per cent of the women obtained a higher occupational level over the four years; the largest proportion of both sexes remained at the same level, and 14 per cent of the men and 12 per cent of the women reported a lower level. Moreover, as seen in Table 7, advancement to a higher occupational level was achieved mostly by workers who began at the semiskilled and unskilled levels in 1959. Within the time period of this study, very little mobility was reported by those at the semiprofessional levels; by 1963, only one woman had advanced to another level, and no one at the semiprofessional levels in 1959 reported having advanced beyond jobs such as medical technician and engineering aide. None of the subjects was employed at the highly professional Level 1 by 1963.

At the skilled level, 28 per cent of the men and 5 per cent of the women reported an advancement. Over 40 per cent of the subjects reported advancement from the semiskilled level, Level 5; a majority advanced from the lowest level, Level 6.

Of the two occupational groups that employed the vast majority of the graduates, business Organization and Technology, the former included proportionately more men and women at the semiprofessional level at both time periods. In order to examine the careers of the same individuals in the same occupational group over the four-year period, only those subjects were included who reported having persisted throughout the four-year work history in the same occupational area.

Table 7

CHANGES IN OCCUPATIONAL LEVEL BY 1963 OF THE
CONSISTENTLY EMPLOYED, IN PERCENTAGES

Occupational level, 1959			*Change* Men				*Women*	
	(N)	Up	Same	Down	(N)	Up	Same	Down
1 Highly professional	(0)	0	0	0	(0)	0	0	0
2 Professional, managerial	(2)	0	50	50	(3)	0	0	100
3 Semiprofessional	(12)	0	67	33	(5)	20	40	40
4 Skilled	(67)	28	46	26	(121)	5	70	25
5 Semiskilled	(76)	44	51	5	(156)	40	59	1
6 Unskilled	(36)	67	33	0	(9)	55	45	0
Total	(193)	39	47	14	(294)	26	62	12

At neither time period did any of the subjects in the Technology group have a job at a level which called for semiprofessional training and responsibility; but 15 per cent of the men in business Organization did have jobs at this level in 1959, and 25 per cent with such jobs did in 1963. Although none of the men with business Organization jobs were ever at an unskilled level, 21 per cent of the men who persisted in technological jobs were at this low level in 1959, and 14 per cent were at this level four years later. The considerable majority of both groups of men were at the skilled and semiskilled levels at both time periods.

The distribution of the ten women in Technology remained the same at both time periods: nine were at the semiskilled level, and one at the unskilled level. Few of the women in business occupations ever reached a semiprofessional level, but 46 per cent were at the skilled level in 1959, and 59 per cent were at this level in 1963.

Not in table form are data showing that, of the youths who changed occupational groups by 1963, nearly one-third of the men were at the semiprofessional level or better, as were nearly one-fifth of the women. A major shift in occupational group evidently meant advancement for some, but indications were that occupational advancement as determined by Roe's levels was enjoyed by only a minority of the young workers over four years. Many could have advanced in this time, however, without reaching another level, and perhaps this is all that could be expected, in the first four years, of initiates in the work world with little or no vocational training.

Table 8

THE CONSISTENTLY EMPLOYED AND COLLEGE WITHDRAWALS BY
OCCUPATIONAL LEVEL IN 1963, IN PERCENTAGES

College experience	(N)	*Occupational level—1963*					
		1	2	3	4	5	6
Men							
Some college	(219)	0	8	19	37	28	8
No college	(181)	0	2	15	35	39	9
Women							
Some college	(297)	0	17	8	49	24	2
No college	(294)	0	1	5	50	42	2

Men: $X^2 = 10.67$, $p < .05$; Women: $X^2 = 55.79$, $p < .01$.

In a final assessment of the occupational advancement of these young workers four years after high school, it was apparent that their peers who had some college training before working had advanced more by 1963. This may be seen in Table 8, which compares the occupational levels of the working men and women who had attended college for some period before 1963, and those who had not. By this time, 27 per cent of the men who had had some college training were at the equivalent of a semiprofessional level or better, compared with 17 per cent of noncollege working men. Thirty-six per cent of the men who had some college experience were at the semi- and unskilled levels, compared with 48 per cent of the noncollege men. Among the women, 25 per cent with some college and 6 per cent with no college experience were at the semiprofessional level or better; these figures include a number of nurses and teachers who were given credentials and positions without the requisite training or a baccalaureate degree. Twenty-six per cent of the women with some college and 44 per cent of the women with no college experience were at semi- and unskilled occupational levels in 1963. The overall chi square treatment of the data, significant for both sexes, indicated greater differences in occupational level between the two groups of women than between the groups of men.*

There was little difference in the occupational levels of the two main occupational groups—business Organization and Technology—or between the group of workers who had some college education and the group that had none. Sixty-two per cent of the men in business Organization with some college were at semiprofessional and skilled levels (including 5 per cent coded at a professional level), compared with 64 per cent of the noncollege men; comparable figures in this group among the women were 65 and 59 per cent (with very few women in either case at a semi-professional level). Eight per cent of the men working in techno-logical areas who had attended college for some time were at a semiprofessional level or better; none of the noncollege men were. Fifty per cent of the men who had some college were at a skilled level, compared with 42 per cent of the noncollege men. Of the few women in Technology, none reached a semiprofessional level, but 57 per cent of the women who had some college training were at a skilled level, compared with 14 per cent of the noncollege women.

* Tests of statistical significance have been computed throughout when inferences have been drawn from *differences* between two or more groups on a particular variable. A difference significant at the 5 per cent level or better (p < .05) indicates that it could have occurred by chance only 5 out of 100 times at most; a difference at the 1 per cent level or better (p < .01) could have occurred by chance no more than 1 out of 100 times. Overall chi square analyses, used more than any other technique in the report, indicate the significance of the difference between the observed versus the expected frequencies (based on the law of probability) across the entire table. Ideally, any two cells compared for differences, or any two relationships (as between tables showing sexes separately), would be examined by further statistical treatment, especially where large numbers inordinately enhance the possibility of statistical significance. Because of the great amount of data considered in this volume, however, definitive statistical treatment of this kind was possible only in a limited number of cases. Therefore, many of the differences discussed are indicative, but not necessarily confirmed.

Although most of these differences were small, they indicated that the workers with even a minimum of college training achieved higher occupational levels, as a group, than did those who did not attend college at all. If this was the case within the period covered by the present study, the occupational levels of the two groups of youths might well have become even more disparate later, when the subjects who had taken out time for some college would have had more time to achieve higher job levels.

Even by the end of the study, the future vocational choices and attainments of these youths were, of course, still in question. However, certainly at the point of graduation, and even four years later, many of these young adults expressed hopes of following careers they could not feasibly realize, and were in fact not engaged in by 1963. This may be seen in Tables 9 and 10, which compare the actual occupations of the workers in 1963 with the occupations they expressed as their ultimate choice in 1959 and 1963. Table 9 shows the preferred and actual occupational groups of men and women college withdrawals and nonattenders; Table 10 shows their preferred and actual occupational levels.

Table 9

PREFERRED OCCUPATIONS AND ACTUAL EMPLOYMENT OF THE
CONSISTENTLY EMPLOYED, BY OCCUPATIONAL GROUP,
IN PERCENTAGES

Occupational groups	Men (N = 181)			Women (N = 294)		
	Choice (1959)	*Choice (1963)*	*Job (1963)*	*Choice (1959)*	*Choice (1963)*	*Job (1963)*
Service	3	4	4	7	3	8
Business contact	4	1	4	1	0	2
Organization	8	21	23	61	19	80
Technology	38	29	61	2	0	5
Outdoor	3	6	3	0	0	0
Arts, science	13	9	5	12	5	5
Unsure or unstated	31	30	0	17	73	0

Once again, only those subjects consistently employed throughout the duration of the study were studied. As has been observed, in 1963 most of the working men held nonprofessional technological jobs, and most women held business jobs. This was true as well for the subsample of consistently employed youths.

However, in 1959 only 38 per cent of the men had expressed a preference for technological jobs, a figure reduced to less than 30 per cent by 1963. A majority of the women had expressed a preference for business work in 1959, but only 19 per cent of these women repeated this preference in 1963. These data add to Lipset and associates' (1955) finding that a majority of their non-college respondents took jobs not as a result of informed choice, but on the basis of availability.

Nearly three-fourths of the women in 1963 failed to list an occupational preference, compared with 17 per cent four years before. By 1963 most working women may have had their hopes set on becoming housewives and mothers, a consideration which would not have been noted in Table 9.

Both in 1959 and 1963, approximately 30 per cent of the men failed to express an occupational choice—a large number to be so unsure of themselves four years after entering the world of employment. Comparatively few men or women chose cultural occupations in 1959 (science, general culture, teaching, and arts and entertainment). Fewer yet expressed this choice in 1963, and still fewer (at least among the men) reported holding jobs in this area in 1963. Service, sales, and outdoor jobs were relatively unpopular and unoccupied. More men expressed a choice for business Organization jobs in 1963 than in 1959; an additional proportion held such jobs by 1963.

Data not here in table form showed that: of the 69 men who preferred jobs in Technology in 1959, 80 per cent remained in this job area in 1963; fifty-seven per cent of the 14 men who preferred business Organization jobs held such jobs in 1963; and ninety per cent of the 180 women who early had preferred business Organization jobs, reported being in such jobs in 1963. Otherwise, a small minority of men and women in 1963 held the type of job for which they had expressed a preference in 1959. For example, only 1 of the 23 men and 7 of the 35 women who had expressed a preference for jobs in science, general culture, or arts and entertainment were actually working in these areas in 1963.

Many of the youths had not obtained jobs in the general areas they preferred by 1963, and as might be expected in this time period, even greater numbers of them had failed to reach the occupational levels they ultimately hoped to attain. In Table

10, it may be seen that 28 per cent of the consistently employed, noncollege men hoped for professional and semiprofessional occupations in 1959. This proportion increased to 38 per cent four years later, although only half of that proportion reported holding jobs at such levels by 1963, and most of these were at the semiprofessional Level 3. At the other extreme, only 8 per cent of the men expressed a preference for semi- and unskilled jobs (Levels 5 and 6) by 1963, even though nearly 50 per cent of the men held such jobs at that time.

Table 10

PREFERRED OCCUPATIONAL LEVEL AND ACTUAL EMPLOYMENT OF THE
CONSISTENTLY EMPLOYED, BY OCCUPATIONAL LEVEL,
IN PERCENTAGES

Occupational level	Men (N = 181)			Women (N = 294)		
	Choice (1959)	Choice (1963)	Job (1963)	Choice (1959)	Choice (1963)	Job (1963)
1 & 2. Highly professional, professional, and managerial	20	10	2	12	3	2
3. Semiprofessional	8	28	15	3	6	5
4. Skilled	34	23	35	39	13	15
5.–6. Semiskilled and unskilled	5	8	48	30	5	43
Unsure or unstated	33	31	0	17	73	0

Nearly 70 per cent of the working women expressed preferences for skilled, semiskilled, and unskilled jobs in 1959. This proportion was reduced to less than 20 per cent by 1963, even though 93 per cent of the women then held jobs at these levels. Fifteen per cent of the women preferred semiprofessional and professional occupations in 1959, compared with 9 per cent of the women who stated this preference in 1963, and the 7 per cent who actually held such jobs. It is known from additional data that only in the case of those few men and women who expressed a choice for semiskilled and unskilled jobs in 1963 did a majority hold the jobs of their choice.

At both time periods women were less prone than men to choose occupations of a professional nature. The 1963 data for the women are difficult to interpret, however, since so few of them listed an occupational choice. Nevertheless, whether the men or women were under consideration, whether the year was 1959 or 1963, whether occupational area or level was in question, a disparity existed between the occupational aspirations and attainments for a majority of the young adults. For many, any change in this situation would at the least necessitate much more time and training.

There is some indication that many of the young people were aware of their unfulfilled potential and goals. Long before the present study, Bradley (1943) and Byrns (1939) had found that the higher their subjects' intelligence, the higher were their vocational goals. It is evident from the much more current data in Table 11, which shows the relationship between level of ability and the level of vocational choice, that the problem of unfulfilled potential still exists. Ability level in Table 11 was determined on the basis of the original sample's ability test scores converted to equivalent School and College Ability Test scores. Students who scored in the uppermost 30 per cent of the sample's distribution were classified at the high ability level; in the middle 40 per cent of the distribution, at the middle ability level; and in the lowest 30 per cent, at the low ability level. This system provided a broad group of "average" ability and two groups distinctly above and below average in academic ability.*

A greater proportion of youths at the high level of ability, who could be expected to reach a professional occupational level (Levels 1 or 2), did express a desire to work at such levels. However, this was more true for employed college withdrawals than for nonattenders. Fifty-four per cent of the men and 68 per cent of the women withdrawals desired a profession, compared with 34 per cent of the men and 39 per cent of the women of high ability who did not enter college. At the low ability level, no less than 40 per cent of those who withdrew from college desired a profession, as did (combining figures) over 17 per cent of the noncollege subjects at the low ability level. The chi squares in Table 11 indicate a significant relationship between level of ability and occupational choice for both sexes regardless of college

---

* However, grossly categorical groups of this kind are likely to mask extensive ability differences related to other traits and behavior. Expediency prohibits the further refinement of classification, and therefore this system of ability differentiation is used throughout this report.

experience. Chi square tests also show statistically significant differences at each ability level when the occupational choices of the college withdrawals and the youths with no college experience are compared. On this basis, it is evident that both ability and post high school education are related to vocational aspiration.

Table 11

LEVEL OF OCCUPATIONAL CHOICE REPORTED IN 1963 BY COLLEGE WITHDRAWALS AND NONATTENDERS, BY ABILITY LEVEL, IN PERCENTAGES

Sex and ability level	*College experience and level of choice*								*Chi square—some college vs. no college*
	Some college				*No college*				
	(N)	1–2	3–4	5–6	(N)	1–2	3–4	5–6	
Men									
High	(160)	54	46	0	(123)	34	55	11	22.19 **
Middle	(141)	41	58	1	(164)	23	71	6	17.17 **
Low	(58)	40	53	7	(88)	19	62	19	10.27 **
(X^2—ability vs. occupational choice)		(16.86 **)				(17.11 **)			
Women									
High	(124)	68	31	1	(86)	39	48	13	24.23 **
Middle	(95)	58	40	2	(122)	33	51	16	19.80 **
Low	(45)	40	44	16	(71)	16	59	25	8.96 *
(X^2—ability vs. occupational choice)		(26.99 **)				(12.42 **)			

* $p < .05$.
** $p < .01$.

Different values and goals have traditionally been found to be related to socioeconomic status ("class," or social and economic position in society). Berelson and Steiner (1964), drawing heavily upon Ginzberg and associates (1951), concluded that lower class youths are much more restricted in occupational choice than upper class youths because of differences in education, expectations, awareness, need for immediate gratification, amount of advice, and the operation of chance. In this context they also quote a passage from an unpublished paper by Lazarsfeld:

The socially underprivileged young person has seen less, read less, heard about less, has experienced less variety in his environment in general, and is simply less aware of the world's possibilities than is the socially privileged young person [p. 404].

Other conclusions of Berelson and Steiner are: that only through college education can lower class youths avoid manual occupations; that, as Davidson and Anderson (1937) found, their first jobs are "prophetic" of their future careers; that the further they progress in school the less vocationally oriented their education becomes; and that the higher their level of education, the less fortuitously determined their occupations and the wider the range of their occupational opportunities.

Therefore, it was expected that the occupational aspirations of the high school graduates would be related to their level of socioeconomic status, just as their aspirations were related to their level of ability. To test this assumption, the occupational aspirations of the graduates classified at three levels of socioeconomic status were compared (Table 12).

Table 12

LEVEL OF OCCUPATIONAL CHOICE REPORTED IN 1963 BY COLLEGE
WITHDRAWALS AND NONATTENDERS, BY SOCIOECONOMIC LEVEL,
IN PERCENTAGES

Sex and socio- economic level	*College experience and level of choice*								*Chi square—*
	Some college				*No college*				*some college*
	(N)	1-2	3-4	5-6	(N)	1-2	3-4	5-6	*vs. no college*
Men									
High	(59)	51	49	0	(19)	31	69	0	2.15 +
Middle	(222)	46	53	1	(228)	25	64	11	29.87 **
Low	(56)	53	43	4	(104)	22	65	13	17.18 **
(X^2—SES vs. occupational choice)		(3.68 +)				(3.07 +)			
Women									
High	(43)	56	37	7	(20)	40	50	10	1.37 +
Middle	(166)	62	36	2	(173)	36	46	18	37.51 **
Low	(36)	42	50	8	(70)	27	59	14	2.56 +
(X^2—SES vs. occupational choice)		(8.66 +)				(3.89 +)			

+ p = not significant.
** p < .01.

In this report, socioeconomic status is based on father's occupation, one of the few best known single indicators of this variable (see Atherton, 1962; Berelson and Steiner, 1964; Gordon, 1958; Kahl, 1957; Warner, Meeker, and Eels, 1957). Students in the original sample whose fathers' occupations were reported to be professional or managerial and whose training required at least the equivalent of a baccalaureate degree were classified at a high socioeconomic level; students whose fathers' occupations were reported to be semiprofessional, lower white collar, or skilled were classified at the middle occupational level; students whose fathers' occupations were semiskilled or unskilled formed the low socioeconomic group. This grouping affords meaningful and convenient differentiation across the sample on an important variable. However, this system, as does the ability grouping, very likely masks many differences in socioeconomic status between individuals within each group.

The finding was contrary to expectations: there was no statistically significant relationship found between socioeconomic status and occupational choice for any of the groups. Although in general the youths at the high socioeconomic level did appear somewhat more disposed to prefer a professional occupation in 1963, it was evident that the relationship between socioeconomic status and vocational choice was nominal compared with the relationship between ability and vocational choice.

This is not to say that the arguments of Lazarsfeld (see Berelson and Steiner, 1964), Lipset and associates (1955), and others do not hold. It is probably true that more privileged youths are aware of more vocational opportunities, more motivated to gain them, and better able to prepare for them. The data in the present case may reflect vague, wishful, unrealistic thinking on the part of lower class high school graduates who would not or could not avail themselves of a college education. However, many of the bright college withdrawals from financially able families also seemed to have forfeited their opportunity to attain a profession, many of their peers of lesser ability evidently could not master the required material, even when given the opportunity, and over 10 per cent of the brightest noncollege youths chose a semiskilled or unskilled occupation, hardly commensurate with their ability. Thus many youths, out of lack of realism, squandered opportunity, or circumstance, no doubt will be disappointed. This disappointment may become especially acute for the brighter youths who failed to complete college. At the same time, many youths of all ability levels chose semiprofessional and skilled occupations, and these may offer them reasonable satisfaction and security for the future.

Vocational patterns are not marked only by choice or achievement of a certain occupational level. For many youths vocational progress is impeded by the impasse of unemployment. Among the subjects in the present sample who did not go to college, 11 per cent of the men and 9 per cent of the women were unemployed the fall following their June graduation from high school. These figures may be compared with the 5.3 per cent of the total labor force reported as unemployed in 1959 by the U. S. Bureau of the Census (1964). The graduates were then just entering the job market and were largely untrained for work. And, as previously noted, many of them reported difficulties finding jobs, especially the kind they wanted. Under these circumstances, at first glance the initial rate of their unemployment might be considered low; after 1959, no more than 3 per cent of the workers reported unemployment at any time interval that they were surveyed during the course of the study, compared with the 5.3 to 6.5 per cent of the entire labor force during the same periods (U. S. Bureau of the Census, 1964).

However, to note that only a very small proportion of the working subjects were unemployed at any one time obscures the fact that 22 per cent of the workers, including those with some college experience, were unemployed at some time during the course of the study. Proportionately more college nonattenders than college withdrawals experienced unemployment (24 versus 19 per cent, respectively). One interpretation might be that the training received in college made them more desirable employees. A second interpretation might be that those who went to college had less time in the labor market to feel the bite of unemployment. Also, more men than women who did not persist in college were unemployed at some time during the four years (25 per cent versus 15 per cent). Rate of unemployment was highest among the noncollege men: 34 per cent were unemployed sometime during the four years of the study. These men, like most of the other subjects, were generally unemployed between one month and one year; however, 4 per cent of the noncollege men were unemployed a total of more than one year.

Unemployment was also found to be more characteristic of the less able among the subjects. Although it became clear in interviews that the men of high academic aptitude who did not attend college very much resembled their less able peers in interests and attitudes, their work histories showed that the bright noncollege subjects were much more consistently employed than their classmates who in 1959 manifested less academic aptitude. In light of this observation, variables within the data collected for the longitudinal sample were then examined, to determine if a similar relationship between ability and consistency of employment existed for the entire sample (Table 13).

Table 13

COLLEGE WITHDRAWALS AND NONATTENDERS UNEMPLOYED AT ANY
TIME BETWEEN 1959 AND 1963, BY ABILITY LEVEL

	Men				*Women*		
	Some college	*No college*	*Chi*		*Some college*	*No college*	*Chi*
Ability level	*(N)* [a] %	*(N)* [a] %	*square*		*(N)* [a] %	*(N)* [a] %	*square some college vs. no college*
High	(213) 21	(161) 26	< .01		(296) 11	(340) 15	< .01
Middle	(197) 21	(256) 31	< .01		(251) 15	(535) 20	< .01
Low	(79) 21	(157) 40	< .01		(98) 22	(334) 25	< .01
(X^2 by ability)	(.006 +)	(7.50 *)			(8.56 *)	(10.88 **)	

[a] The numbers represent the longitudinal sample exclusive of those who persisted in college and those for whom ability scores were unavailable.

+ p = N.S.
* p < .05.
** p < .01.

There was no correspondence between level of ability and unemployment among the men who had had some college experience, but this relationship did exist for all other groups. For example, unemployment was reported by 26 per cent of the noncollege men at the high ability level, 31 per cent at the middle level, and 40 per cent at the low level. The data in Table 13 also suggest several other items for consideration. Even when the subjects were matched for level of ability as defined on page 56, those who had had some college experience consistently reported less unemployment than the noncollege subjects. Regardless of level of ability, proportionately more men than women reported having been unemployed.

The high rate of unemployment found among the non-college men of low ability suggests that it may become increasingly difficult for society to provide them with useful jobs. The changing nature of the work world demands specialized skills and by 1963, many fewer subjects than in 1959 reported holding jobs as unskilled common laborers (Table 6). Some may have been promoted to better jobs, but the figures also may have reflected the decreasing number of unskilled jobs in the labor market. However, although skilled jobs are both more in demand and more available than semiskilled jobs, they require the ability to learn a skill, and to be proficient, not always possible for the individual of limited intelligence.

The data also suggested a relationship between socioeconomic level and rate of unemployment, inasmuch as the smallest proportion of unemployed youths was at the high socioeconomic level, and the greatest proportion at the low level, regardless of any college experience. But again, this appeared to be paramount among the noncollege men; unemployment was reported by 19 per cent of these at the high socioeconomic level and 37 per cent at the low socioeconomic level. Moreover, for no group was a statistically significant relationship found between unemployment and socioeconomic level on the basis of the chi square treatments of the data, although significant differences in amount of unemployment did exist for both sexes between the college withdrawals and nonattenders at the middle socioeconomic level, and for the men alone, at the low socioeconomic level.

The statistics indicate that unemployment is more related to level of ability than to socioeconomic status. But were ability and socioeconomic status to be examined simultaneously in this context, interaction between the two variables might be expected, and it is therefore to be concluded that the association of the two variables with unemployment is not altogether clear. The rate of unemployment may be related to socioeconomic status to some extent, regardless of differences in ability. But what specific traits, attitudes, and opportunities are constituted in different levels of socioeconomic status, and what their relationship to amount of unemployment may be, was not discernible from these data. It is clear, however, that the prevalence of unemployment is widespread enough to limit vocational choices of many young adults, particularly those of low ability who do not attend college.

GEOGRAPHICAL AND OCCUPATIONAL MOBILITY

Considering the extent to which the youths shifted locations and jobs, there was less unemployment than might have been expected. The young adults in the sample in many respects illustrated a mobile America. The data as examined did not delineate the social mobility of the sample of high school graduates, but they did indicate their geographic and occupational mobility.

In 1963, of the 182,000,000 persons living in the United States, 19 per cent had given a different address the previous year (Popenoe, 1966). It is therefore interesting to note that within four years after graduation, 27 per cent of the men and 32 per cent of the women college withdrawals and nonattenders reported an address outside of the community in which they were originally surveyed. Twenty-three per cent of these youths reported addresses at least 30 miles beyond their high school communities, and another 14 per cent addresses outside of the state.

Differences in geographical mobility between the men and women were nominal, although the women with some college experience showed a relatively great amount of mobility. Thirty-seven per cent of these women listed addresses outside their high school communities, mostly 30 miles or more beyond that locale, possibly because they married men from other communities whom they had met in college.

During the course of the study, occupational mobility, or simply changing of jobs, was more prevalent than geographical mobility. A little over half of the men and women changed jobs at least once by 1963, and these were not merely title changes within the same type of occupation, but changes to jobs so different that they were given different Census classification codes. Only for women were statistically significant differences indicated in this respect between those who attended college but withdrew, and those who did not attend at all. However, men changed jobs proportionately more than women; nearly 15 per cent of the men made major changes in jobs three or more times within the four years.

Considering the amount of geographical movement found, and the possibility that many of the subjects might have to leave their hometowns to find jobs, it was hypothesized that the workers who were living more than 30 miles away from their high school communities by 1963 would report having worked in the largest number of different occupations, and would also have the highest rate of unemployment.

The high school graduates showed extensive geographical and occupational mobility, but there was little obvious relationship between their moves and job changes or unemployment. What relationship did exist between change of locale and number of job changes with any statistical significance at all pertained only to the women; the small differences found for the men were contrary to what had been expected. A statistically significant relationship was indicated, however, between geographical mobility and the proportion of men (but not women) who reported having been unemployed at any time between 1959 and 1963. Some of these findings may, of course, have been related to certain aspects of the different communities which are discussed later in this chapter.

The relationship between the number of times the subjects changed their occupations and their rate of unemployment was much more decided than the relationship between occupational change and geographical mobility or between geographical mobility and unemployment. As may be seen in Table 14, those men and women who changed jobs most frequently were also unemployed in greatest proportion. For instance, 21 per cent of the men who held only one job and 44 per cent of those who held three or more jobs during the first four years after their high school graduation reported having been unemployed at least once during that period. The subjects who had some college experience were combined with those who had none because in this context the groups resembled one another almost exactly. But the statistical differences in rate of unemployment between the various job categories were extensive for both sexes.

Table 14

COLLEGE WITHDRAWALS AND NONATTENDERS UNEMPLOYED AT ANY
TIME BETWEEN 1959 AND 1963, BY NUMBER OF
OCCUPATIONS HELD

Number of occupations	*Men*		*Women*	
	(N) [a]	*%*	*(N)* [a]	*%*
One	(348)	21	(790)	12
Two	(235)	27	(528)	19
Three or more	(266)	44	(350)	32
(Chi square)	(40.42 **)		(61.97 **)	

[a] Base N is composed of those who held a full-time job any time between 1959 and 1963.
** p < .01.

Lay-off's, job dissatisfaction, attempts at bettering one's situation, and marriage are plausible reasons for shifting occupations. In this instance, the reasons for changing jobs were not evident although it was clear that most youths in the employed group made at least one major change in occupation, and that a large proportion of them were also unemployed at some point.

It has been established that level of ability was related to unemployment, and that there was an apparent if not statistically confirmed relationship between socioeconomic status and rate of unemployment. This led to the hypothesis that the least able youths and those lowest in socioeconomic background would also be the most likely to change jobs. However, this did not prove to be true. It was also hypothesized that occupational mobility could be related not only to lack of available and permanent jobs, but also to the upward mobility of young people who aspired to jobs at higher levels than those they were originally able to find. And it was expected that those who in 1959 had expressed interest in relatively high level occupations would have changed jobs more by 1963 than their peers with less ambitious goals. No relationship was shown to exist, however, between occupational mobility and preferred level of occupation as defined in this chapter. Neither was any relationship found between number of job changes and level of occupation held in 1963. Frequency of job change was consistently related only to length of employment.

Whatever the aspirations of America's young adults, it is certain that for many military service represents an interim experience to be undertaken before they can begin to move toward ultimate personal and vocational goals. This was largely the case for the men in the present sample, even during the relatively peaceful lull between the Korean and Vietnam wars. By four years after graduation from high school, 46 per cent of the noncollege men and 36 per cent of the men who had withdrawn from college had entered military service.

Most of the noncollege men who entered military service did so soon after high school; over 60 per cent by December, 1959, and over 80 per cent within a year after graduation. Of the men who withdrew from college and entered military service, approximately one-third did so within the first year after high school, another third did so in the second year after high school, and the remainder in the third or fourth years after high school—the year of entry probably determined by the length of their stay in college.

Doubtless many of the graduates who entered military service received some special training applicable to later employment, and 23 per cent of the women and 17 per cent of the men who did not attend college reported getting training in some kind of special school other than a bona fide college. These included, for the most part, technical schools, beauty colleges, and business schools.

Table 15 shows the occupational levels of those subjects who were employed in 1963 and had undertaken various types of post high school training prior to that time. Only those subjects in the longitudinal sample were included whose educational and work histories were available throughout the duration of the study; the military service group was composed of men who had not been employed by December, 1959. Although the relationship suggested by the data in Table 15 between type of post high school training and subsequent occupational level is not direct or entirely consistent, those who attended special vocational schools (exclusive of the men who took vocational training in 1959) or who went to college for a limited period, apparently achieved, as a group, higher occupational levels than did those who had no special training.

Table 15

OCCUPATIONAL LEVELS OF THOSE EMPLOYED IN 1963, BY TYPE OF
POST HIGH SCHOOL TRAINING, IN PERCENTAGES

Post high school training	Men				Women			
	(N)	1–3	4	5–6	(N)	1–3	4	5–6
Began in military service [a]	(52)	23	21	56	(0)	0	0	0
Special school in 1959	(20)	10	45	45	(114)	42	36	22
Special school after 1959	(40)	28	35	37	(40)	13	48	39
Some college	(219)	27	37	36	(123)	13	59	28
No college or special school	(197)	13	32	55	(409)	5	46	49

[a] This group is composed exclusively of the high school graduates who entered military service by December, 1959, without any intervening employment.

Men: $X^2 = 29.60$, p < .02; Women: $X^2 = 177.07$, p < .01.

Among the men, those who entered military service were the only ones who, in 1963, were represented by a majority (56 per cent) at the semiskilled and unskilled occupational levels (Levels 5 and 6). Other than those with no training. However, their representation in the professional-semiprofessional category surpassed that of the men with no post high school training. Few men entered a special school immediately after high school, and those that did were the least represented at the semiprofessional or higher levels by 1963. Men who either attended special schools after 1959 or had some bona fide college experience were most represented at the more professional levels.

Among the women, those who entered special schools immediately after high school graduation in 1959 had the highest representation (42 per cent) at the semiprofessional and professional levels (mostly in nursing), with only 22 per cent at semiskilled or unskilled levels in 1963. Also at semiskilled and unskilled levels in 1963 were 28 per cent of the women who had had some college, 39 per cent who had attended special schools after 1959, and 49 per cent with no special training. Thirteen per cent of the women who entered special schools at some point after 1959 or attended college for a limited period, had jobs at semiprofessional or professional levels in 1963, compared with 5 per cent of the working women at this level who had had no special training.

That a limited period in college does not clearly bear on vocational preparation was seen in records of the 183 men in the sample who entered California junior colleges. Although these schools give special attention to sub-baccalaureate vocational education, and most of the California men in the sample did not transfer from their junior colleges, only 14 per cent of them were enrolled in non-baccalaureate programs, and only 15 per cent were reported by the colleges to have taken vocational programs. Even fewer of these students obtained an associate of arts degree or a certificate of completion in any curriculum.

Nevertheless, the men who had attended junior colleges attained occupational levels equivalent to those of men who had gone to special schools with specific vocational orientations, and the members of both these groups fared better occupationally than did those who either had no post high school training or training limited to what they got during military service. How much of this occupational pattern is attributable to selective ability, type of training, or specific circumstance goes unanswered at this time. But the implications of these data in the context of this report point to one more area for further investigation.

MARRIAGE AND MONEY

A primary adult role—and vocation—so far not discussed, is that of marriage. By 1963, marriage had become a fact of life for a majority of the women who either had not attended college, or had not persisted (62 per cent). Another 3 per cent of these women were divorced or separated by this time, and a few others had remarried. In 1963, of the 35 per cent who were unmarried, 14 per cent of the noncollege women were engaged or "going steady," and 21 per cent were single and unattached. The proportion of unmarried men among those who had not attended college or persisted (58 per cent) was large. Of the students who persisted in college, 16 per cent of the men and 15 per cent of the women were married.

A majority (54 per cent) of the married women were full-time housewives in 1963. Sixty-three per cent of the married women had at least one child, and of these mothers, 80 per cent were full-time housewives. (A majority of the divorced women also had children, but nearly three-fourths of these women were working.) Of the married women who did not yet have a child, 33 per cent were housewives. The evidence is, therefore, what one might anticipate. Although, according to the U. S. Department of Labor (1966), there has been an increasing proportion in the labor force of married women of the age group under consideration (approximately 35 per cent in 1965), relatively few of the women under study who had preschool children were working.

Eight per cent of the husbands of the employed married women were in the military service, 10 per cent were college students, 2 per cent were unemployed, and the remainder had jobs. These pursuits and percentages were essentially duplicated by the husbands of the full-time housewives in 1963. This finding was contrary to our expectations that working wives would be found to be compensating for lack of income from husbands either in college or unemployed.

Table 16

COLLEGE WITHDRAWALS AND NONATTENDERS BY INCOME
REPORTED IN 1963, IN PERCENTAGES

College experience	(N)	Less than $3,000	3,000– 4,999	5,000– 7,499	7,500 or more
Men					
Some college	(457)	48	29	18	5
No college	(548)	37	33	23	7
Women					
Some college	(590)	28	36	27	9
No college	(1138)	17	36	31	16

Men: $X^2 = 14.25$, p $< .01$; Women: $X^2 = 35.70$, p $< .01$.

In 1963, marriage existed on a stringent economic basis for many youths in the sample. The median family income reported in 1963 for the nation was $6,249 (U.S. Bureau of the Census, 1965); from the combined data in Table 16, the median income that year of those in the sample who did not persist in college was less than $4,250. Women reported a higher income than men, in part probably because more of them were married and shared a double income, or had older, well-established husbands. The young adults who never attended college also reported a higher income than did those with some college experience. But, as noted earlier, the noncollege subjects had had longer to work up the labor ladder and would therefore be more likely to report a higher income than those who had spent some time in college. Also, a greater proportion of them were married and had joint incomes. At the same time, it will be remembered that in 1963 the workers who had some college experience were, as a group, at a higher occupational level than the noncollege subjects.

In 1962, the minimum income reported as necessary for a "reasonable" standard of living for a family of four was $3,000 (*Congressional Quarterly Almanac*, 1964). The fact that 42 per cent of the men and 21 per cent of the women—most of whom were married and had children—reported a total income of less than $3,000 in 1963 indicates that young adults do not immediately enter the mainstream of affluent American living. The experiences of the many who earned less than $3,000 a year go unspecified at this time, but deserve further attention. It would be interesting, too, to examine the history of the relatively few who were earning a fairly good living by the fourth year after their high school graduation, to see how they had been able to manage their economic lives to such advantage.

COMMUNITY DIFFERENCES

Whatever the work history and vocational development of the youths during the first four years after they left high school, there was every indication that they varied from community to community, as illustrated in Table 17. The table shows the smallest and largest proportions of men from all the communities surveyed who pursued various post high school activities.

Although the data obtained were not meant to provide a systematic assessment of variations in employment patterns as related to community characteristics, they do suggest some clues. The highest proportions of men who reported being in military service in 1963 came from Port Huron, Michigan; South Bend, Indiana; and Altoona, Pennsylvania, in that order. The lowest proportions were men from Freeport, Illinois; Lorain, Ohio; and

Table 17

EMPLOYMENT PATTERNS OF MALE COLLEGE WITHDRAWALS AND
NONATTENDERS COMBINED, BY RANGE OF REPRESENTATION
IN COMMUNITIES STUDIED, IN PERCENTAGES

| | Community representation | |
| | Least | Greatest |
Employment pattern	*proportion*	*proportion*
In military service, 1963	11	39
Prof., tech. and kindred employment, 1963	0	14
In business Organization, 1963	4	26
In Technology, 1963	16	47
Left high school community by 1963	13	42
Changed jobs	30	58
Ever unemployed	6	51

Muncie, Indiana. The high percentage from Port Huron and Altoona might be explained by local economic problems and limited
employment opportunities in both cities. Major industries such
as the brass and ship works in Port Huron and the Pennsylvania
Railroad Carworks in Altoona had been radically cutting down in
production over the 10 years or so prior to 1963. South Bend was
undergoing a series of economic shifts caused by the tightening up
of its automotive industries and the eventual shut-down of the
Studebaker plant. The communities from which the smallest proportions of young men entered the service—Freeport, Lorain, and
Muncie—appeared to have fairly stable economies, although at
the time of the study Muncie was regarded by the Federal government as a depressed area. The lack of local colleges, considered a
possible factor in young men's decisions to enter the military
service, did not figure in these instances, since neither Lorain nor
Freeport had public colleges at the time of the study.

The highest percentages of professional workers in the
sample were in Joplin, Missouri; Lorain, Ohio; and Racine, Wisconsin. The lowest percentages were in Freeport, Illinois; San
Francisco, California; and Eau Claire, Wisconsin. At first glance,
this finding, especially as it related to San Francisco, where more
professional opportunities should be available, seems surprising.
But perhaps the higher percentage of professional people in the
relatively small and economically depressed communities can be

accounted for by a comparative lack of competition that would leave the lower level professions open to those with a minimum of post high school education. Some support for this theory was provided by the interviews with subjects in Altoona, where young women who had not completed their baccalaureate degrees had nevertheless been promoted into full-time teaching jobs. However, in communities such as San Francisco, where there are more educated people vying for positions, a greater premium may be placed on more highly educated people. In Eau Claire, which evidently cannot absorb its college graduates, a representative of the Chamber of Commerce pointed out that the ". . . high school graduate who doesn't go to college has more job opportunity here than the college graduate." In the Freeport Chamber of Commerce interview, it was also pointed out that the community lost many of its professional young people because it had few vocational opportunities to offer them.

San Francisco and Freeport employed the largest proportion of the youths in business organizations. San Francisco was the largest city in the sample, and noted for a great deal of industrial and financial activity which would call for a corresponding force of office workers. The highest percentages of technical workers were in Muncie and Hutchinson, Kansas. The reasons for this were not clearly suggested by the data.

The highest percentages of men who were still in their home communities four years after graduation were in Muncie, Racine, and San Francisco—all cities that seemed to offer fairly good job opportunities to young men on their way up. The lowest percentages were in Eau Claire, Wisconsin; Bakersfield, California; and Zanesville, Ohio. These communities appeared fairly restricted in occupational opportunities and the Chamber of Commerce representatives in these communities indicated that their college graduates went to the larger cities nearby. There was no accounting for the differences in proportion of women who had left their home communities, nor was it possible to explain the differences between the cities in number of job changes and amount of unemployment. But it was evident that community environment is yet another factor related to vocational development.

These data suggest that vocational steps are often taken in contexts which can highly restrict choices. Among the factors found to have bearing on vocational choice and development were community characteristics, educational opportunity, level of ability, and job availability. Much fluctuation was found in employment patterns. Many of the young people approached work in a vague and unrealistic manner and many worked at jobs different from what they would have chosen. By 1963, few had attained an income of much substance. A large proportion had left their high school communities and many had changed jobs, especially the large group that had experienced unemployment. Although unemployment at any single period was not great, viewed over the four years of the study it was seen to have affected an appreciable number, especially the noncollege men of relatively low academic aptitude.

Perhaps the most salient findings are that most men who did not have any college experience (and a great many who withdrew from college) were limited to factory types of jobs, that most women held clerical jobs, and that most of these young adults did not prefer these jobs but had not changed or improved them. Considering the confining nature of so many semiskilled and even skilled technical and clerical occupations, this situation does not suggest much opportunity for occupational role-testing, exploration of identity, or broadening of important potentials. Factors such as these deserve special attention in any consideration of the vocational and personal development of young adults, particularly of those who do not go to college.

V

Patterns of Flow
in College

The contribution a college education can make to the personal and career development of young adults makes it important to make inquiry into students' progress as it relates to patterns of college attendance. This chapter traces the educational mobility of those who entered college at any time during the four years subsequent to their graduation from high school. The variations, patterns, and flow of college attendance were examined, with focus on: 1) the rates of college entrance and persistence; 2) the patterns of withdrawal from college; 3) the incidence of transfer and the relative persistence of transfer students; 4) part-time and delayed college attendance; and 5) plans for graduate school attendance compared with actual attendance.

Description of the flow of students in and out of college is based almost entirely on complete records of youths who attended college at any time between 1959 and 1963, including those of students who did not return the various follow-up questionnaires. This was possible since college records were made available on over 99 per cent of the college students in the sample. Records were obtained from all the colleges the students were known to have attended, in addition to those from their college of origin.

If the fact of actual transfer was in doubt, all colleges were contacted to which students had their transcripts sent from their previous colleges.

Nationally, it was estimated that approximately 40 per cent of the 1959 high school graduating class would attend college, and there was no reason to expect that the present sample would depart from this norm. Previous research led to the expectation that half of the beginning college students would withdraw in four years and that the rate of persistence and achievement of baccalaureate degrees of students who did not transfer from their colleges of entrance would be higher than that of students transferring from two-year colleges (Hills, 1965; Summerskill, 1962). It was expected that this would be, particularly true in private colleges and universities, which are more likely than "open door" public institutions to recruit selected students for their high level of ability and academic motivation.

Without any evidence to go on, it was speculated that for financial reasons many of the youths would work for a short time before entering college and others would dispose of their military obligations before undertaking college studies. Therefore, it was hypothesized that there would be an influx of college attendance after a period of work, military service, and—for many—also a period of part-time college attendance. A majority of the college seniors were also expected to have plans to attend graduate school, in line with the plans of most college seniors since about 1959. There was no reason to assume, however, that these plans would be matched by actual graduate school attendance. No doubt many professional careers now require a minimum of a year or two of postgraduate training. Still, marriage, the need to work, military service, inadequate undergraduate college grades, weariness with college after four years, and the lack of motivation for serious graduate study seemed plausible reasons for not expecting a sudden surge to graduate school by the great majority of college graduates.

COLLEGE ENTRANCE

An overview of the sample's college entrance patterns between 1959 and 1963 may be seen in Table 18. Forty per cent of the sample entered a bona fide college full time in the September following high school graduation, compared with Cooper's (1960)

nationwide estimate of 42 per cent for 1959. Over 10 per cent
more men than women in the sample entered college. Three per
cent of the entire group entered part time immediately after high
school, another 2 per cent part time between 1960 and 1963, and
4 per cent full time after 1959.

Table 18

HIGH SCHOOL GRADUATES WHO ATTENDED COLLEGE FULL TIME AND
PART TIME, 1959–1963, IN PERCENTAGES

College entrance	Men (N = 4676)	Women (N = 5102)	Total (N = 9778)
Never attended	43	58	51
Full time, 1959	46	35	40
Part time, 1959	4	3	3
Full time, after 1959	5	3	4
Part time, after 1959	2	1	2

During the four years subsequent to high school, nearly
half of the graduates had some exposure to college, and almost all
of these students entered college the semester following their high
school graduation. Nearly 60 per cent of both men and women
students entered local colleges, and as would be expected, most
of them entered public institutions. However, over 20 per cent
entered private colleges, usually outside their communities, and
nearly 25 per cent entered public colleges outside their communities.

Table 19 shows the types of colleges the high school graduates entered directly out of high school. The colleges were classified according to educational level and administrative control as
defined in the *Education Directory* (U.S. Department of Health,
Education and Welfare, Office of Education, 1963). Of the public
institutions, two-year extension centers were distinguished from
community junior colleges, and four-year colleges from universities. Distinctions were also made between public and private institutions, and the latter were further classified according to
whether or not they were church-related.

Over half of the students entered public two-year colleges
and state colleges, in about equal proportions. Nearly 20 per cent
of the students enrolled in public universities, but only 6 per cent

Table 19

HIGH SCHOOL GRADUATES ENTERING COLLEGE FULL TIME, 1959, BY
TYPE OF COLLEGE, IN PERCENTAGES

Type of college	Men (N = 2136)	Women (N = 1777)	Total (N = 3913)
Two-year college			
Public	29	28	28
Extension center	8	4	6
Private	1	2	1
Four-year college			
Public	23	29	26
Church-related	10	13	11
Private nonsectarian	4	4	4
University			
Public	19	16	18
Church-related	3	2	3
Private nonsectarian	3	2	3

enrolled in university extension centers. This finding may reflect enrollment trends at large, but it may also be related to an artifact of the sampling in the forerunner to the present study. In that investigation, 25 per cent of the students in the sample were first surveyed in communities with junior colleges, and 25 per cent in communities with state colleges. Since it has been shown that students in communities with public junior colleges and four-year colleges enter college at a higher rate than do students in communities without such facilities, the figures in Table 19 may reflect response to educational opportunity, not only educational choice.

The largest proportion of students who entered private institutions chose church-related colleges. Six per cent of the students enrolled in private universities, both church-related and nonsectarian, in equal proportions. Combining figures, more than twice as many students entered private colleges as private universities.

RECORDS OF PERSISTENCE AND WITHDRAWAL

Data from the present study reflect the same tendency shown by Summerskill (1962) in his review of 35 studies which presented attrition rates in hundreds of colleges and universities since 1913. He concluded that, on the average, approximately half of the students who enter American colleges withdrew within four years, which corresponds with the data shown in Table 20. Another finding, however, departs from one of Summerskill's, which was that an average of 40 per cent of students who enter college receive degrees within four years. In the present sample, nearly half of the students who entered college full time in September, 1959, had withdrawn before June, 1963, and 23 per cent of the students remained in college for four years without obtaining their baccalaureate degree, leaving 28 per cent who obtained degrees within a conventional four-year period. Although the data presented in this chapter are based on precise records of a wide variety of students, it is unknown, at this point, whether or not the data indicate a changing trend in college patterns.

Table 20

EDUCATIONAL STATUS IN JUNE, 1963, OF STUDENTS WHO ENTERED
COLLEGE FULL TIME SEPTEMBER, 1959, IN PERCENTAGES

Sex	(N)	Bachelor's degree	In college; no degree	No longer in college
Men	(2136)	24	31	45
Women	(1777)	33	16	51
Total	(3913)	28	24	48

Table 20 shows that proportionately more men than women persisted in college for four years, but proportionately more women than men obtained their degrees in this time. While one-third of the women obtained degrees as against slightly less than one-fourth of the men, nearly twice as many men as women remained in college consistently without obtaining a degree within a conventional four-year period (31 per cent versus 16 per cent, respectively).

Demos (1961) has deplored the fact that high school students are encouraged to believe the myth that only those deficient in academic aptitude should take more than four years to obtain a baccalaureate degree. There are, of course, many reasons which have nothing to do with ability for stretching college studies beyond four years. Common reasons may be assumed to be the need to finance one's own education, delay occasioned by changing majors as the result of discovering one's interests or "identity," and personal problems. This is not to say, however, that many college students do not also terminate or delay their education out of lack of ability or motivation. For whatever reasons, the data in the present study indicate not only the expected and considerable attrition, but also a widespread tendency, among those who persist in college for four years, to take more than four years to get a degree. Under the circumstances, Demos' recommendation, that counselors suggest a "stretch-out" approach for certain students, may have merit. At least, many students might then be prepared for the eventuality that their college career might be prolonged beyond their initial expectations.

Table 21

EDUCATIONAL STATUS IN JUNE, 1963, OF STUDENTS WHO ENTERED
DIFFERENT TYPES OF COLLEGES FULL TIME
SEPTEMBER, 1959, IN PERCENTAGES

Type of college entered in 1959	*(N)*	*Bachelor's degree*	*In college; no degree*	*No longer in college*
Two-year college				
Public	(1104)	11	22	67
Extension center	(241)	17	29	54
Private	(58)	21	12	67
Four-year college				
Public	(1000)	27	23	50
Church-related	(446)	48	20	32
Private nonsectarian	(167)	44	22	34
University				
Public	(694)	36	30	34
Church-related	(103)	58	24	18
Private nonsectarian	(100)	52	25	23

There were also differences in rate of persistence and attainment of degrees among students who attended different types of colleges (Table 21). The highest proportion of students who received degrees within four years after graduation from high school were those who had entered church-related universities (58 per cent). Of the students who entered public universities, 36 per cent graduated in four years and 34 per cent withdrew within that period. Of the students who enrolled in public four-year colleges, a little over one-fourth obtained degrees in four years and one-half withdrew. Combining figures, 49 per cent of the students who entered private four-year colleges and universities obtained baccalaureate degrees, and only 30 per cent withdrew within four years. Students who entered two-year colleges had the lowest persistence rates of any of these groups; those in public four-year colleges had the second lowest.

Relatively few students attended private nonsectarian or church-related colleges and universities, but compared with students in public institutions, their performance records were high: They remained in college for four years and obtained their degrees in this time in greater proportion than the other students. It is known from the previous report on this sample that, compared with other students, the students who entered private colleges were higher in academic aptitude and socioeconomic status, and generally manifested greater interest in college and working with ideas (see Medsker and Trent, 1965).

In addition, inasmuch as they entered a special kind of college, they showed a special interest. They may also have had more need to finish college "on schedule," since to prolong education in a private college is costly. These differences, both observed and conjectured, in ability, background, and disposition, although not great in all cases, may be enough to account for the differences in performance. Without controlling for such key factors as ability and socioeconomic status, it cannot be said that the experiences offered in different types of colleges were related to the observed differences in performance. Considering the advantages with which the students in private institutions came to college, it might even be argued that their records should have been better than they were. Additional research is needed to learn whether or not this is true. What is known at this point is that students grouped by type of college entered differed in important characteristics and in their subsequent performance, as determined by the criteria of persistence and completion of a baccalaureate degree.

As could be anticipated in view of the terminal function of two-year colleges and the limited goals of many of the students who enter them, students who enrolled in junior colleges and extension centers, either public or private, obtained the lowest proportion of bachelor's degrees within four years (12 per cent) and had the highest rate of attrition.

The rate of withdrawal from college varied widely with the type of college entered in 1959, but attrition was high for the total group of entering students, regardless of type of college entered. In their previous study of college attendance, the authors noted that 83 per cent of the students who entered college in 1959 remained through their first year, showing a first-year attrition rate of only 17 per cent. Since the attrition rate was as high as 48 per cent by 1963, however, it was suspected and proved to be true that a very large proportion of students did not return to college for a second year.

Although the College Attendance Study had shown persistence to be high the first year in college, 49 per cent of the withdrawals first left college before their second year of studies, 30 per cent withdrew before their third year, 17 per cent before their fourth year, and 4 per cent during the fourth year. Although withdrawal was not necessarily a one-time event, it tended to be permanent within the time limits of the present study. Fourteen per cent of the men and 10 per cent of the women withdrew from college twice or more within four years, but only a little over 10 per cent who withdrew were re-enrolled by June, 1963. From the interviews with the representative sample of these youths, it was evident that, although many of the withdrawals wanted to return to college, most of those who did indicate a desire to return expressed no hope of doing so in the foreseeable future.

Jex and Merrill (1962), in their consideration of persistence rates of students at the University of Utah, take an optimistic view toward attrition. Their conclusion is that since World War II, the "dropout" pattern of higher education has shifted to one of "interruption." In several instances, this optimism has been demonstrated as warranted. Eckland's (1964) 10-year follow-up of the men in the 1952 freshman class at the University of Illinois revealed that approximately 50 per cent of the class obtained degrees after a period of uninterrupted attendance, and only 33 per cent received degrees within four years. Within 10 years, however, 70 per cent of the class had obtained baccalaureate degrees. This proportion is appreciably higher than the 59 per cent of the 1950 nationwide class that Iffert (1957) projected, on the basis of his four-year follow-up of dropouts, would ultimately graduate. In Eckland's study of the 594 students who withdrew before graduation, approximately 55 per cent obtained degrees. This figure does not include an additional 10 per cent of these students who were on the verge of graduating as the study terminated. Much the same situation was reported for the entering class of 1955, at Pennsylvania State University (Ford and Urban, 1965) and for the entering class of 1961, at the University of California (Suczek and Alfert, 1966).

Jex and Merrill (1962) reported a 13-year follow-up of the freshman class which entered the University of Utah four years prior to the Illinois class studied by Eckland. Only 20 per cent of the class graduated on schedule; 45 per cent graduated from the university within 13 years, and an estimated additional 15 per cent graduated from some college. The known figure of 45 per cent is over twice that of the proportion of students who graduated within four years, and is enough to justify the contention that—at least for many students—withdrawal constitutes an interruption rather than a termination of college studies. But it does not indicate that college entrants eventually complete their studies to the extent indicated by Eckland's (1964) study. Nor is the fate of dropouts revealed by the Jex-Merrill data since no distinction is made between transfer students and actual withdrawals other than by interpolated figures based on estimates rather than follow-up.

The differences in the findings of the studies may be related to the different periods during which students entered college. Since the Utah students had three more years than the Illinois students in which to get their degrees, they may have reflected differences in opportunity or motivation more characteristic of that age group. On the other hand, the University of Illinois, a major public university of particularly good academic reputation, may have attracted students of exceptional motivation and aptitude, who would be likely to return to college after an interruption. This was probably the case when Illinois students were compared with students in general at the time, even if entering students at the University of Illinois are now more select than they were 15 years ago. It is indicative that today freshmen at major universities are generally drawn from the upper ranks of their high school graduating class. This was certainly true of the

University of California students studied by Suczek and Alfert, and the contemporary Pennsylvania students were, no doubt, also relatively select.

However, since Eckland, Ford, and Urban, and Suczek and Alfert dealt with students at relatively select and large universities, their research included neither four-year colleges nor two-year colleges, which are enrolling increasingly greater proportions of the nation's lower division students. As a group, two-year college students are less academically oriented than other college students, and it is possible that the academic fatality of withdrawals from two-year colleges is greater than that of withdrawals from four-year colleges and especially from universities.

The present study is based on a contemporary and broadly based sample. It includes a large number of entering junior college students and makes a careful distinction between actual withdrawals from college and transfer students who, as will be shown, performed much differently from the withdrawals. Within the limits of a four-year follow-up, therefore, the data at hand indicate that the record of the University of Utah students is representative of the situation at large. Here again, the findings regarding proportions of students at different kinds of colleges who obtain their degrees cannot be resolved without additional research based on a long-term follow-up of a large representative national sample of college students.

However, attrition figures in general cannot categorically be regarded as a sign of student mortality. Although a number of the high school seniors indicated that they did not intend to complete a four-year college program, their withdrawal need not always be interpreted as failure to achieve educational goals. The students' stated educational purposes are matched with their subsequent persistence in college in Table 22.

Educational status in 1963 is shown for those students who, prior to entering college, had planned a two-year program or a four-year program, or had been undecided or unspecific about their intentions. Of the men who originally planned to attend college for four years, 62 per cent persisted that length of time; of those who had left their plans unstated in 1959, forty-eight per cent of the men persisted; and of the men who had originally reported planning on a two-year program, 32 per cent persisted for

Table 22

COLLEGE PLANS REPORTED IN 1959, COMPARED WITH EDUCATIONAL
STATUS IN JUNE, 1963, IN PERCENTAGES

		In college			No longer in college		
Plans	(N)	Bach-elor's degree	No Bach-elor's degree	A.A.	Cer-tifi-cated	2 yrs. or more com-pleted	Less than 2 yrs. com-pleted
Men							
2-year program	(284)	7	25	9	4	20	35
4-year program	(1328)	28	34	2	0	16	20
Undecided a	(524)	22	26	2	0	19	31
Women							
2-year program	(210)	7	9	9	7	17	51
4-year program	(1127)	39	16	3	1	15	26
Undecided a	(440)	31	18	4	1	16	30

a Number of "undecided" responses includes the few who gave no answer.

four years. Thirty-two per cent of the men who had either planned
a two-year program or did not state any plans, failed to complete
two years of college. Associate of arts degrees and certificates of
completion were obtained by only 13 per cent of the men who had
planned to complete a two-year program, and by only 2 per cent
of the other men in the sample.

Of the women who had planned a two-year program, 16
per cent persisted in college four years, but half of them withdrew before completing two years. A slight majority of women
(53 per cent) who had planned to complete a four-year program
remained in college through 1963. This was 7 per cent less than
the proportion of men who achieved this stated goal. However,
proportionately more women than men who had been undecided
about their plans in 1959 got baccalaureate degrees (31 per cent
and 22 per cent, respectively). Although persistence seemed clearly
related to a student's original educational intent, the relationship
between them was far from perfect. During the four-year follow-
up period, it became apparent that there was a decided discrep-

ancy between educational plans and their accomplishment. At the same time, the young people who from the outset indicated a strong intention to persist in college were the ones most likely to realize their plans. This early show of incentive suggests a degree of motivation possibly not shared by the others.

THE TRANSFER STUDENT

Transfer students represent another important pattern in flow through college. Transferring from one institution to another has become common both in two-year and four-year colleges. Furthermore, since in many regions two-year colleges are assuming a major responsibility for lower division education, the incidence of transfers from two-year to four-year institutions is likely to increase.

Among the students in the present sample who entered college full time in 1959, twenty-eight per cent changed institutions at least once, and 5 per cent changed twice or more. As might be expected, the percentage of transfers from two-year colleges was greatest—54 per cent from university extension centers and 42 per cent from all other two-year colleges. Thirty-five per cent of all university students and 23 per cent of all four-year college students who entered either public or private institutions transferred. Of the students who entered four-year state colleges full time, 15 per cent transferred to other colleges.

The data indicate a somewhat greater rate of transfer from two-year to four-year institutions since Medsker (1960) surveyed a large sample in 1956. The data in the present study do not confirm a growing tendency to transfer from two-year colleges, however, since another study of Medsker's now underway shows that proportionately slightly fewer students transferred between 1961 and 1965 than in 1956. It is also clear that a large proportion of four-year college and university students also transfer, with the university students transferring in greater proportion than the college students. On the other hand, although very few university extension centers—in contrast to junior colleges—emphasize self-contained two-year terminal curricula, 46 per cent of the students in extension centers did not transfer and thus became, in effect, "terminal" students.

The data, relating only to students who attended college

full time consistently throughout the four years after graduation from high school, suggest a tendency for students to transfer from a given type of institution to one of a similar nature. Students who entered public institutions gravitated almost exclusively to other public institutions, and the largest proportion of students who transferred from universities continued in a university. However, by 1963, fifty per cent of the students who had entered private nonsectarian colleges were in public institutions, as were nearly half of the students originally in denominational colleges, who were in 1963 equally divided between public colleges and universities. Thirty-seven per cent of the students who transferred from private, church-related or nondenominational colleges were enrolled in these same types of colleges in 1963. Of the students who transferred from state colleges, a large proportion (41 per cent) were in public universities by 1963. Less than 10 per cent of transfers from all private four-year colleges were in both types of private universities by 1963.

Of the students who transferred from public junior colleges and were still in college in 1963, ten per cent were still attending some type of two-year college in 1963. Eleven per cent of those students who originally transferred from state colleges were attending two-year colleges in 1963, as were 10 per cent of those students who originally transferred from a public university. These proportions are relatively small, but large enough to indicate that students not only transfer from one two-year college to another, but also from four-year colleges and universities to two-year colleges.

The reasons for transferring from a four-year to a two-year college were not investigated, but the necessity to reduce either costs or academic difficulties might be involved. As data to follow show, transferring in general extends the period needed to complete college, and "reverse" transferring, from a four-year to a two-year college, may be responsible for even further extension of this period. Consequently, it is worth looking into the reasons for "deviant" transfer patterns and their results.

Transfer students showed a propensity for persisting in college; relatively few withdrew within their first two years. Less than 10 per cent of the students who transferred failed to complete two years of college, whereas nearly 40 per cent of the students who did not transfer failed to complete two years of college. Over-all, 70 per cent of the transfer students remained in college through 1963, and only 7 per cent withdrew before completing two years of college.

Proportionately more of the students who transferred at least twice persisted in college than did the students who trans-ferred once or not at all. Only a negligible number of multiple-transfer students failed to complete two years of college, and 9 per cent more of these students than those who transferred only once remained in college four years.

Table 23

EDUCATIONAL STATUS IN 1963 OF NATIVE AND TRANSFER STUDENTS
WHO PERSISTED AT LEAST TWO YEARS BY TYPE OF COLLEGE
LAST ATTENDED, IN PERCENTAGES

Type of college last attended	(N)	Bachelor's degree	In college; no degree	No longer in college
Four-year college				
Public				
Native	(529)	45	33	22
Transfer	(363)	22	56	22
Church-related				
Native	(236)	67	17	16
Transfer	(135)	41	36	24
Private nonsectarian				
Native	(72)	60	16	24
Transfer	(51)	41	45	14
University				
Public				
Native	(367)	53	29	18
Transfer	(449)	38	40	22
Church-related				
Native	(72)	71	21	8
Transfer	(32)	50	38	12
Private nonsectarian				
Native	(58)	71	17	12
Transfer	(37)	38	48	14
Total colleges				
Native	(1334)	55	26	19
Transfer	(1067)	33	45	22

The greatest proportion of withdrawals were students who neither transferred nor completed two years of college. But once the factor of early withdrawal was eliminated, the rate of persistence of the native and transfer students was essentially the same. As may be seen in Table 23, 3 per cent more native students than transfers with at least two years of college, persisted for four years. Table 23 compares, by type of four-year college or university last attended, persistence records in 1963 of native students with at least two years who transferred from two-year or four-year colleges. Those who had less than two years of college or remained in a two-year college or had transferred to one were eliminated from the analysis.

However, it is also evident in Table 23 that a majority of the persisting native students, 22 per cent more than the transfer students, obtained degrees in four years. The differences between the two groups varied by type of institution, from 15 per cent in public universities to 33 per cent in private nonsectarian universities. One implication of this finding is that it may take transfers more time to fulfill requirements in some types of institutions than in others. But regardless of type of institution, it is evident that transferring is more a matter of extending the time it takes to graduate than a matter of attrition. It is also obvious that a large proportion of transfer students were included in the nearly 50 per cent of the persisters who took more than four years to graduate from college.

Data presented earlier in Table 21 indicated that the smallest proportion of students in four-year colleges to receive degrees were those in state colleges, and data in Table 23 show that this was true for transfers to state colleges as well as for native persisters in these colleges. Of all types of four-year colleges or universities, state colleges graduated the smallest proportion of transfer students (22 per cent within four years). Compared with all other students, the largest proportion of students who received baccalaureate degrees in four years (71 per cent) were native students in private sectarian and nonsectarian universities. Of all transfer students, those relatively few students who transferred to church-related universities received their bachelor's degrees in greatest proportion (50 per cent). The comparatively superior record of the private college transfers may be related to the economic and academic advantages noted previously for private college students in general.

Differences in persistence between native and transfer

students are shown more specifically in Table 24. The following analysis is of full-time students who had attended college for at least one semester more than two years; a majority of these were presumed to have reached junior standing. Educational status in 1963 is here based on a comparison of native students and transfer students (excluding transfers from four-year colleges or universities) who had entered either a junior college or extension center in 1959 and transferred at any time up to 1963.

Table 24

EDUCATIONAL STATUS IN 1963 OF FULL-TIME NATIVE STUDENTS AND
TRANSFERS FROM TWO-YEAR COLLEGES WHO PERSISTED MORE
THAN TWO YEARS, IN PERCENTAGES [a]

Student group	(N)	Bachelor's degree	In college; no degree	Did not complete college
Native	(1214)	59	29	12
Transfers from junior colleges	(397)	33	46	21
Transfers from extension centers	(113)	33	50	17

[a] Chi square = 102.2, $p < .01$. Z ratio, no longer in college, junior college transfers vs. natives = 4.00, $p < .01$; extension center transfers vs. natives = 1.37, p = not significant.

Many of the data shown in Table 24 resembled those reported in the previous table. Nearly 60 per cent of the native students who attended college more than two years completed work toward a degree by 1963, in contrast to 33 per cent of the transfers from two-year colleges. However, the attrition rate was significantly higher among the transfers from junior colleges even though they all attended college for at least two and one-half years. Twelve per cent of the native students dropped out some time after two and one-half years of college, compared with 21 per cent of the transfers from junior colleges and 17 per cent of the transfers from extension centers who withdrew after this time. The records of junior college and extension center transfer students were similar: the attrition rate of junior college transfers who attended college for more than two years was only 4 per cent higher than that of transfers from extension centers.

The data point to the probability that the records of transfers from four-year colleges and universities differ from those of transfers from two-year colleges. When transfers as a whole were considered, they differed only nominally from native students in rate of attrition. But when the two-year college transfers were considered separately, they not only took longer than native students to obtain baccalaureate degrees, they also withdrew from college after two and one-half years in somewhat greater proportion. The differences found in rates of attrition and college completion between two-year college transfers and four-year college and university native students confirm the findings of numerous earlier and contemporary studies reviewed by Hills (1965).

UNCONVENTIONAL COLLEGE ATTENDANCE

Patterns of college attendance may reflect important aspects of decision-making on the part of young adults. In view of the large number of high school graduates in the present sample who did not attend college full time or who did not enter college at all, questions arise about whether any of them did eventually enter college after a period of work, and also whether part-time students became more deeply involved with college studies and shifted to full-time programs.

Through college records and a follow-up questionnaire, contact was maintained with the small proportions of students who entered college part time in 1959, and on any basis after 1959. Their rate of attrition was found to be high. Three per cent of the entire sample had entered college part time in 1959. By 1963, eighty-four per cent of the original part-time students had dropped out of college altogether, 7 per cent remained in college part time, and only 9 per cent were in college on a full-time basis. Six per cent of the entire sample entered college after 1959, one-third of them part time. Of the full-time students who entered college after September, 1959, over 75 per cent enrolled before the end of the second year after high school, 17 per cent during the third year following high school, and 6 per cent still later. The vast majority of graduates who entered colleges did so upon graduation from high school, and the numbers of college enrollees gradually diminished over the next few years. No great post-military or post-employment influx into college was observed during the four years under study.

The few students who entered college full time after 1959 enrolled in the different types of colleges in the same proportions as did the larger group that entered college immediately after high school, except that after 1959, seven per cent more of the students who entered college full time enrolled in private two-year colleges and extension centers and 6 per cent fewer entered public universities. The majority of the part-time students entered two-year institutions, mostly junior colleges.

Sixty-five per cent of the students who entered college full time after September, 1959, had withdrawn by 1963, and this was true even of those students who enrolled as late as the third year after high school graduation. If college success is defined as persisting in college, then according to the picture which evolved during the time limit of the study, the prognosis for success is not good for students who delay going to college.

GRADUATE SCHOOL ATTENDANCE

Recently a great deal of attention has been given to graduate students (see Berelson, 1960; Carmichael, 1961; Cartter, 1966; Heiss, 1967; Heiss, Davis, and Voci, 1967; and Mechanic, 1962). There is good cause for this interest. Between 1955 and 1965, the proportionate increase in graduate school enrollments was twice that of undergraduate enrollments, and at least two surveys have shown that a majority of contemporary college seniors plan to enter graduate school at some time (Davis and Bradburn, 1962; Gropper and Fitzpatrick, 1959).

A number of reasons may account for the apparent surge to graduate school, among them: the widespread emphasis on specialization, a greater drive towards affluence in society, avoidance of the draft, and increased intellectual involvement. Since there is as yet little definitive research on graduate students, and complete and accurate enrollment data are not available, not much is known about the predominant reasons for graduate school attendance or the characteristics of college graduates who persist through various levels of graduate school and those who do not. This study supplements existing data on the plans of college persisters to attend graduate school, their rate of entrance, and their goals. It is not, however, designed to examine the differential progress and characteristics of graduate students.

On the basis of the spring 1963 questionnaire administered to the college sample that had entered college full time in 1959, postgraduate plans were obtained from 77 per cent of those who were graduating that spring, and from approximately 71 per cent of those who were still in college but had not yet earned a degree. Information also was obtained about the postgraduate activities of over 80 per cent of the college persisters from answers to a postcard mailed during the fall of 1963, and again one year later to those who did not respond in 1963.

Table 25

REPORTED PLANS FOR POSTGRADUATE EDUCATION BY
EDUCATIONAL STATUS IN 1963, IN PERCENTAGES

		Plans for graduate or professional school, 1963			
Educational status, 1963	(N)	Right after college	After work/or military	Some other time	No plans [a]
Men					
Bachelor's degree	(362)	54	25	6	15
In college; no degree	(479)	28	34	8	30
Women					
Bachelor's degree	(461)	20	45	8	27
In college; no degree	(237)	13	33	6	48

[a] "No plans" includes the less than 2 per cent of the responding sample who did not answer the question.

Table 25, based on the percentages mentioned above, shows the proportion of persisters who in the spring of 1963 planned on postgraduate education. The table also distinguishes between those persisters who graduated by June, 1963, and those who did not. There was a great difference in the postgraduate educational plans reported by these two groups. A considerable majority of the responding students who received baccalaureate degrees reported plans to extend their education; 85 per cent of the men and 73 per cent of the women indicated their intention to do graduate work. These figures nearly duplicate those found by Davis (1963) in his large sample of college seniors. Over half of the men in the present study reported plans to enter graduate or professional school immediately. Only 20 per cent of the graduating women shared these plans, but 53 per cent planned on graduate work at some point, principally after a period of employment.

As noted, going on to graduate school figured much less in the plans of responding students who had spent four years in college without having obtained a degree. Thirty per cent of these men and nearly half of the women had no intention of doing graduate work, although 28 per cent of the men did plan on graduate school directly after college. There was no clear indication of why the two groups of persisters differed in their postgraduate plans, but some clues are suggested by the differences between the groups shown by the data and by previous research. The persisting students who did not receive their degrees by June, 1963, were at a somewhat lower level of ability and socioeconomic status as a group than their peers who received degrees within four years. In addition, data reported elsewhere (Trent and Ruyle, 1965) indicated that persisters who failed to obtain their degrees within four years were also at a lower level of intellectual disposition, as determined by various personality scales discussed in the next chapters, than those who did. It may be, therefore, that since the students who did not receive their degrees in four years were less intellectually inclined and less academically and financially able than their peers who did, they were also less oriented toward graduate work. These factors may also help account for the differences in postgraduate plans of students in different types of colleges. Postgraduate plans were closely in line with the academic performance of students noted when they were classified by type of college attended.

The smallest number of graduating seniors who reported plans to enter graduate school immediately after graduation were those from state colleges (25 per cent). Thirty-four per cent of the seniors in church-related colleges, 30 per cent in church-related universities, and 39 per cent in public universities planned to enter graduate or professional school immediately after college. The greatest number of students with plans for immediate postgraduate study were those from private, nonsectarian colleges (44 per cent) and private, nonsectarian universities (59 per cent). Among the responding men who obtained baccalaureate degrees in 1963, forty per cent from state colleges, 45 per cent from church-related universities, and 57 per cent from church-related colleges expressed plans to attend graduate school directly after college. Sixty per cent of the graduating men from state universities, 67 per cent from private, nonsectarian colleges, and 76 per cent from private, nonsectarian universities planned to enter graduate school right after college.

Figures for the women were quite different: Of the graduating women in all types of colleges, only 17 per cent planned to undertake graduate studies immediately after college. Twenty-four per cent of the women in church-related and public universities and 45 per cent of the women in private, nonsectarian colleges planned to engage in graduate studies immediately after college.

Although the vast majority of the college graduates in the sample reported plans to do graduate work, most did not plan on going beyond the master's degree. Of the men who answered the project questionnaire prior to graduation in the spring of 1963, 42 per cent reported plans to obtain master's degrees, 12 per cent law degrees, 10 per cent professional degrees at the doctoral level (mostly in medicine), and 16 per cent Ph.D. degrees. Nearly half of the responding women who obtained bachelor's degrees in 1963 planned to take postgraduate work toward a teaching credential, and one-third planned to work toward a master's degree. (At least one state in the sample requires a master's degree of permanently certificated teachers.) Six per cent of the women planned on a doctoral degree of some kind; none of them reported plans to work towards an M.D. degree.

In order to compare the plans of the college graduates who obtained their degrees in 1963 with their pursuits after college, the graduates were asked to return a postcard questionnaire reporting their current activities. Colleges to which graduates were known to have sent transcripts were also contacted in an attempt to gather information on the 20 per cent of this sample who did not return their postcards. Graduate schools returned information on all but 3 per cent of these. Although postcard and transcript records were not complete in all cases, information was obtained about the postgraduate activities of most of the college senior sample (Table 26).

Table 26

DISTRIBUTION OF COLLEGE GRADUATES BY POSTGRADUATE
EDUCATION, IN PERCENTAGES

		Postgraduate status, September, 1963			
Sex	*(N)*	*Graduate school: academic*	*Profes- sional school/ teaching*	*Other post- graduate education*	*Not in graduate school*
Men	(492)	15	23	4	58
Women	(582)	8	8	2	82
Total	(1074)	11	15	3	71

Twenty-nine per cent of all the college graduates were known to have engaged in some kind of postgraduate studies by June, 1964 (42 per cent of the men and 18 per cent of the women). Of the graduating students who, as college seniors, had indicated the intention to attend graduate or professional school at some time, 52 per cent of the men and 26 per cent of the women were known to have done so by the time of the final follow-up. Although it is not evident from the table, of those who had planned to enter graduate school immediately after college, 71 per cent of the men and 65 per cent of the women did so. There was no record of attendance for a number of students who reported that they were in graduate school. Many of these may have considered summer school, an evening course, or work toward a teaching credential as graduate status whereas some of the graduate schools may have used other criteria.

Of those known to have gone on to graduate work, proportionately more of the men entered professional school (60 per cent) than graduate school (40 per cent), but approximately the same proportion of women entered professional school (49 per cent) as graduate school (51 per cent). For present purposes, academically oriented fields, such as the humanities and social sciences, are referred to as being within graduate schools, and applied fields, such as business, engineering, education, law, and medicine, are considered as being within professional schools. The majority of women in professional schools, however, were completing teaching credential requirements.

Sixty-six per cent of the responding women who were known to have undertaken postgraduate work by June, 1964, were working on master's degrees, and a majority of the men in this group were also working on master's degrees (53 per cent). Nineteen per cent of the men were working toward a bachelor of laws degree, 7 per cent toward an M.D. degree, 7 per cent toward a Ph.D. and 3 per cent toward a bachelor of divinity degree. A larger proportion of men were planning on medical and law degrees than had so reported a few months earlier, and fewer men were contemplating working for a Ph.D. However, many of these men may have wished to complete master's requirements before deciding about the Ph.D. degree.

But regardless of the college origin of graduate students, the point at which they enter graduate school, or what their specific postgraduate educational goals might be, graduate school enrollments will doubtless continue to increase. Precisely what the outcome of these enrollments may entail in scholarly and vocational attainment is yet to be known. What is known is that a majority of the men in the present sample who undertook postgraduate education entered professional schools rather than the more academically oriented graduate schools, and that most men and women did not plan to go beyond a master's degree.

The one survey known on the subject suggests that most of these graduate students will not go beyond the master's degree, and many will not get that far. In his 11-year follow-up of 176 graduate students, Wright (1964) found that of the 115 master's candidates in his sample, approximately 50 per cent received a master's degree, 40 per cent received no degree, and 10 per cent obtained a doctorate; of the 61 Ph.D. candidates, less than 33 per cent obtained a doctorate within the 11-year limit of the study. In spite of plans, serious graduate studies, particularly at the doctoral level, do not appear to be prevalent.

CONCLUSION

Whether the pattern of the flow of graduate students is as diverse and complex as that of undergraduates remains to be seen, just as the causes of these diverse patterns are yet to be discovered. Of particular concern is the great loss of young adults who leave college without realizing their educational and related vocational goals. The 40 per cent of the sample that entered college immediately after high school graduation followed the trend found nationally in 1959. That approximately half of the college entrants withdrew from college within four years without obtaining a degree parallels the findings of research over the last three decades.

On the whole, since private institutions enroll students somewhat more select in academic potential than students in public colleges, it is not surprising that the record of persistence and attainment of degrees was higher among students in the private colleges and universities. A larger proportion of private college and university students also expressed plans to attend graduate school immediately after college, although a considerable majority of all graduating college seniors expressed plans for postgraduate work at some time in the future. It is not at all clear, however, to what degree the institutions themselves had any influence on the superior records or educational plans of the students. Factors of ability, financial opportunity, and motivation, not examined in this chapter, very likely have a great bearing on the patterns of college attendance found.

This is no doubt equally true of the different performances of transfer and native students. The records of transfer students contributed largely to the finding that nearly half of the students who persisted in college for four years did not secure their degrees within that conventional period of time; the native students in considerably greater proportion than the transfers completed their college studies "on schedule." On the basis of this and related comparable research, the evidence is that transference from one college to another extends the time it takes to get a degree. The causes of this delay and its effect on the development of the students involved call for analyses beyond the limits of this study and apparently beyond that of previous research.

Two distinctions are necessary: First, transfers from four-year colleges apparently differ to some extent from transfers from two-year colleges. Indications were that the two-year college transfers had a statistically higher rate of attrition than the other students even after having attended college at least two and one-half years, although this might not have been the case had the factor of ability been controlled. Second, transfers in general must be distinguished from students who actually withdraw from college. The pursuits of the two groups, carefully traced in the present analysis, yielded quite different results. Most of the transfers were found to have persisted in college for four years, and presumably most of them went on to obtain their degrees. Most withdrawals did not persist for more than two years, very few returned to college within the duration of the study, and of those who did, most were no longer enrolled in college at the termination of the study.

Within the four-year period of the study, it was found that the prognosis for graduation from college was not good for youths who delay entrance to college or withdraw. This differs, however, from Eckland's (1964) conclusion on the basis of his 10-year follow-up of students at the University of Illinois. Neither was it the conclusion of Ford and Urban (1965) or Suczek and Alfert (1966) in their respective examinations of students at Pennsylvania State University and the University of California. The differing findings—one based on a broad sample studied for a relatively limited period, and the others based on limited samples followed for a longer time—must be resolved through research on both a broad sample and a long follow-up. The issue of how many students complete college is important if it is assumed that a long term exposure to college makes an appreciable difference in personal and career development. Different patterns of college attendance also may make a great difference in subsequent personality development, whether or not the student obtains a degree.

Up to this point, generalizations about the vocational and educational development of the young adults in the sample have been based on simple marginal descriptions of the pursuits of the subjects in the sample. In the following chapter, a number of background and personality variables are presented in an attempt to delineate factors which distinguish students who persist in college from those who withdraw without completing their programs.

VI

Factors Related to
Persistence in College

At a time when society is in great need of the fully
realized potential of its able youth, higher education is increasingly considered an important factor in the development of personality which leads to successful assumption of adult roles. It is,
therefore, important to understand the characteristics of young
people who persist in college, those who enter and withdraw, and
those who do not attend at any point.

The concept of attrition needs clarification at the outset.
The research of Eckland (1964), Jex and Merrill (1962), and
Suczek and Alfert (1966) is enough to indicate that for many
students leaving college is a temporary interruption rather than
a final dropping out. There is also evidence that there are differences between voluntary withdrawals and dismissals, and also
between withdrawals with passing grades and those with a record
of failure (Rose, 1965; Rose and Elton, 1966; Suczek and Alfert,
1966). Ample evidence remains, however, that withdrawals, whatever their academic status or whatever their length of interrupted
study, differ in many ways from students who persist in college
(Sexton, 1965; Summerskill, 1962).

Differences go beyond ability and finances. If attrition

could be accounted for solely on the basis of lack of ability, then a solution might lie in identifying those college aspirants clearly incapable of college work, and finding other means to foster their self-development. But data from the present sample and elsewhere consistently indicate that academic aptitude, as such, does not account for most of the withdrawals from college, and that the same may be said for financial status (Iffert, 1957; Sexton, 1965; Slocum, 1956; Summerskill, 1962; Yoshino, 1958).

One very important factor found to be related to persistence in college was family values, especially those of parents (Levenson, 1965; Sexton, 1965; Slocum, 1956). Generally, children tended to enter college and graduate if their parents were very much interested in their doing so. This held even for the comparatively few students of low socioeconomic status who reported that their parents showed a great deal of interest in college. Another factor highly related to persistence in college, academic motivation, also no doubt derives in part from family climate. Motivation may be manifested in such diverse forms as the quality and quantity of study outside of class (Holmes, 1958; Sexton, 1965), willingness to persist, or desire to achieve (Heilbrun, 1962).

Personality factors, too, have been found to be related to persistence in college, but not with consistency or clarity. Sexton (1965) concluded from her review of the literature that maladjustment is not very evident among withdrawals, but a number of researchers have identified nonconformity or resistance to authority or dependency and irresponsibility as more characteristic of college withdrawals than persisters (Brown, 1960; Chambers and associates, 1965; Rose, 1965; Rose and Elton, 1966; Suczek and Alfert, 1966). Prediger (1965) compared unspecified biographical data of passing and failing persisters with passing and failing withdrawals, and found no differences. Williams (1966) used the Bell Adjustment Inventory and Guilford-Zimmerman Temperament Study to compare two small samples of persisters and withdrawals matched for ability, but found that none of the variables which distinguished the persisters and withdrawals in the first sample distinguished the two groups in the second sample. Studying University of Kentucky freshmen, Rose (1965) compared voluntary withdrawals, successful persisters, and unsuccessful persisters who were matched for ability and found that, although a factorial measure of tolerance and autonomy drawn from the Omnibus Personality Inventory distinguished statistically between the groups at the 5 per cent level, a measure of scholarly orientation taken from the same inventory did not.

Neither tolerance and autonomy nor scholarly orientation distinguished the groups when first-year "dropouts" were added in subsequent analyses (Rose and Elton, 1966). Suczek and Alfert (1966) compared withdrawals in good academic standing and persisters at the University of California, Berkeley, using a variety of scales, primarily including six of the Omnibus Personality Inventory scales presumably used by Rose and Elton, and the measure of Ethnocentrism and Authoritarianism devised by Adorno and associates (1950). Unlike Rose and Elton, Suczek and Alfert found that their sample of withdrawals in good academic standing were significantly more intellectually oriented, autonomous, complex, open to the ambiguous, and innovative in their thinking than were those who persisted at the university for four years. Least autonomous and intellectually oriented were the "dropouts" who were failing.

The Suczek and Alfert research can be considered as having some limitations. With few exceptions, differences in response to individual items were considered in favor of scale scores, even though the available scales presumably would have represented validated and reliable measures of the traits under consideration. With such large numbers, even differences significant at the 1 per cent level could easily be artifacts, yet most differences were divided between the 5 and 10 per cent levels. Also, out of nearly 600 items, the statistical differences that did occur might often have been a matter of chance. Reification resulted when students were considered "mature," without the benefit of cross-validation. Transfer students were generally included among the withdrawals. However, both the Suczek and Alfert research and the Rose and Elton study represent commendable efforts to examine characteristics of meaningful groupings of withdrawals from college in a more than ordinarily innovative and comprehensive way. It nevertheless seems evident from this brief review of the research findings that they corroborate Waller's (1964) and Knoell's (1960) more comprehensive reviews of persistence in college, which also indicated that the factors related to college attrition need more precise delineation and study.

The present chapter is a further inquiry into the extent to which persistence in college is related to academic aptitude and financial resources, and the extent to which it is related to internalized "presses," such as values and aspirations, which affect motivation. It was expected that withdrawals, compared as a group with persisters, would be at a lower level of ability and socioeconomic status, but that, as has been indicated in past research, neither academic aptitude nor financial status would account for the majority of the withdrawals. It was also expected that before entering college, those who became persisters would indicate a greater interest in college than withdrawals and have less utilitarian expectations of education and, conflicting research notwithstanding, would manifest more autonomous and intellectual attitudes and interests. It was further expected that after their entrance into college, the persisters would choose academic majors in greater proportion than would the withdrawals, and register greater academic motivation, as reflected in the relative amounts of time spent, by the two groups, in study and social life.

The analyses to follow compare students in the sample who persisted in college with those who did not, with respect to: 1) personal and academic factors such as academic aptitude, socioeconomic background, reported problems, choice of type of college, major subject, and reported reasons for leaving college, and 2) academic motivation as reflected by interest expressed in college, reasons for choice of college, hours spent studying, and measured attitudes. Only students who entered college full time in 1959 and responded to both the 1959 and 1963 comprehensive research batteries are included. Responding persisters are defined as students who remained in college consistently for four years and were in college in the spring of 1963, whether or not they obtained a baccalaureate degree. Withdrawals are defined as students who neither completed four years of college nor were enrolled in the spring of 1963. Transfers were included among the persisters if they remained in college through the spring of 1963, and among the withdrawals if they did not. Unfortunately, however, it was not possible to distinguish between voluntary withdrawals and dismissals, or between withdrawals in good academic standing and those on probation or failing.

The persisters and withdrawals in the longitudinal sample considered included approximately 2,300 subjects. Combining figures, approximately 61 per cent of the responding sample persisted in college and 39 per cent withdrew. As noted in the previous chapter, the college records of nearly all of the students who entered college and the postcard responses obtained in addition to the 1963 survey questionnaire showed that approximately 52 per cent of the students persisted in college and 48 per cent withdrew. Fifty-five per cent of the men and 49 per cent of the women in the original sample persisted in college, compared with 67 per cent and 55 per cent respectively in the present responding longitudinal sample. Therefore, because the proportion of persisters that responded to the comprehensive survey both in 1959 and 1963 was larger than the proportion of persisters in the total sample that entered college full time in 1959, there is an over-representation of persisters (particularly men) in the subsample now under study. Of the total sample, 6 per cent more women than men withdrew from college, whereas 12 per cent more women than men were among the withdrawals who responded to the 1963 comprehensive survey.

Other differences between those in the original 1959 sample who participated in the 1963 survey and those who did not, may be noted in Appendix D. A significant chi square was obtained for the college students when the respondents and nonrespondents were compared by level of socioeconomic status, but not for the youths who did not enter college. College and noncollege respondents were also significantly higher in level of ability than nonrespondents. However, when the respondents and nonrespondents were compared on the three attitudinal scales related to intellectual and academic motivation (discussed later in the present chapter) there was no systematic, significant difference between the two groups. Whatever the variable, there was great overlapping of the 1963 respondents and nonparticipants, and since there were differences between respondents and nonrespondents among both college persisters and withdrawals, neither group was more selective than the other on any variable considered.

Since approximately 70 per cent of all persisters and 48 per cent of all withdrawals were heard from, so large a longitudinal sample warrants examination, and their patterns of behavior and opinions may be regarded as suggestive of what would be found for the total sample. Nevertheless, generalizations drawn from the data provided by the subsamples in this chapter should be considered with the special characteristics of these samples in mind.

PERSONAL AND ACADEMIC FACTORS RELATED TO PERSISTENCE

Although intellectual ability or, more specifically, academic aptitude is related to college entrance, other factors, such as socioeconomic status and parental encouragement, were found to be even more related to the young adult's decision to attend college. The relationship between ability and college attendance is evident in Table 27, but it is also evident from the table that lack of ability cannot account for the large proportions of the withdrawals.

Table 27

ABILITY LEVELS OF COLLEGE PERSISTERS AND
WITHDRAWALS, IN PERCENTAGES

Ability level	Men		Women	
	Persisters (N = 793)	Withdrawals (N = 386)	Persisters (N = 620)	Withdrawals (N = 504)
High	66	44	60	46
Middle	27	40	34	39
Low	7	16	6	15
(Chi square)	(52.63 **)		(36.97 **)	

** $p < .01$.

Levels of ability in Table 27 were based on the distribution of SCAT score equivalents obtained by the total 1959 high school senior sample. The highest and lowest groups included the scores of students in the uppermost and lowest 30 per cent of the distribution, respectively. The middle group included scores in the middle 40 per cent of the distribution. At the high level of ability there were 22 per cent more persisters than withdrawals among the men and 14 per cent more persisters than withdrawals among the women. Combining figures, less than 7 per cent of the persisters were at the low level of ability, compared with 15 per cent of the withdrawals. But these differences did not represent the whole picture: Only half the proportion of withdrawals that could have been expected on the basis of the total sample were at the low level of ability—approximately 15 per cent, compared with the normative representation of 30 per cent. Thirty per cent of the total original sample were at the high level of academic aptitude, but 44 per cent of the men and 46 per cent of the women who withdrew were at this level. In fact, the largest proportion of withdrawals was at the high level of ability. Nevertheless, ability continued to be an important factor, particularly for the women. When looking at all those of low ability who entered college, it was apparent that while slightly over half of these men withdrew (52 per cent), an even greater percentage of the women withdrew (68 per cent).

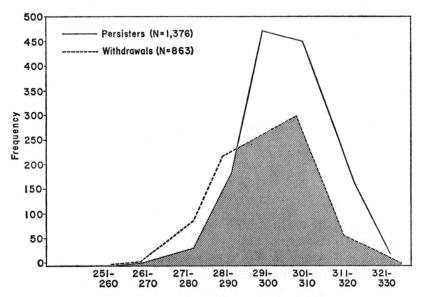

Figure 3. DISTRIBUTION OF SCAT SCORE EQUIVALENTS FOR PERSISTERS AND WITHDRAWALS.

In spite of the differences shown in Table 27, it is evident that the academic aptitude scores of a considerable majority of the persisters and withdrawals overlapped. The extensiveness of the overlap may be seen graphically by the nearly complete imposition of the ability distribution curve of the withdrawals over that of the persisters, indicated by the shaded area in Figure 3.

But the significance of the differences in ability between the two groups indicated in the table was considered great enough that, in order to assure that differences in ability alone did not account for other differences found between the two groups, level of ability was held constant when the two groups were compared on other variables in subsequent analyses.

The socioeconomic levels of the two groups, based on the occupations of the students' fathers as reported in 1959, are shown in Table 28. Professional and managerial occupations were classified as high; semiprofessional, small business owners, sales, clerical, and skilled occupations were classified as middle; and semiskilled and unskilled occupations were classified as low.

Table 28

FATHER'S OCCUPATIONAL LEVEL OF COLLEGE PERSISTERS AND
WITHDRAWALS, IN PERCENTAGES

Father's occupational level	Men		Women	
	Persisters (N = 793)	Withdrawals (N = 386)	Persisters (N = 620)	Withdrawals (N = 504)
High	28	15	34	19
Middle	61	64	58	64
Low	11	21	8	17
(Chi square)	(34.97 **)		(41.41 **)	

** p < .01.

Socioeconomic level, like ability, can be seen to be related statistically to persistence. However, among the men differences in socioeconomic level were less marked than differences in ability between the persisters and withdrawals. The majority of both the persisters and withdrawals were at the middle socioeconomic level for both sexes. At the high socioeconomic level, there were 13 per cent more persisters than withdrawals among the men and 15 per cent more persisters than withdrawals among the women. And at the low socioeconomic level there were, combining figures, 9 per cent more withdrawals than persisters. The significance of the overall chi squares notwithstanding, there were more similarities between the two groups than differences.

Similarities between the persisters and withdrawals were

also evident in their reported sources of income. Data not in table form showed that the largest proportion of both persisters and withdrawals, while in college, considered their parents the source of at least half of their income. Members of both groups, particularly the men, also reported part-time work as a major source of income. At the same time, although differences generally were not great, more withdrawals than persisters did report receiving proportionately less income from parents and more from part-time work: Five per cent more of the persisting men than withdrawals reported that over half of their financial support came from their parents (a difference not statistically significant), while 10 per cent more male withdrawals than persisters reported that wages from part-time work accounted for over half of their income (a difference significant beyond the 1 per cent level). Approximately 25 per cent of the persisters and 13 per cent of the withdrawals reported receiving scholarships (differences whose Z ratios were significant beyond the 1 per cent level), and 3 per cent of both persisters and withdrawals received scholarships which provided over half of their income.

Although withdrawals appeared to be at some economic disadvantage, it is of interest that fewer withdrawals than persisters sought loans. They may have considered themselves ineligible for any of a variety of reasons, but indications from the interviewed students were that the main reason was indifference. In any event, 13 per cent of the persisters and 5 per cent of the withdrawals reported receiving loans. Students who subsequently became withdrawals did work somewhat more than persisters at part-time jobs, but evidently did not go so far as to explore all the financial avenues open to them.

The overlap in socioeconomic status between the persisters and withdrawals noted in Table 28, and more specifically the overlap in the amount and type of financial support reported by the students, were all the more remarkable since socioeconomic status was found to be so highly related to initial college entrance. Apparently socioeconomic status is more associated with entering college than remaining there, a finding of other research as well (see Gottlieb, 1962; Munger, 1954; Smith and Penny, 1959). But since degree of persistence did vary to some extent with socioeconomic level, in subsequent comparisons of persisters and withdrawals, socioeconomic level was held constant, as was ability level.

It was previously reported that ability, socioeconomic status, and even measured level of intellectual disposition were found to be related to the type of college entered (Medsker and Trent, 1965). Students who entered private four-year colleges and universities, followed by students who entered public universities, came from the highest socioeconomic backgrounds and were the most able and intellectually oriented of all the students. It could be predicted that these students would be the most likely to persist in college, and this was borne out both by the data in the previous chapter for the total college sample and also by the data in Table 29, which includes only those students who responded to the 1959 and 1963 survey batteries.

Table 29 shows that among the respondents who attended four-year colleges, the largest proportion of persisters last attended private colleges, particularly those under denominational control. However, the difference in rate of persistence was negligible between men attending public and private nondenominational colleges (70 versus 71 per cent, respectively), and although 77 per cent of the men in denominational colleges persisted for four years, the overall chi square was not significant. Differences in rate of persistence among women in various types of four-year colleges were somewhat more marked. Of those who last attended denominational colleges, 72 per cent persisted, compared with 66 per cent in private colleges, and 57 per cent in public colleges.

There were proportionately more persisters among students who were last in universities than among those who were last in four-year colleges, regardless of type of institutional control. At least 80 per cent of the responding university student group were persisters. However, paralleling the finding for four-year college students, the rate of persistence was higher for private than public university students. Table 29 gives data for the longitudinal sample, not for the more complete sample which includes junior college students and for which college records were obtained. However, in the total sample, the number of withdrawals from private and church-related universities were markedly few compared with withdrawals from other types of colleges and universities, just as is indicated for the longitudinal sample in Table 29. One hundred per cent of the responding men and women last in

Table 29

TYPE OF COLLEGE LAST ATTENDED BY COLLEGE PERSISTERS AND
WITHDRAWALS, IN PERCENTAGES

Type of college last attended	(N)	Men Per-sisters	With-drawals	(N)	Women Per-sisters	With-drawals
College						
Public	(348)	70	30	(394)	57	43
Private	(56)	71	29	(41)	66	34
Church-related	(153)	77	23	(161)	72	28
(Chi square)		(3.02 +)			(11.50 **)	
University						
Public	(324)	85	15	(251)	80	20
Private	(33)	100	0	(22)	100	0
Church-related	(43)	100	0	(23)	100	0
(Chi square)		(12.49 **)			(11.04 **)	

+ p = not significant.
** p < .01.

attendance at denominational or other private universities persisted in college for four years, compared with 85 per cent of the men and 80 per cent of the women who last attended public universities. With the exception of the four-year college men, the overall chi squares indicate significant differences between the persistence rates of the groups in Table 29. However, the greatest difference in persistence—15 per cent—was between women in public colleges and those in church-related schools. Considering the preponderance of students in public institutions, the differences in rates of persistence of students grossly grouped by type of college last attended are noteworthy but not large.

Although these data were based on a more limited sample than that reported on in the previous chapter, the patterns of both sets of data indicate that rate of persistence varied somewhat by type of college. But it has also been noted that the characteristics of entering students varied by the type of college they enrolled in, and that persistence varied with ability and socioeconomic status, which differed for students attending different types of colleges. Consequently, at this point little can be said about the direct influence of the type of college on the persistence of its students, since traits leading to persistence may have been deter-mined before students entered college. It may at least be said, however, that whether or not students' behavior is influenced by the college after matriculation, those who persist are somewhat more likely to choose certain types of colleges to enter. This may account in part for the very high rate of persistence found by Eckland (1964) and Suczek and Alfert (1966) among students who matriculated at two major public universities.

The predisposing factors that may operate in the relation-ship between type of college chosen and persistence may also operate in the relationship between choice of major subject and persistence. It is nevertheless worth noting the pattern that emerged when the factor of major field was considered. Respond-ing students of both sexes who majored in academic subjects (natu-ral science, social science, and the humanities) persisted in college to a greater degree than students who majored in applied sub-jects (primarily education, business, and engineering), even when subjects known to be in two-year terminal programs were elimi-nated from analyses. Of the students who in 1959 planned on a four-year curriculum, 83 per cent of the men and 71 per cent of the women who majored in academic subjects persisted, compared with 73 per cent of the men and 65 per cent of the women who majored in applied subjects. These figures are somewhat higher than those found for the total sample described in Chapter V. Differences in persistence between students in academic and applied majors were even greater for women who had originally planned on a two-year curriculum. Fifty per cent of these women who majored in academic subjects persisted in college, compared with 18 per cent of the women originally enrolled in two-year applied curricula. Chi squares were significant for the men in four-year curricula and for the women in two-year curricula.

Persistence also varied by field within the academic and applied areas. Among the men in applied areas, the rate of per-sistence was highest in engineering and medical sciences (72 and 75 per cent respectively), although few (52 in number) in the sample were in medicine; the rate was lowest in business and in forestry and agriculture (63 per cent and 62 per cent respectively), again based on the very few (26) in the latter two fields. Among the women in the applied areas, the rate of persistence was highest in education (68 per cent) and the lowest in business (16 per cent).

Differences in persistence among students in academic majors were not as marked as among the applied majors, but were nevertheless apparent. The highest persistence rate for both sexes was found among the social sciences (87 per cent of the men and 77 per cent of the women) and the lowest among the humanities majors (72 per cent of the men and 63 per cent of the women). The persistence rate of the natural science majors fell between the other two groups, although it was much the same for women in this field as in social science.

Type of college, major field, socioeconomic status, and level of ability were all factors which appeared to be related to persistence in college. However, not only are these factors likely to be interrelated, but the finding of the present research was that they did not distinguish between the majority of persisters and withdrawals. This assessment is also in line with what emerged from the responses by the future college persisters and withdrawals while they were still high school seniors, to the questions about what their most likely reasons would be for not finishing college (Table 30).

Table 30

ANTICIPATED REASON FOR WITHDRAWAL AS REPORTED IN 1959 BY EVENTUAL COLLEGE PERSISTERS AND WITHDRAWALS, IN PERCENTAGES

Anticipated reason for withdrawal	Men			Women		
	Per-sisters (N = 793)	With-drawals (N = 386)	Z ratio	Per-sisters (N = 620)	With-drawals (N = 504)	Z ratio
Academic	37	39	0.73 +	16	14	0.61 +
Financial	41	32	2.87 **	29	25	1.35 +
Circumstantial [a]	15	16	2.73 **	50	50	0.17 +
No answer, don't know	7	13	3.22 **	5	11	2.80 **
(Chi square)	(14.71 **)			(8.92 *)		

[a] Circumstantial includes "marriage, health, catastrophe, and other."
+ p = not significant.
* p < .05.
** p < .01.

There were essentially no differences between the two groups in expectancy of academic problems as a cause of withdrawal from college, and the circumstantial reasons, which for the most part included marriage, health, and catastrophe, also did not distinguish between the two groups. Only anticipation of financial problems appeared to differentiate the persisters from the withdrawals at all. However, contrary to expectations, proportionately more persisters than withdrawals reported financial problems as the most likely reason for not finishing college. These data, together with previous research and more specific data to follow, suggest there is reason to challenge the popular myth that finances account for a large proportion of college withdrawals.*

The only other notable differences in Table 30 were between sexes rather than between withdrawals and persisters. Combining figures, over twice as many men (38 per cent) as women (approximately 15 per cent) listed academic problems as their most likely reason for leaving college prematurely, and proportionately more men than women anticipated financial problems as a likely cause for withdrawal (38 per cent versus 27 per cent). On the other hand, over three times as many women as men (50 per cent versus 15 per cent) felt that circumstantial reasons would account for their withdrawing from college, and the largest proportion of these mentioned marriage as the specific circumstance.

The differences between the persisters and withdrawals reflected in Table 30 remained essentially the same when the students' responses were examined by ability and socioeconomic level. On the basis of chi square analyses, only in the case of the women at the low ability level ($p < .05$) and middle socioeconomic level ($p < .01$) and the men at the middle and low socioeconomic levels ($p < .05$) were there statistically significant differences between the persisters and withdrawals in anticipated reasons given for withdrawal.

In 1963, when the students in the sample were asked about the difficulties they experienced in college, there were statistically significant—but not remarkable—differences between the men persisters and withdrawals but not between the women in the two

* It may be, however, that some of the withdrawals, less sure than the persisters that they would enter college, failed to complete the college section of the questionnaire in 1959.

groups (Table 31). There was some tendency for the withdrawals to list more problems (an average number approaching 3) than the persisters (an average of 2). But the difference in this respect between the two groups, slight in itself, was one only of quantity, not type, and the quantity only referred to numbers of problems, not numbers of students experiencing difficulties in college. Essentially as many persisters (84 per cent of the men, 78 per cent of the women) as withdrawals (85 per cent of the men, 75 per cent of the women) reported having had academic problems in college. However, the data in Table 31 contain no information about the extent or kind of academic problems reported by the subjects, and it may be that there are factors of intensity or complexity of problems that contribute to attrition. From the data at hand, however, the differences between the two groups appear to be nominal.

Table 31

ACADEMIC PROBLEMS IN COLLEGE REPORTED BY COLLEGE
PERSISTERS AND WITHDRAWALS, IN PERCENTAGES

	Men		Women	
	Persisters	*Withdrawals*	*Persisters*	*Withdrawals*
Academic problem	*(N = 793)*	*(N = 386)*	*(N = 620)*	*(N = 504)*
Learning how to study	60	66	50	50
Keeping up with high academic standards	27	23	23	18
Overburdened by combined work and study	22	26	19	20
Left on own too much	3	8	3	6
Inability to express self	18	21	21	19
Lack of faculty interest	9	6	8	11
Lack of high school preparation	25	31	24	25
(Chi square)	(20.77 **)		(10.74 +)	

+ p = not significant.
** p < .01.

Proportionately more men who withdrew from college reported such problems as lack of high school preparation and having to learn how to study although differences between group responses did not exceed 6 per cent. Moreover, the differences were not entirely one-sided: Proportionately more persisting men than withdrawals reported lack of faculty interest and difficulty in keeping up with high academic standards. Only 4 per cent more of the men withdrawals than persisters reported being overburdened by a combination of work and study, which again suggested that the two groups were very little differentiated by the economic factor. Differences between the two groups of women on these variables were even more negligible.

The data in Table 31 apparently reflect characteristics of all college students, rather than any which distinguished withdrawals from persisting students or men from women. Reporting on the difficulties experienced in college, the majority of them indicated "learning how to study" was a primary problem. Next, and in decreasing importance, were, "lack of high school preparation," "keeping up with high academic standards," "overburdened by combined work and study," and "inability to express self."

Not shown in table form is the fact that among the personal problems students reported experiencing in college, finances were mentioned by about 25 per cent. The financial factor did not differentiate the two groups of women at all; 20 per cent of the persisters and 19 per cent of the withdrawals reported financial problems. Among the men, 6 per cent more of the withdrawals than persisters reported financial problems (34 per cent versus 28 per cent), interesting in view of the 38 per cent of the men who anticipated, while still in high school, that lack of money would be their most likely obstacle to continuing in college.

The one personal factor that did differentiate the two groups to some degree was social life. Among the men, 15 per cent more withdrawals than persisters reported too much social life as a problem encountered in college (33 per cent versus 18 per cent, respectively); among the women, nearly 10 per cent more of the withdrawals than the persisters reported the same problem (23 per cent versus 14 per cent). Differences between the persisters and withdrawals on this variable were at the 1 per cent level of significance for both the men and women. That reports of too much participation in social life distinguished withdrawals from persisters more than reports of academic or financial problems suggests that a clue to a basic difference between the groups was the phenomenon of motivation, which is discussed more fully in the next section of this chapter.

What becomes increasingly evident is that lack of interest

and motivation account for attrition as much or more than ability or financial resources. When the withdrawals in the sample were questioned about their specific reasons for leaving college, only about one-half of the men and considerably less than one-third of the women listed academic or financial reasons, and the proportions of withdrawals who listed these reasons varied relatively little by socioeconomic or ability level. When such variations did become apparent, they were neither systematic nor in the anticipated directions. Twenty-two per cent of the men at the high ability level reported withdrawing from college because of poor grades, compared with 19 per cent of the men at the low ability level. "Poor grades" were given as a reason for withdrawal by 16 per cent of the withdrawals, and "finances" by 12 per cent. Employment, marriage, and lack of motivation, specifically stated, accounted for the majority of the other reasons listed.

ACADEMIC MOTIVATION

Since the data thus far observed suggested a relationship between academic motivation and persistence in college, a variety of factors likely to reflect academic motivation were examined: reported feelings about the importance of college, degree of anticipation about pursuing a college education, and willingness to study. On the basis of these items, it was found that both before and after they entered college, motivation to persist in college differentiated those who were to become persisters from those who were to become withdrawals (Table 32).

Table 32

IMPORTANCE OF COLLEGE AS REPORTED IN 1959 BY COLLEGE
PERSISTERS AND WITHDRAWALS, IN PERCENTAGES

| | Men | | Women | |
| | *Persisters* | *Withdrawals* | *Persisters* | *Withdrawals* |
Importance of college	*(N = 793)*	*(N = 386)*	*(N = 620)*	*(N = 504)*
Extremely important	72	44	69	40
Important	21	36	24	39
Not very important [a]	7	20	7	21
(Chi square)	(90.65 **)		(100.87 **)	

[a] Approximately 2 per cent of the students in this group did not respond to this item.

** $p < .01$.

Although most of the students, when they were seniors in high school, felt college was important, the majority of those who became persisters in college felt that college was "extremely important." Nearly 30 per cent more of the persisters than withdrawals, regardless of sex, held this opinion. On the other hand, combining sexes, 20 per cent of those who became withdrawals reported indifference about the importance of college, in contrast to 7 per cent of the persisters.

These initial differences in attitude about the importance of college were found to be just as remarkable when viewed by ability and socioeconomic level. Of men at the high ability level, 74 per cent of those who became persisters thought of college as extremely important, compared with 48 per cent of those who became withdrawals. At the high socioeconomic level, 84 per cent of the persisting men and 55 per cent of the withdrawals had felt college was extremely important. The difference in attitude was paralleled at the middle and low ability and socioeconomic levels, and was similar for women.

The extent to which the students reported liking high school in 1959, and even more, the extent to which they thought it likely they would graduate from college, also differentiated the withdrawals from the persisters. While still in high school, 64 per cent of those who later became persisters in college reported liking high school very much, compared with 52 per cent of those who later withdrew. Forty-three per cent of the students who became persisters felt it extremely likely they would graduate from college, compared with 18 per cent of the withdrawals. The differences between the persisters and withdrawals on these variables were consistently significant beyond the 1 per cent level.

More persisting men than women had felt it extremely likely they would graduate from college, but again differences existed between the persisters and withdrawals regardless of sex. Forty-six per cent of the persisting men had reported, in 1959, that it was extremely likely they would graduate from college, compared with 16 per cent of the withdrawals; corresponding figures for the women were 39 per cent versus 20 per cent. Again, these differences existed regardless of level of ability or socioeconomic status.

Motivation as determined by expectation of graduating

from college was also related to persistence in college even among students who attained similar grades in high school. The distribution of the students' high school ranks (available for most of the students in the sample), was categorized, like their ability distribution, into the uppermost and lowermost 30 per cent and middle 40 per cent. In general, whatever their ability level, the withdrawals had not obtained as high a grade rank in high school as the persisters. This finding met expectations, but the interrelationship between prior achievement, expressed motivation, and persistence, could not be predicted. It was found that differences in motivation existed between the college persisters and withdrawals even among those students in the upper 30 per cent of the distribution of high school ranks. Fifty-eight per cent of the men who became persisters, and were at the high level of high school rank, had felt it extremely likely they would graduate from college, compared with 32 per cent of the withdrawals; corresponding figures for the women were 42 per cent versus 24 per cent.

From the begining of the study, the future persisters manifested themselves as more academically and intellectually oriented than the future withdrawals. As high school seniors, they not only saw college as being more important than did the withdrawals, and were more able to conceive of themselves as completing a college curriculum, they also had a different perception of the purpose of education four years later.

Forty-five per cent of the persisters saw the main purpose of education as the gaining of knowledge and appreciation of ideas, compared with 31 per cent of the withdrawals. Forty-two per cent of the withdrawals viewed the main purpose of education as vocational training, compared with 28 per cent of the persisters. Once again, these differences were significant beyond the 1 per cent level. The respondents' evaluations of education are discussed more fully in Chapter IX.

However, although the persisters also were aware of the vocational advantages associated with higher education, they had more reasons, altogether, for entering college (Table 33). In order to summarize the students' reported reasons for their college of choice (not necessarily the one they attended) their reasons were categorized according to whether they had to do with academic factors, opportunities other than academic, or factors incidental to the purely academic or opportunistic. Academic factors included the school's reputation and programs offered; factors related to opportunity included the school's proximity to home, the possibility of part-time work or a better job after graduation, compatibility of the institution, and a scholarship offer; incidental factors included parents' previous attendance at the school, the attendance of friends, social life, adventure, athletics, campus atmosphere and features, and church relationship. The students were permitted to check as many reasons for their choice of college as they felt were applicable.

Table 33

REASONS FOR CHOICE OF PREFERRED COLLEGE REPORTED BY COLLEGE
PERSISTERS AND WITHDRAWALS, IN PERCENTAGES

Reasons for choice [a]	Men			Women		
	Per-sisters ($N = 793$)	With-drawals ($N = 386$)	Z ratio	Per-sisters ($N = 620$)	With-drawals ($N = 504$)	Z ratio
Academic	78	60	6.36 **	82	67	5.81 **
Opportunity	85	78	2.74 **	83	82	0.31 +
Incidental	77	71	2.14 *	84	74	4.36 **

[a] Since students could check more than one reason, percentages do not add to 100.
+ p = not significant.
* $p < .05$.
** $p < .01$.

Every category was checked by a larger proportion of persisters than withdrawals, but the difference between the groups was particularly marked in the responses to the category relating to academic reasons, and especially to the item about "academic reputation." It was found in the more specific data which contributed to the academic category in Table 33 that 67 per cent of the persisters reported choosing their college for its academic reputation, compared with 47 per cent of the withdrawals; nearly 10 per cent more persisters than withdrawals chose their college for the program it offered.

Some differences in choice of college related to "opportunity" also existed between the persisters and withdrawals. Although the differences seldom exceeded 6 per cent, proportionately more persisting men than withdrawals reported that the choice of their preferred college was at least partially influenced by available scholarships, employment prospects after graduation, and undefined personal needs. Consistent with data observed earlier in this chapter, proportionately more withdrawals (no more than 10 per cent in any instance) reported the relative lack of expense, proximity to home, and part-time employment opportunities as reasons for their choice. "Closeness to home" was the opportunity most often listed as important to the women, and this was the only reason given by women which seemed to distinguish between the persisters (41 per cent) and withdrawals (50 per cent).

Proportionately more persisters than withdrawals reported incidental reasons as relevant to the choice of their preferred college. Generally, at least a third of the students noted "attendance by friends," "size of the college" (not specified), and "campus atmosphere" as reasons for college choice. But attendance of friends was the only reason for college choice noted by proportionately more withdrawals than persisters. "Social life" was reported as more important to the women, and "athletics" somewhat more important to the men, by both persisters and withdrawals. Women also appeared to be more influenced by friends and family. The persisters of both sexes in greater proportion than the withdrawals considered previous attendance by members of their family, church affiliation, and especially campus atmosphere as factors that figured in their choice of college. Although differences between the persisters and withdrawals in reasons reported for choice of college rarely exceeded 7 percentage points, all the reasons differentiated between the two groups at a statistically significant level, with the exception of the women's reasons dealing with opportunities.

It is to be noted, once again, that the persisters had more reasons and a wider variety of reasons for their college choices than did the withdrawals. In particular, they seemed to be more academically motivated in their choice of college. The persisters' greater propensity for academic life was also reflected in their significantly greater academic involvement, as shown by amount of study done after entering college (Table 34).

Table 34

NUMBER OF STUDY HOURS PER WEEK REPORTED BY COLLEGE
PERSISTERS AND WITHDRAWALS, IN PERCENTAGES

| | Men | | Women | |
| | *Persisters* | *Withdrawals* | *Persisters* | *Withdrawals* |
Hours of study	*(N = 793)*	*(N = 386)*	*(N = 620)*	*(N = 504)*
9 or fewer	18	36	21	28
10 to 19	38	34	44	34
20 or more	43	14	34	16
No answer	1	16	1	22
(Chi square)	(101.49 **)		(35.32 **)	

** $p < .01$.

Among the men, three times as many persisters as withdrawals reported studying over 20 hours a week outside class (43 per cent versus 14 per cent); twice as many withdrawals reported studying less than 10 hours a week (36 per cent versus 18 per cent). Differences in amount of study hours reported by women persisters and withdrawals were not as great, but the pattern of differences remained the same as that found among the men.

Since a somewhat larger proportion of the withdrawals than the persisters were dependent upon part-time work for support, it was postulated that the number of hours the future withdrawals had to work might have prevented them from being able to study as much as the persisters. But when the number of hours worked was held constant (more or less than 10 hours a week), the differences tabulated between the withdrawals and persisters were marked. Of the men who worked less than ten hours a week, 35 per cent of those who became withdrawals reported studying less than 10 hours a week, compared with 19 per cent of the persisters; 18 per cent of the withdrawals who worked less than 10 hours reported studying 20 hours or more, compared with 45 per cent of the persisters. Even greater differences in hours spent studying distinguished the two groups of men who worked more than 10 hours a week. Once again differences were not as great between the women persisters and withdrawals, but the pattern remained the same and continued to be highly significant.

Through the administration of various attitude scales, the academic motivation of the persisters and withdrawals was assessed

Table 35

STANDARD MEAN SCORES ON INTELLECTUALITY SCALES IN
1959 OF COLLEGE PERSISTERS AND WITHDRAWALS

| | Men [a] | | Women [a] | |
| | Persisters | Withdrawals | Persisters | Withdrawals |
Scale	(N = 696)	(N = 309)	(N = 595)	(N = 413)
Thinking introversion	48.82	44.67	50.22	47.39
Complexity	51.00	51.34	49.07	49.33
Nonauthoritarianism	46.09	44.34	44.80	43.56

[a] The numbers do not equal those in previous tables in this chapter because some students did not complete the Omnibus Personality Inventory.

in a systematic way not possible through the opinion survey referred to in this chapter. The scores obtained by the persisters and withdrawals on several scales measuring dimensions of intellectual disposition and attitudes are shown in Table 35. Each of the scales, taken from the Omnibus Personality Inventory, was administered to the students before they entered college. The three scales were: Thinking Introversion, which measures preference for reflective, abstract thinking; Complexity, which measures extent of intellectual curiosity and tolerance for ambiguity; and Nonauthoritarianism, which measures tendency towards independent, unbiased, open, and flexible thinking. The scales are described briefly as follows:

Thinking Introversion (TI); 60 items. High scorers are characterized by a liking for reflective thought. Their thinking tends to be less dominated by external conditions and generally accepted ideas than that of extroverts (low scorers). High scorers display an interest in a variety of ideas for their own sake, whereas low scorers tend to evaluate ideas for their practical, immediate application. This scale also appears to measure general appreciation of and interest in scholarly activities.

Complexity (Co); 27 items. High scorers are tolerant of ambiguities, fond of novel situations and ideas, and aware of subtle variations in patterns of stimuli. Low scorers prefer sure, simple, and structured situations. This orientation is principally a perceptual style of viewing and organizing phenomena, and may be viewed as a gauge of intellectual curiosity.

Nonauthoritarianism (Na); 20 items. High scorers on this dimension are generally flexible and realistic in their relationships, unromantic and uncynical, tolerant, objective, and free of dependency on rules or rituals for dealing with ideas, objects, and people. Low scorers are more rigid and conventional in their thinking, tending to see numerous situations in a black-or-white fashion.

As noted in Appendix C, all the scales have been validated in a variety of ways, and each scale possesses an acceptable reliability coefficient. The twenty-item Nonauthoritarianism scale is relatively brief and heterogeneous compared with the other scales, and therefore should not be expected to have high coefficients of equivalence. The test-retest correlation coefficient for the scale is high (.92). Further technical details of the three scales may be found in the OPI manual (Center for the Study of Higher Education, 1962).

The standard mean profiles obtained by the groups on these scales may be seen in Figure 4. The means were standardized by reference to the Omnibus Personality Inventory, whose freshman norm groups possessed a mean of 50 on each scale, with a standard deviation of 10. It will be noted that the means of the persisters and withdrawals were generally lower than would have been predicted on the basis of the norm groups. At the same time, as expected, the persisters in general had shown a greater degree of measured intellectuality than the withdrawals before they entered college. The persisting men and women scored significantly higher on the Thinking Introversion and Nonauthoritarianism scales as noted by the significance tests in Appendix Table E-2. Differences between the persisters and withdrawals on the Thinking Introversion scale were well beyond the 5 per cent level, but they just reached this level of significance on the Nonauthoritarianism scale. The Complexity scale, however, did not distinguish between persisters and withdrawals.

In 1959, the future withdrawals, in contrast to their relative scores on the other two measures, scored slightly higher than the persisters on the Complexity scale. Although not statistically significant, this finding was surprising, especially since there is considerable intercorrelation among the three scales (see Appendix

C). The finding is also curious in light of the reversal in the mean Complexity scores of the two groups in 1963, a phenomenon which will be explored in the next chapter. It can be said at this point, however, that after four years the mean Complexity score of the persisters increased and the mean Complexity score of the withdrawals decreased. At that point, the scores of the persisters were higher in measured Complexity than the withdrawals.

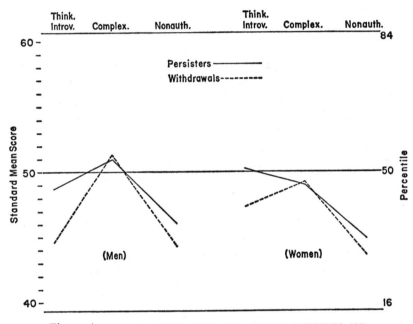

Figure 4. STANDARD MEAN SCORES OF COLLEGE PERSISTERS AND WITHDRAWALS ON INTELLECTUALITY SCALES IN 1959.

The Thinking Introversion and Nonauthoritarianism scales significantly distinguished the men of the two groups only at the high ability level, the Thinking Introversion scale distinguished at each socioeconomic level, and the Nonauthoritarianism scale only at the low socioeconomic level (Appendix Table E-2).

Among the women, the Nonauthoritarianism scores ceased to distinguish the persisters from the withdrawals significantly when levels of ability and socioeconomic status were held constant.

The two groups of women differed significantly on the Thinking Introversion scale only at the high ability level and middle socio-economic level.

All significant differences for men and women were at the 5 per cent level, but tests for significance of differences on individual scales were not computed when general analyses of variance failed to show significant differences between the persisters and withdrawals across all three scales.

In sum, while the students were seniors in high school, two out of the three measures of intellectual and autonomous attitudes distinguished the eventual college persisters from the withdrawals, but mostly for students at a high level of ability. One of the measures distinguished the two groups in the reverse direction from that expected, although the differences were not statistically significant. Differences in distribution of scores between the two groups were not great, whatever their statistical significance or direction. The evidence is that these measures on the whole were poor predictors of persistence in college. This unexpected finding warrants further consideration, since four years later there was a great and consistent difference between the same persisters and withdrawals on these and other very reliable measures of intellectual disposition and academic motivation.

It may be that the persisters were more ready for growth in intellectual disposition, or at least for the type of opportunity for intellectual growth provided by the colleges they attended. It may be, too, that many of the withdrawals, slightly higher than the persisters to start with in complexity of outlook, intellectual curiosity, and tolerance for ambiguity as measured by the Complexity scale, sought more from their college experiences than did many persisters. They may also have felt less compelled than the persisters to obtain their degrees when they found college irrelevant to their needs and lacking in the stimulation they sought. This possibility has been corroborated to some extent in other research.

Heist (1967) identified a number of potentially highly creative students in several select liberal arts colleges and found that a majority withdrew from college before their senior year. It will be recalled that Rose and Elton (1966) found that freshmen at the University of Kentucky who withdrew in good standing were less conforming and no less autonomous and intellectually oriented than students who persisted through the first year of college. Early in this chapter questions were raised about the significance of the differences and the inclusion of transfers in the samples of University of California persisters and withdrawals studied by Suczek and Alfert (1966). Nevertheless, it may be said that, unlike the failing withdrawals, withdrawals in good standing were at least as autonomous and scholarly in orientation as the persisters, and tended to be somewhat more intellectual and autonomous. Under the circumstances, it is regrettable that achieving and failing withdrawals could not have been examined separately in the more broadly based sample studied in this chapter.

However, in the present sample, the data do not consistently point to the withdrawals as being, on the average, an exceptionally autonomous, intellectually committed, and creative group seeking a unique, enriched education. As high school seniors, they had indicated as great an intellectual disposition as the eventual persisters on one scale; but otherwise, both before and after entering college, they showed less ability, less interest in college, and less intellectual disposition and academic motivation than the persisters.

CONCLUSION

A diversity of individuals was doubtless included among the withdrawals—from those who needed a special challenge to those who needed special assistance to prepare them for the exigencies of college life. And doubtless, too, many colleges failed to meet their different needs. Eckland (1964) and Yates (1954) may be correct in their suggestion that when students are not properly stimulated to self-development and attainment of identity in college, for some, interruption of college studies can represent a moratorium more conducive to self-development than "sticking it out." The causes of attrition and the individual characteristics of withdrawals certainly deserve further study. The finding in the present research was that withdrawals began with at least as great a complexity of outlook as the persisters, and subsequently decreased in this trait, whereas the persisters increased. If this finding is replicated with another sample, then research into its meaning would seem essential.

In addition to the specific problem raised by the relative degrees of measured Complexity of persisters and withdrawals, it is evident that more needs to be learned about the conjunction of elements which influence decisions about college attendance, persistence, and withdrawal.

According to the data at hand, the persisters entered college with considerably more intent than the withdrawals to attend and graduate. They were more selective in choosing their colleges and saw more reasons for attending. They studied harder and were less prone to allow social life to interfere with their studies. They tended to be more intellectual, self-reliant, and open-minded before entering college, and even more intellectually oriented and autonomous after four years. None of these findings could be attributed to differences in ability or socioeconomic status to any major extent. Therefore, a tenable interpretation of the findings is that the persisters entered college with the necessary predisposition, or what Sanford (1962c) has termed the state of readiness, to persist and develop in college.

Rose and Elton (1966) and Suczek and Alfert (1966) found some signs that persisters were more conforming than withdrawals in good standing, although their findings were not generally confirmed by measures of autonomy drawn from the Omnibus Personality Inventory. Williams' (1966) hypothesis has some bearing here: Those who come to resemble their environment are more likely to persist in college than those who fail to resemble it. Heilbrun's (1962) conclusion, that persisters show more endurance and will to achieve than withdrawals, also seems relevant.

The expectations of most colleges are that students will develop intellectually and become more autonomous in attitude, and regimens are established for this purpose. Students disposed to conform to such procedures may develop in the way intended by the college; a few may become autonomous enough to transcend the regulations. Students not so disposed to adjust, even the relatively few who are initially more autonomous and complex than the eventual persisters, may be the ones most likely to withdraw. At least temporarily, the withdrawals thereby forego experiences which are at first unpleasant but which ultimately could provide the opportunity for greater development and satisfaction. Evidently, many of these withdrawals return to college disposed to persist; however, it may be worth questioning why means already available could not have been used to ameliorate the college environment so as to avoid repelling so many students. Moreover, we should investigate whether those who return to college after withdrawing develop in the same manner as those who persist in college without interruption.

Since the data in this chapter have repeatedly indicated the importance of early academic motivation to persistence in college, it is important to inquire into possible sources of academic motivation. Previous research, such as that of Bloom (1964), Jaffe and Adams (1964), and Little (1959) suggest that one prime source of academic motivation is parental influence. This was also indicated in the present research, which studied parental influence on college persistence and found it comprised several factors. In addition to communicating their educational values and encouragement, parents' temperaments and interactions with their children, as perceived by the subjects, also figured importantly. The relationship between family background, academic motivation, and persistence in college is discussed more fully in Chapter IX, which in part deals with the subjects' evaluations of their families' influence (see also Trent, Athey, and Craise, 1965; Trent and Ruyle, 1965).

The indications are strong that the academic orientation necessary for successful completion of college is extensively derived from very early family environment and beginning school experiences. Although this phenomenon was not examined directly in the present study, data observed support the view that the influence of early environment, especially that provided by parents, is of critical importance. This is not to say that school and college have no influence on students. The data in the following chapter show a distinct relationship between persistence in college and change in attitudes and values.

VII

Values and Attitudes
Four Years After High School

Although relatively little is known about the dynamics of individual differences in decision-making, it can be assumed that an individual's attitudes and values underlie his aspirations, decisions, and choices. Persistence in college has been shown in this study to be related to disposition toward learning in addition to ability and financial status. Thus, when examining the career decisions and life styles of young adults, an understanding of the development of their values and attitudes becomes important. Social scientists have given much attention to the study of values, particularly to the role of higher education in the development of students' values (Eddy, 1959; Jacob, 1957; Sanford, 1962c). However, no consensus has been gained about the role college should take in the changing of values, the effect of a college education on values, or how to assess the impact of college on values.

Dressel (1965) raises questions as to whether colleges should consider it their function to attempt to change students' values and in the end argues that ". . . the answer to the question, 'Is change in the values of college students desirable?' must be the

128

well-qualified one that *some* changes are desirable in *some* students [p. 108]." Ethical considerations aside, a number of researchers have claimed that college does little to affect students' attitudes and values. Bloom's (1964) position is that basic values are formed for the most part by early childhood, although important change can take place afterwards. Sontag and Kagan (1963) have concluded that motivation for intellectual mastery is established by the sixth grade. Perhaps best known is Jacob's (1957) summary of research on this subject, which led him to assert that college has little influence on students' values other than to make them more homogeneous, which for many means moving them in a slightly more liberal direction. Freedman (1965) is more optimistic on this point, primarily as the result of his research on Vassar students. He has stated:

> The situation of the college student, particularly the situation of the freshman, would on the face of it appear to be highly favorable to change [p. 27].

Some researchers have found considerable change in students' values even after one or two years of college attendance, especially changes toward more critical thinking, greater autonomy, and less ethnocentrism (Dressel and Lehmann, 1965; Lehmann and Dressel, 1963; Howard and Warrington, 1958; Plant, 1958). Other researchers, however have found no change (Corey, 1940; Whitely, 1938). On the other hand, it also has been argued that not only can value changes be observed in individuals but, as changes in the culture take place, between generations (Barton, 1959; Freedman, 1961). Barton (1959), however, suggested that inadequate research methodology lies behind such differences in findings and conclusions. Shortcomings in the conduct of much research, such as use of limited samples and lack of reliable and valid instruments and design are evidently widespread.

In light of these considerations, a great deal remains to be known about the effect of college on students. The general consensus of the research is that students do change in college; they become less stereotyped and prejudiced in their judgments, more critical in their thinking, and more tolerant, flexible, and autonomous in attitude.* Information is particularly lacking, however, about differences in personality development, within a given period, between college students and peers who do not attend college, and between individuals of varying abilities and socioeconomic backgrounds in both groups. Research to date has centered on individual case studies and on studies of students in selected types of institutions; little research has been done with noncollege comparison groups or with controls for differences in socioeconomic or ability levels.

It is hoped that these deficiencies can be corrected to some extent through a variety of analyses of the broadly based longitudinal sample in the present study. The emphasis will be on the differences between the principal groups compared with respect to change of measured attitudes: high school graduates in the sample who were consistently in college for four years and those who remained consistently employed during this time. In this way, individuals whose exclusive experience was full time in college could be compared with those who experienced the work world full time. Occasional comparative analyses also will be made of two other groups important to the study: college withdrawals who had attended college a minimum of one year and a maximum of three years, viewed as definitely having been exposed to college; and women who became full-time housewives immediately after graduation from high school, with no exposure either to work or college.

In addition to change in measured attitudes between 1959 and 1963, certain other values and attitudes not examined in 1959 will be analyzed, including cultural and esthetic values, and attitudes toward politics, marriage, and religion. Only those subjects described in Chapter III who participated in the study both in 1959 and 1963 were included in the longitudinal analyses. All subjects were examined who responded to questions which were asked only in 1963.

The design of the following analyses are such that the association of length of college attendance with personality development may be assessed by the scores on attitudinal scales

* Four comprehensive reviews of the literature on change of attitudes and values of college students are those of Freedman (1960); Lehmann and Dressel (1963); Newcomb and Feldman (1968); and Webster, Freedman, and Heist (1962).

administered in 1959 and 1963 to high school peers who may be regarded as "experimental" and "control" groups. The experimental group consists of youths who persisted in college for four consecutive years after their high school graduation, and the control group of students who remained employed during this time. The change scores of the two groups were examined at each of three levels of ability and socioeconomic status. Therefore it was possible to compare the change of personality scores of peer groups roughly alike in ability and background but with very different intervening experiences—college or employment—during the first four years following high school.

The two other comparison groups might be considered secondary control groups. The college withdrawals provide an indication of the association of length of persistence in college with extent of personality development or change of attitude. The young women who entered full-time homemaking immediately after high school provided an indication of the comparative personality growth of those high school graduates who experienced neither employment nor college.

These analyses bear directly on two crucial hypotheses: that college students compared with their noncollege peers manifest greater change in intellectual disposition, values, and autonomy; and that greater change occurs among students who attend college for four years compared with college withdrawals.

Sampling bias, as noted previously, continues to require that the data be treated with caution. There is an overrepresentation of students in the longitudinal sample who persisted in college, and the college students are at a disproportionately high socioeconomic and ability level. However, the two major groups analyzed—those who were consistently in college for four years and those who were employed for four years—included a good representation of subjects who did not attend college: 40 per cent of the men and 47 per cent of the women. Moreover, differences in ability and background were minimized in subsequent analyses by holding level of ability and socioeconomic status constant.

DEVELOPMENT OF INTELLECTUAL DISPOSITION

Choosing and mastering a profession, attaining a specialty, shifting easily from one specialty to another, and having zest for ideas and information are in large part dependent upon disposition towards learning and general intellectual interests. Two of the Omnibus Personality Inventory attitudinal scales administered to the sample were designed to reflect degree of intellectual disposition: the Thinking Introversion scale, which assesses attraction for reflective, abstract thought, and the Complexity scale, which assesses tolerance for ambiguity and intellectual inquiry. These scales were administered to the subjects in the longitudinal sample before high school graduation and again four years later. In most of the tables in this chapter, the results shown are for the two principal groups only—the one that remained in college consistently for four years and the one consistently employed during that time (Table 36).

The data in Table 36 are in the form of standard scores made by the same individuals in 1959 and 1963; for each scale, 50 represents the original Omnibus Personality Inventory normative mean and 10 the standard deviation. (As noted in Appendix C, the Social Maturity scale was the only one normed on the present sample, since it constituted an abridged version of that scale contained in the form of the Omnibus Personality Inventory available in 1959.) The differences between the college group and employed group, regardless of sex, are immediately apparent. The college men and women gained significantly as groups in tendency towards reflective thought (Thinking Introversion), and the college women gained significantly in inquiry or tolerance for ambiguity (Complexity), although the statistically significant gain in Complexity manifested by the large numbers of college women was not notable in actual score points.* The only group gain made by the employed between 1959 and 1963 was by the men, on the Thinking Introversion scale. All other group means of the noncollege youths *decreased* in 1963; there was a particularly noticeable and significant decrease in the Complexity scores of the employed men and women. That is, as a group, and in contrast to the college students, the young men and women who entered employment immediately after high school showed, after four

---

* Since the same individuals responded to the same scales in 1959 and 1963, their mean scores were considered correlated. Therefore a *t* test was used which tested the significance of difference between correlated means. The derivation of this statistical test may be found in Appendix E.

Table 36

STANDARD MEAN THINKING INTROVERSION AND COMPLEXITY SCORES OF
COLLEGE PERSISTERS AND THE CONSISTENTLY EMPLOYED,
1959 AND 1963

Scales and Groups

	(N)[a]		Thinking Introversion		Complexity		Ψ values of College vs. Employed[b]	
	College	Employed	College	Employed	College	Employed	TI	Co
Men	(723)	(444)						
1959			48.62	41.31	50.69	50.95		
1963			51.76	43.57	51.28	48.03		
Difference			3.14	2.26	0.59	−2.92		
(t)			(10.47 **)	(5.02 **)	(1.74 +)	(5.62 **)	.88 +	3.51 **
Women	(578)	(478)						
1959			50.24	43.57	48.79	46.44		
1963			53.74	42.88	50.61	44.43		
Difference			3.50	−0.69	1.82	−2.01		
(t)			(9.72 **)	(1.86 *)	(4.79 **)	(4.10 **)	4.19 **	3.83 **

[a] Samples are composed of those who persisted in college full time during the four-year period of the study and those who persisted in employment full time.

[b] Ψ values constitute the differences in mean differences between the scores of the groups being compared in 1959 and 1963. The computation of the statistical significance of these values may be found in Appendix E.

+ p = not significant.
* p < .05.
** p < .01.

133

years, less tolerance for ambiguity and less interest in intellectual inquiry.

The figures in the last two columns of Table 36 further indicate this finding. The Ψ values of the subjects' change scores show the differences between the mean differences of the college and employed groups on the two scales. The rationale, derivation, and computation of the form of analysis used to determine the statistical significance of these values may be found in Appendix E. What is important about the technique used is that it takes into account both the variance of the difference scores as well as the fact that this variance was derived from correlated scores.

Not only did the groups change significantly on the two scales over the four years between test periods in either a negative or positive direction, but they differed from one another in the *amount* they changed. Only on the Thinking Introversion scale did the differences between mean differences of the college and noncollege men fail to reach the 1 per cent level of significance. There were therefore not only statistically significant differences in *direction* of change between the college students and workers, but in *amount* of change on these instruments.

Moreover, at least for the men, their changes in Complexity scores cannot be considered the result of differences at the outset. Although it might be argued that individuals who become more complex in outlook are more complex when first measured, thus showing a greater disposition to change, there was no statistical difference in the mean Complexity scores obtained by the college and employed men in 1959 (critical ratio = .43). The differences found between the college and employed men in 1963 could not therefore have been predicted from their scores in 1959.

The standard mean intellectual attitude scores of the groups by the subjects' ability and socioeconomic levels are shown in Appendix Tables E-4 and E-5. The method used to determine ability and socioeconomic level was described in Chapter IV. The patterns of differences in intellectual disposition found between the college and employed groups persisted when subjects of like ability and from similar family backgrounds were examined. In a number of instances the differences between mean scores obtained in 1959 and 1963 by each group at the different ability and socioeconomic levels were not statistically significant, but the differences in change scores between the college and employed groups did remain significant for the most part.

The trend already observed was present when the mean intellectual disposition scores of the college and employed groups at each ability and socioeconomic level were compared. And on the basis of critical ratios that may be found in Appendix Table E-3, differences in intellectual disposition between the college and employed samples remained clear at both time periods. Differences also generally continued to exist in the amount of change shown by the groups, although the differences in intellectual disposition between the two time periods were somewhat less clear when young adults of like ability, socioeconomic status, and post high school experience were studied. The evidence is that changes in intellectual disposition were related not only to college and work experience, but also to aptitude and background, and no doubt to many other prior and intervening factors impossible to isolate in the present study. And, although there were consistent differences between the college and employed groups in amount and direction of change in disposition, and although most of these differences were statistically significant, questions still may be raised about the actual extent of these differences. Most of the analysis groups comprised fairly large numbers, and only relatively slight differences in distribution of scores are necessary for the statistical significance of these distributions when large numbers are involved. But if the findings do not necessarily indicate large differences in development of intellectual interests and awareness between the college and employed groups over the four years, there is yet a clear and consistent tendency for college students to develop more in this direction and for those who did not experience college to become less complex in outlook and less tolerant of ambiguity.

Assuming college students change more in intellectual disposition than their employed peers, when does this change take place? Is it primarily in the freshman year, or is it a gradual, continuing process? It was noted earlier that Sanford (1967) sees personality development as a continuing process, even beyond college, but that Freedman (1965) argues that changes in values and attitudes among college students take place mostly within the freshman year. Lehmann and Dressel (1963) vary in their conclusions on the subject, according to the particular measurement of personality. They found length of college attendance to be related to increase in flexibility of values for men and women and to increase in objectivity of thinking for women, but all the college students in their sample (mostly at Michigan State University) became less dogmatic and more open to ideas, regardless of length of stay in college. Lehmann's study, however, did not distinguish withdrawal students from transfers and therefore could not examine the relationship between length in college and personality change. Although the findings in the present study are open to more than one interpretation, additional indications of the relationship between length of attendance in college and change of values may be inferred from the data. The mean standard intellectual disposition scores of those subjects who had attended college for more than one year but fewer than three years, and for those who had attended college for four years, are shown in Table 37.

The scores obtained on both scales indicate that with the exception of the men's Thinking Introversion scores, those students with more exposure to college changed most. Four years after graduation from high school, the college withdrawals manifested less development in intellectual disposition than did those students who had attended college consistently for the four years. Following the same pattern as the employed youths, the mean Complexity score in 1963 for college withdrawals was lower than it had been in 1959. Once again, with the exception of the men's Thinking Introversion scores, the college persisters changed significantly more than the withdrawals in an intellectual direction, as noted by the Ψ values in Table 37.

However, several qualifications must be made. Since scores were only obtained in 1959 and again in 1963, it is possible that the students who attended college for four years changed in attitude within the first two years. But it cannot be said that the college persisters exhibited a more intellectual orientation than the withdrawals on both scales before they entered college. From the critical ratios (Appendix Table E-3), it is known that the persisters obtained a significantly higher mean Thinking Introversion score than the withdrawals both in 1959 and 1963, although for the men the gap closed somewhat by 1963. On the Complexity

Table 37

STANDARD MEAN THINKING INTROVERSION AND COMPLEXITY SCORES OF STUDENTS WHO REMAINED IN COLLEGE BETWEEN ONE AND THREE YEARS, AND THOSE WHO REMAINED FOUR YEARS

Scales and Groups

	(N) Persisters	(N) Withdrawals	Thinking Introversion Persisters	Thinking Introversion Withdrawals	Complexity Persisters	Complexity Withdrawals	Ψ values of Persisters and Withdrawals TI	Ψ values of Persisters and Withdrawals Co
Men	(723)	(105)						
1959			48.61	45.06	50.69	52.28		
1963			51.76	48.87	51.28	50.67		
Difference			3.15	3.81	0.59	−1.61		
(t)			(10.50 **)	(4.33 **)	(1.74 +)	(1.56 +)	0.66 +	2.20 *
Women	(578)	(195)						
1959			50.24	46.41	48.79	49.20		
1963			53.74	47.07	50.61	46.42		
Difference			3.50	0.66	1.82	−2.78		
(t)			(9.72 **)	(1.16 +)	(4.79 **)	(4.09 **)	2.84 **	4.60 **

+ p = not significant.
* p < .05.
** p < .01.

137

scale, however, the withdrawals began with a higher mean score than the persisters, although differences were not statistically significant.

The withdrawals, originally with slightly higher Complexity scores, showed a significant decrease on the scale after four years while the scores of the persisters as a group increased to some degree. The result was a reversal of the situation found in 1959: By 1963, the persisters were higher than the withdrawals in Complexity, even if not to a statistically significant degree in the case of the men. Regardless of this reversal, the most dominant fact is that there was essentially no difference in Complexity scores between the two groups. Since the scale measures intellectual curiosity and tolerance for ambiguity, traits supposedly fostered by higher education, it seems unfortunate that the scores of the college persisters were not higher. This is true even if complexity of outlook may be considered a relatively stable trait, formed early in life. This interesting phenomenon was also the subject of speculation in the previous chapter. Even more interesting, a comparison with Table 36 shows that the women who withdrew from college decreased in Complexity even more than the working women who never attended college.

Important as these qualifications may be, they do not alter the evidence that the greater the high school graduates' propensity for persisting in college, the greater their propensity for changing in a more intellectual direction. Once again, however, the statistics observed for groups of this size suggest trends distinguishing the groups, but not greatly differentiating factors. In data not shown in table form, this pattern continued to exist when level of ability and socioeconomic status were held constant, but the significance of the differences between the two groups of men diminished. Only at the low level of ability and socioeconomic status did the women persisters and withdrawals fail to differ significantly in the amount they changed on the two scales. This suggests that college may have more influence in certain areas on students from higher levels of ability and socioeconomic status than on those from the lower levels, or at least that the relationship between persistence in college and intellectual disposition does not operate altogether independently of family background and academic aptitude.

Nor was change in intellectual attitude found to be associated solely with persistence in college, or with ability and socioeconomic status. That different noncollege experiences are associated with differences in change of attitudes and values may be inferred from the comparative analysis of women who engaged in different pursuits during the first four years after high school: college, work, homemaking, or a combination of these pursuits (Table 38). It has already been observed that college women became more intellectually oriented between 1959 and 1963 and working women less so. The combined-pursuits group showed greater intellectual disposition, as measured by the Thinking Introversion and Complexity scales, than the continuously employed women both in 1959 and 1963 (see the critical ratios in Appendix Table E-3). Like the continuously employed women, however, the "combined" group decreased in tendency towards reflective thinking (Thinking Introversion), although again not significantly, and decreased significantly more in mean Complexity score than the continuously employed women.

While still seniors in high school, the women who became housewifes soon after high school and the women who varied their pursuits obtained higher mean Thinking Introversion and Complexity scores in 1959 than the women who were to be continuously employed from 1959 to 1963. But the homemakers who had not had any work experience showed a significantly greater decrease in measured intellectual attitudes on both scales than did any other group of women. All the groups changed significantly between 1959 and 1963 on the two scales except for the combined pursuits group and the employed women on the Thinking Introversion scale. The differences in Complexity scores of the groups of women are graphed in Figure 5 along with those of the employed and college men. Mean levels of Complexity of the various groups at the point of high school graduation and four years later can thus be observed in relation to one another.

Analysis of variance confirms statistically significant differences between the change scores obtained by the various groups of women on both of the scales (Thinking Introversion: $F = 14.21$, $p < .01$; Complexity: $F = 5.76$, $p < .01$). Analyses of the significance of the Ψ values in Table 38 confirm the differences in amount of change manifested by the different groups of women and make it clear that the greatest regression in intellectual in-

Table 38

STANDARD MEAN THINKING INTROVERSION AND COMPLEXITY SCORES,
1959 AND 1963, OF WOMEN WHO WERE CONSISTENTLY
STUDENTS, WORKERS, OR HOMEMAKERS AND
THOSE WHO COMBINED PURSUITS

Groups	(N)	Thinking Introversion [a]	Complexity [b]
College	(578)		
1959		50.24	48.79
1963		53.74	50.61
Difference		3.50	1.82
(t)		(9.72 **)	(4.79 **)
Employed	(478)		
1959		43.57	46.44
1963		42.88	44.43
Difference		−0.69	−2.01
(t)		(1.86 +)	(4.10 **)
Homemaking	(216)		
1959		44.41	49.57
1963		41.91	44.79
Difference		−2.50	−4.78
(t)		(4.24 **)	(7.03 **)
Combination	(1102)		
1959		46.10	48.83
1963		45.75	45.81
Difference		−0.35	−3.02
(t)		(1.46 +)	(10.41 **)

[a] Thinking Introversion: College vs. Employed—$\Psi = 4.19$ *; Employed vs. Homemakers—$\Psi = 1.81$ **; Homemakers vs. Combined—$\Psi = 2.15$ **; Employed vs. Combined—$\Psi = 0.34$ +.

[b] Complexity: College vs. Employed—$\Psi = 3.83$ **; Employed vs. Homemakers—Ψ 2.77 **; Homemakers vs. Combined—$\Psi = 1.76$ *; Employed vs. Combined—$\Psi = 1.01$ +.

+ p = not significant.
* p < .05.
** p < .01.

terest took place among the homemakers, and the greatest growth in intellectual disposition among the college women.

This finding held regardless of ability or socioeconomic status. The homemakers in the uppermost 30 per cent of the sample's ability distribution decreased in Thinking Introversion

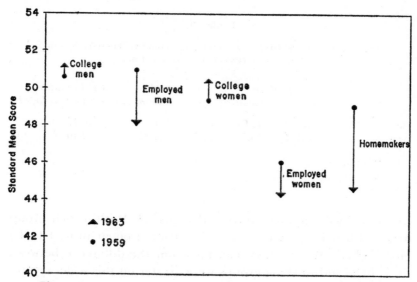

Figure 5. CHANGE ON COMPLEXITY SCALE FROM 1959 TO 1963 BY
POST HIGH SCHOOL ACTIVITY.

by more than 3 standard mean points, and in Complexity by more
than 7 points. At the high socioeconomic level, the homemakers
decreased in Thinking Introversion by nearly 5 standard mean
points and in Complexity by over 6 points. These data suggest
the validity of the concept of the "trapped housewives," who have
figured so prominently in recent sociological studies and popular
publications. Although the scores of the housewives were much
like those of the employed by 1963, it is of interest that of these
two groups, the women who went into employment in 1959 had
lower Complexity scores at that point.

The data in Table 39 indicate how open the subjects were
to esthetic experience, or their interest in the beautiful and artistic
as measured by the Estheticism scale of the Omnibus Personality
Inventory, described as follows:

Estheticism (Es); 24 items. High scorers indicate interests
in diverse artistic matters and activities. The content of the statements in this scale extends beyond references to painting, sculp-
ture, and music, and includes literature and drama.

Since the scale was administered only in 1963, the extent to
which the groups changed on this dimension cannot be determined. But it is clear that the students who persisted in college four
years differed markedly in esthetic appreciation from their peers

Table 39

STANDARD MEAN ESTHETICISM SCORES OF COLLEGE PERSISTERS AND
THE CONSISTENTLY EMPLOYED, 1963

	College		Employed		Critical ratio
	(N)	Mean	(N)	Mean	(College vs. Employed)
Men	(723)	47.94	(444)	41.31	10.87 **
Women	(578)	55.42	(478)	44.82	17.10 **

Critical ratio—
Men vs. women   (13.36 **)   (5.32 **)
** p < .01.

who remained employed during that period. Within each group
distinguished by post high school pursuit, women proved to be
more esthetically oriented than men, but the difference between
the college and working groups were greater on this scale, regardless of sex, than were the differences between the two pursuit
groups on the other intellectual disposition scales. Among the men,
the college students' standard mean Estheticism score was well over
one-half a standard deviation higher than the workers' score;
among the women this difference spanned nearly a whole standard
deviation.

Level of ability was found to be clearly and positively related to esthetic orientation only for the college women. Within
any group of subjects, whether in college or employed, the highest
Estheticism score was obtained by those from a high socioeconomic
level. The standard score of employed women at the high socioeconomic level was nearly 2.6 points higher than that of working
women at the low socioeconomic level. Differences in means between subjects of high and low socioeconomic levels averaged less
than 1.5 standard points; without exception, differences between
Estheticism scores of the college students and workers were much
greater than differences in scores between groups of different socioeconomic or ability levels. Except for men at the middle ability
level, the difference in mean scores between the college and employed groups for both sexes at each ability and socioeconomic
level extended over half a standard deviation at the minimum.
Differences were highly significant in all cases.

Of course, it cannot be said that college attendance caused

the difference in the scores, but only that college persisters registered far greater esthetic appreciation than nonattenders, and that this difference could not be accounted for in this study by differences in ability or socioeconomic background.

The differences in the measured intellectual and esthetic orientation between the college and employed groups were reflected in their reported activities and interests. In 1963, seventy-one per cent of the college men reported having browsed in a bookstore at least three times during the past year, compared with 31 per cent of the employed men; comparable figures for the women were 81 and 36 per cent, respectively. About 35 per cent of the male college students also reported having attended dramatic performances, concerts, public lectures, and art exhibits at least three times during the preceding year, compared with 6 per cent of the employed men. Comparable figures for the women were approximately 50 per cent for the college students and less than 15 per cent for the employed.

Of these cultural activities, only frequency of browsing in book stores had any clear relationship to level of ability, and more for the employed group than for the college students. Frequency with which different cultural activities were pursued varied more consistently with socioeconomic level than with ability level, but differences in regular attendance at these activities, even between the highest and lowest socioeconomic levels, seldom reached as high as 10 percentage points.

As was the case with their Esetheticism scores on the Omnibus Personality Inventory, whether the high school graduates attended college was associated more with the frequency of their cultural activities than with their level of ability or socioeconomic status. For instance, 42 per cent of the college men at the high level of ability attended dramatic performances several times within the last year, compared with 9 per cent of the working men of high ability. Comparable figures at the middle level of ability were 29 and 7 per cent and at the low level of ability 38 and 8 per cent. Statistical differences between the college and employed youths existed on these variables without exception for both sexes, and regardless of ability and socioeconomic status.

Of course, that there were differences in esthetic and cultural interests between the two groups does not necessarily imply that college was the influencing factor; the statistical differences found may reflect what were initial differences in disposition between the members of the two groups. Also, differences in cultural pursuits of college and noncollege youths might in part be accounted for by the college students' relatively easy access to numerous cultural activities typically found on college campuses. It was in order to rule out this factor of proximity that two cultural interests not linked to locale or environment were chosen as discriminating items. The graduates' preferences in magazines and music were noted at the two time periods in an attempt to discover, through their shifts in reading and musical interests, any changes in intellectual interests. In 1959, the largest proportion of the high school graduate sample, regardless of sex or later pursuit, expressed preferences for general interest magazines such as the *Saturday Evening Post* and sports magazines. These magazines remained favorites of the employed graduates in 1963 but in much smaller proportions than in 1959. In 1959, only 9 per cent of the students listed "no preference," compared with 35 per cent in 1963. Few of the college-bound students preferred cultural and scientific magazines such as *The Atlantic Monthly* and *Scientific American* at the point of their high school graduation, and almost none of the noncollege group preferred magazines of this calibre. The only notable change four years later was a substantially increased interest in newsmagazines among the college students ($Z = 6.82$; $p < .01$), who also showed a significantly greater interest in cultural and newsmagazines than the employed youths. (Cultural magazines: $Z = 4.88$, 1959; $Z = 5.13$, 1963. Newsmagazines: $Z = 6.41$, 1959; $Z = 19.83$, 1963; $p < .01$ in all cases.) But the latter percentages involved were small, and as manifested by their reading habits, the college students did not appear to have increased markedly in intellectual interests more than the employed youths.

"A great liking for classical music" was taken as another indicator of cultural interests. In both 1959 and 1963, fifty per cent of the college women reported liking classical music a great deal; in 1959, thirty-one per cent of the college men shared this interest, and in 1963, thirty-seven per cent. Proportionately fewer of the employed in the sample liked classical music a great deal at either time period compared with the college students, and this difference was even more pronounced in 1963. Twenty-six per cent of the employed women liked classical music a great deal as high school seniors, compared with 13 per cent of the same group four years later; among the employed men, 16 per cent shared this interest in 1959 and 14 per cent in 1963. With respect to cultural interests, tastes in music differentiated between college students and their working peers more than magazine reading; over the four-year period a larger proportion of the former than the latter maintained and developed their interest in music. The college men changed significantly toward a greater liking for classical music and the employed women reported significantly less interest. The working men maintained the least interest and the college women, without changing on this variable, the most.

The graduates' intellectual interests were further investigated through their evaluation of different types of occupations. In the questionnaire, 10 occupations were designated by job title or description of function, and the subjects were instructed to rate them according to the "amount of *respect* they are given by the general public," and also according to how much *"appeal"* the different job areas had for the subjects themselves. The owner of a hardware store served as the example of a small businessman, a biologist as the example of a scientist in an applied field, and a college professor as the example of a professional in an academic occupation.

The opinion reported by the majority of the youths, both in 1959 and 1963, was that the public holds a great deal of respect for the academic profession, but less for the applied scientist and least by far for the businessman (Table 40). Less than 10 per cent of the college youths and less than 15 per cent of the employed thought the public had a "great deal" of respect for the small businessman. Much less than half of the sample considered any of the ocupations personally appealing, but the largest number of the youths, including the workers, reported the academic profession as the most appealing.

However, proportionately fewer of the workers found the academic profession of great appeal by 1963, whereas proportionately more college youths than in 1959 reported this occupation as having great personal appeal (Table 41). There was a significant decrease both in college and employed youths who

Table 40

COLLEGE PERSISTERS AND THE CONSISTENTLY EMPLOYED REPORTING ON
OCCUPATIONS HELD IN GREAT RESPECT BY THE PUBLIC,
1959 AND 1963, IN PERCENTAGES

	(N)		Business		Occupations and Groups Scientific		Academic	
	College	Employed	College	Employed	College	Employed	College	Employed
Men	(793)	(537)						
1959			9	15	28	33	64	58
1963			5	13	19	22	56	64
Women	(620)	(540)						
1959			7	14	39	42	68	64
1963			2	13	33	29	60	66
(Z ratio—1959 vs. 1963) [a]			(4.83 **)	(.92 +)	(4.54 **)	(6.08 **)	(4.27 **)	(1.90 +)

[a] Sexes combined.
+ p = not significant.
** p < .01.

found the occupation of the applied scientist or businessman greatly appealing. By 1963 only a little over 12 per cent, combining all groups, reported that an occupation within the field of biology had this much appeal, and less than 2 per cent of the employed and college youths found business very appealing.

It is not surprising that college students would identify more with an occupation generally presumed to be intellectual, but the rejection of the "practical" occupations traditionally held in great respect in American society is of interest. It will be seen in the next chapter that this rejection of practical business interests went beyond the specific occupations listed in this context and that the more inclined the individual was to change in measured attitude over the four years, the less likely he was to share the interests of businessmen such as accountants and salesmen.

The data reviewed to this point indicate that the college student is more likely than his working peer to increase in intellectual disposition whether the criterion is measured attitudes, leisure activities, or opinions about careers, although the differences are not always great.

ATTAINMENT OF AUTONOMY

Since there is a significant positive correlation between intellectual disposition and autonomous, nonauthoritarian attitudes as assessed by the Omnibus Personality Inventory (see the intercorrelation matrix in Appendix Table C-1), it can be inferred that there is also a logical relationship between intellectualism and autonomy. Those high in measured intellectual disposition manifest a great interest in a variety of ideas, and openness to complex and even conflicting ideas. This attitude toward life and learning necessitates an open, flexible, critical, objective, and nonjudgmental way of thinking in general. It is, of course, this kind of intellectual orientation that is purportedly measured by the various autonomy scales of the Omnibus Personality Inventory, including the Autonomy scale itself, the Social Maturity scale, and its derivative, the Nonauthoritarianism scale.

It is also this orientation that is so important for the individual to develop, whether or not he attends college, if he is to cope effectively with the tensions, changes, and complexities of contemporary society. The hypothesis was that those with the

Table 41

COLLEGE PERSISTERS AND THE CONSISTENTLY EMPLOYED REPORTING VARIOUS OCCUPATIONS THAT HAVE A "GREAT DEAL" OF APPEAL TO THEM, 1959 AND 1963, IN PERCENTAGES

| | (N) | | Occupations and Groups | | | | | |
| | | | Business | | Scientific | | Academic | |
	College	Employed	College	Employed	College	Employed	College	Employed
Men	(793)	(537)						
1959			4	12	16	18	26	22
1963			2	2	10	9	37	14
Women	(620)	(540)						
1959			3	5	21	21	32	25
1963			1	1	17	11	44	20
(Z ratio—1959 vs. 1963) [a]			(3.36 **)	(7.56 **)	(3.74 **)	(6.31 **)	(6.24 **)	(3.64 **)

[a] Sexes combined.

** $p < .01$.

least exposure to college would show the least development in this direction four years after high school. It is, after all, an avowed purpose of many colleges to provide a general, liberating education designed to promote critical, autonomous, and informed thinking. If colleges succeed at all in this purpose, then students should show a positive change in autonomy after four years. In contrast to the goals of higher education, nonprofessional jobs are rarely calculated to develop autonomous thinking. Whether the job is filing in an office or riveting on an assembly line, the work is most often more constricting than liberating.

The data to follow provide a closer examination of the association between varying amounts of exposure to college and development of autonomy, since the data present differences in autonomy scores obtained between 1959 and 1963 by the groups under consideration. The Social Maturity and Nonauthoritarianism scales were used because they were the only Omnibus Personality Inventory scales of this type available at both time periods.

The Nonauthoritarianism scale, described in Chapter VI, is composed of 20 items, the majority of which are included in the much longer Social Maturity scale, described as follows:

Social Maturity (SM) (67 items): A personality syndrome, having its origin in responses to nonauthoritarian items and their correlates. In college populations, it is correlated with age. High scorers tend to be uncompulsive, nonpunitive, independent, and not subject to feelings of victimization. They also possess genuine curiosity and interest in intellectual and esthetic matters. Low scorers tend to be more judgmental, intolerant, and conventional in their thinking.

Although the shorter scale has a lower internal consistency reliability than the longer one, it measures the syndrome of authoritarianism more specifically. Together, the scales provide a broad assessment of the subjects' openness, objectivity, and flexibility of thinking.

The data in Table 42 indicate that just prior to high school graduation, the mean Nonauthoritarianism score of the college-bound men was a little over 3 standard points higher than that of their male classmates who entered employment, a difference significant at the 1 per cent level (C.R. = 5.37). By 1963, the difference in mean scores between the two groups spanned over 10 standard points—beyond a whole standard deviation. Over the four years, the college men increased by 6 points, whereas the employed men showed a decrease of 1 standard point. The highly significant and decidedly observable increase in the college men's mean Nonauthoritarianism score and the working men's regression in mean score (although not at a statistically significant level) were further corroborated by the statistical significance of the difference in change between the two groups.

The pattern of differences found between the college and employed men on the Nonauthoritarianism scale also existed for the women, and with equally great statistical significance. In 1959, however, the men were generally less authoritarian than the women, regardless of later pursuits. By 1963, this difference between the sexes still held for the employed in the sample, but not for the college students.

On the more complex Social Maturity scale, all groups showed an increase in mean scores between 1959 and 1963. The increase made by both men and women college students was much greater, however, than the increase made by the employed group, and the college women's mean Social Maturity score in 1963 was significantly higher than the college men's (C.R. = 3.80). Combining sexes, the college students' mean score increased by nearly 10 standard points, and the employed graduates' score by approximately 3.5 points. The statistical significance of the Ψ values in Table 42 testify to the large differences between the college students and their employed peers in change of mean Social Maturity score. The differences on both Autonomy scales far exceeded those found on the Thinking Introversion and Complexity scales. In a study of University of California and Stanford University students between 1961 and 1965, Korn (1968) also found that of all variables examined, including traits measured by Omnibus Personality Inventory scales, the students at both universities changed most in autonomy as measured by another version of the Social Maturity scale.

Data in Appendix Table E-6 show a relationship between autonomy and degree of ability, as measured by the two Omnibus Personality Inventory scales. For example, the standard mean Nonauthoritarianism scores obtained by the employed men in

Table 42

STANDARD MEAN NONAUTHORITARIANISM AND SOCIAL MATURITY SCORES,
1959 AND 1963, OF COLLEGE PERSISTERS AND
THE CONSISTENTLY EMPLOYED

Scales and Groups

Sex and Year	(N) College	Employed	Nonauthoritarianism College	Employed	Social Maturity College	Employed	Ψ values of College vs. Employed Na	SM
Men	(723)	(444)						
1959			46.26	43.02	53.34	50.00		
1963			52.28	42.03	62.50	53.76		
Difference			6.02	−0.99	9.16	3.76		
(t)			(15.71 **)	(1.62 +)	(28.32 **)	(7.67 **)	7.01 **	4.15 **
Women	(578)	(478)						
1959			44.52	40.78	52.85	47.82		
1963			52.60	40.46	63.37	51.16		
Difference			8.08	−0.32	10.52	3.34		
(t)			(19.16 **)	(0.60 +)	(30.04 **)	(7.77 **)	8.40 **	7.18 **

+ p = not significant.
** p < .01.

151

1959 at the high, middle, and low ability levels were, respectively: 44.2, 43.5, and 40.8. The corresponding means in 1963 were: 44.5, 41.4, and 40.4. The relationship between socioeconomic level and autonomy was much less marked and consistent, except for that found in the mean Nonauthoritarianism scores of the employed men in 1963 (Appendix Table E-7). This varied from high to low socioeconomic levels as follows: 44.2, 42.7, and 40.6.

Only at the high ability level did the employed of either sex increase in their mean Nonauthoritarianism score, and the increase was nominal (less than one point, combining sexes). College students increased approximately 7 points. Using the men as the example, on the Social Maturity scale the change scores of the college students varied with ability levels from 8.7 to 11.0, and with socioeconomic levels from 8.4 to 10.7. Corresponding ranges of change scores for the employed group were 2.4 to 4.1 among ability levels, and from 2.6 to 6.0 among socioeconomic levels. The women's change scores followed the same pattern.

As was generally the case with the scores that indicated intellectual disposition, the differences between the college and employed graduates' mean autonomy scores at each ability and socioeconomic level were consistently greater than the differences between mean scores of the graduates at high and low ability and socioeconomic levels. Whatever their ability or background, those in the sample who had been employed, compared with the college students, showed considerably less growth in autonomy after four years. The Ψ values in Appendix Tables E-6 and E-7 show that the change scores of the college and employed groups on both scales were significantly different—mostly beyond the 1 per cent level—at each ability and socioeconomic level with the exception of the Social Maturity scores of the high socioeconomic women. In fact, as measured by the Nonauthoritarianism scale, the employed as a group tended to become less open-minded and flexible in their thinking after high school.

Persistence in college was associated with amount of increase in autonomy, again regardless of sex, ability, or socioeconomic level. On the average, the college persisters increased their mean Nonauthoritarianism scores by nearly 7 standard points, and the withdrawals by 3 points (Table 43). On the Social Maturity scale, the presisters increased their mean scores by 9.8 standard

Table 43

STANDARD MEAN NONAUTHORITIANISM AND SOCIAL MATURITY SCORES OF STUDENTS WHO REMAINED IN COLLEGE BETWEEN ONE AND THREE YEARS, AND THOSE WHO REMAINED FOUR YEARS

Scales and Groups

Sex and Year	(N) Persisters	Withdrawals	Nonauthoritarianism Persisters	Withdrawals	Social Maturity Persisters	Withdrawals	Ψ value of Persisters and Withdrawals Na	SM
Men	(723)	(105)						
1959			46.26	45.23	53.34	53.78		
1963			52.28	47.08	62.50	58.72		
Difference			6.02	1.85	9.16	4.94		
(t)			(15.71 **)	(1.85 +)	(28.32 **)	(6.12 **)	4.17 **	4.22 **
Women	(578)	(195)						
1959			44.52	43.84	52.85	52.68		
1963			52.60	47.47	63.37	58.32		
Difference			8.08	3.63	10.52	5.64		
(t)			(19.16 **)	(4.60 **)	(30.04 **)	(8.92 **)	4.45 **	4.88 **

+ p = not significant.
* p < .05.
** p < .01.

153

points, and the withdrawals by 5.4 points. The computation of the highly significant difference in change in autonomy between the college persisters and withdrawals may be found in Appendix Table E-1. The resultant Ψ values in Table 43 show that for both sexes the college persisters changed more than the withdrawals on the two scales.

These data present the same problem of interpretation as did the data from the measures of intellectual disposition discussed earlier. Without scores from intermittent tests, it cannot be affirmed that the students increased in autonomy in direct proportion to the length of their exposure to college. However, since the college students with four years in college and those with less had obtained the same Social Maturity scores when they were high school seniors, it can be said that the group of students who persisted in college made the greatest change in level of autonomy as measured by this scale.

The evidence does not necessarily contradict Freedman's (1960) or Lehmann's and Dressel's (1962, 1963)—that the greatest change of values of college students takes place during their freshman and sophomore years. It is to be noted in the present instance, however, that the difference in change is greater between the withdrawals and persisters than it is between the withdrawals and those who did not enter college. Moreover, the difference of .4 of a standard deviation significantly exceeds the standard error of measurement between the persisters and withdrawals. The extent of these differences is too great to dismiss the strong possibility that the college persisters continued to develop throughout college in a way that the withdrawals did not. The only other conceivable possibility is that the persisters developed that much more than the withdrawals at the outset of college.

If persistence in college is related to personality development, then it may be argued that the longer the exposure to college the more change in attitudes and values is fostered or at least facilitated by the college. If change takes place early, then it may be argued that the eventual persisters are from the beginning more open to change than the eventual withdrawals. Related research does not clearly point to the greater validity of one interpretation over the other. The decisive differences found here in measured change in attitudes and values after four years between

those who attended college and those who did not, and between
those who persisted in college four years and those who attended
for shorter periods, corroborate the findings of an early study of
Plant (1958), but they disagree at first reading with the findings
of Telford and Plant (1963), and are at some variance with the
findings of Lehmann and Dressel (1962, 1963).

For their study of the impact of public two-year colleges
on values, Telford and Plant administered Rokeach's Dogmatism
scale (Rokeach, 1960) and the Allport-Vernon-Lindzey Study of
Values (Allport, Vernon, and Lindzey, 1951) to a sample of 4506
subjects who applied to six California public junior colleges in the
summer and fall of 1960. The scales correlate significantly with
the Omnibus Personality Inventory's intellectuality and autonomy
scales (Center for the Study of Higher Education, 1962). All the
scales were again administered to as many of the sample as could
be reached by mail two years later. The subjects in the longitudinal sample were then classified into three categories: those
who applied for admission but did not actually attend classes,
those who attended one or two semesters, and those who attended
for three or four semesters. The mean scores obtained by the three
groups at the time of application and two years later were then
compared and tested for significance of differences through the
use of the *t* test. The mean differences between the groups were
not impressive. However, the difference in means was statistically
significant for each group. The authors concluded that students
who attended junior college for three or four semesters did not
change in attitude any more than those who had not attended at
all.

This result, however, was affected by a number of limitations. Telford and Plant's sampling loss after two years was greater
than that in the present study after four years: Only 38 per cent
of their entire original sample responded two years later, and only
32 per cent of their subjects who did not attend college responded.
Thus the problem of dealing with a possibly biased sample, which
was mentioned in reference to the present report, was even more
crucial in the Telford and Plant study. Other possible sources of
sampling bias in the Telford-Plant study were that only students
who were motivated to enroll in a college were surveyed, and then
only those drawn to the junior college.

Additional factors to be considered in evaluating the Telford-Plant study are: that nonattendance figures were based only on the responding subjects' self-report; that the AVL scales measure hierarchy and not intensity of values; that scales like Rokeach's may be subject to response bias when their items are not "scrambled" with other types of items; and that the t technique used by Telford and Plant is inadequate to test the significance of group differences on scales that are intercorrelated, and should have been supplemented by measurement of differences between the group differences. Even according to the t values obtained, the three groups in the study exhibited marked differences in amount of change.

Despite these shortcomings, Telford and Plant's work is useful in pointing up the problems inherent in research of this kind and provides a means for discussing the differences in the findings of the two studies. By confining themselves to junior college students, however, Telford and Plant were seriously limited because their sample was thus followed only for two years and suffered from a high loss of subjects.

Limitations of another sort affect Lehmann and Dressel's (1962, 1963) studies, referred to earlier. Only students at Michigan State University were studied and although they were classified by year of withdrawal, they were tested only in 1958 and 1962. Persisters were defined as students who entered the university in 1958 and were enrolled there 9 out of 11 terms (including spring term of 1962) where 12 terms constitute four academic years and transfer students were included with the withdrawals.

In reference to the first limitation, there is evidence that students attending major universities are at the outset more select in personality than other students. The fact that students were re-tested only after four years presents precisely the same problems of interpretation that affect the present study. Students who persist consecutively through four years of college may be different from students who withdraw for a term or more in ways as yet unknown. Finally, the most serious limitation is that transfer students were included among the withdrawals. This makes it impossible to generalize on the relationship between length of stay in college and change of personality, because transfers are not really withdrawals. This is an especially important factor, considering the differences observed in Chapters V and VI between transfers and withdrawals as well as between withdrawals in good academic standing and those with failing status.

These limitations aside, Lehmann obtained a good response from his subjects in 1962. Usable pre- and post-study data were obtained from 57 per cent of the "withdrawals" classified by length of stay in college, and 68 per cent of the persisters. As noted above, the persisters became significantly more "emergent" in their values as measured by the Differential Values Inventory. There was a significant relationship between the mean Critical Thinking scores obtained in 1962 and the length the women stayed at Michigan State University, suggesting that the longer they remained at the university the more perceptive and less stereotypic they became in their thinking. There was a significant change in the Critical Thinking scores of the men but it was not significantly related to their length of stay in college. The students, as a whole, became significantly more open-minded and objective in their thinking as measured by the Dogmatism scale. The longer the students stayed in college the higher their mean scores on the scale, but not enough to distinguish between the persisters and withdrawals with statistical significance. Since the withdrawals included transfer students—and since it is indicated from research cited in Chapter V that so many withdrawals from major universities continue their studies—it may be remarkable that Lehmann and Dressel found as many differences as they did.

In other research, Plant (1962) found that four-year college students changed in attitudes and values after two years far more than the three- and four-semester junior college students he studied with Telford. This finding is consistent with the findings of the present study in reference to students who attended college four years or less, and in reference to junior college students specifically. In the report preliminary to the present study (Medsker and Trent, 1965), evidence was presented which showed that junior college students were from lower and more culturally limited backgrounds than students enrolled in four-year colleges and universities, and were less autonomous in measured attitude and more restricted in intellectual disposition.

In light of the disparate findings on the subject, more research must be conducted before the relationship between the length of college experience and personality development can be further delineated. Ideally, the research should include testing not only at entrance to college and four years later, but also at the end of the first, second, and third year. It should also include a wide variety of students examined in a variety of educational settings. For a final measure it should control for level of initial scores, academic aptitude, and socioeconomic status.

At the present time, it may at least be said that the findings in the present study of differences in personality change between the persisters and withdrawals were based on students of tested ability and socioeconomic status who attended a diversity of institutions and were known to have persisted in college for four years or to have withdrawn and not returned to college within the period of the study.

Differences in attitude were not only apparent between those who entered junior colleges and those who entered four-year colleges or universities, but also between students who persisted in various types of four-year colleges (Table 44). Men and women in private nonsectarian colleges and universities in 1963 had entered college with the least show of authoritarianism in 1959, and students in church-related colleges with the most (except for students in two-year colleges, not shown in the table). In between were students who in 1963 were in public universities and colleges. The results on the correlated Social Maturity scale were essentially the same.

The differences among students who entered various types of colleges in 1959 continued to exist in 1963. The students, grouped by type of college they attended, who obtained the highest mean autonomy scores in 1959, also obtained the highest mean scores in 1963, and the student groups with the lowest mean autonomy scores in 1959 had the lowest scores in 1963. This correspondence of the ranks of the college groups between the two time periods was confirmed statistically; when the ranked Nonauthoritarianism means of 1959 and 1963 obtained by the students in the different types of colleges were correlated, the men had a rho coefficient of .89 and the women a perfect correlation of 1.00.

At least among the women, the higher the mean scores of these groups in 1959, generally the greater were their changes in

Table 44

STANDARD MEAN NONAUTHORITARIANISM AND SOCIAL MATURITY SCORES OF COLLEGE PERSISTERS, 1959 AND 1963, BY TYPE OF COLLEGE ATTENDED IN 1963

Scales	Public	College Church-related	Private nonsectarian	Public	University Church-related	Private nonsectarian
Men						
(N)	(214)	(114)	(37)	(250)	(39)	(31)
Nonauthoritarianism						
1959	45.48	45.44	49.54	46.51	42.92	54.48
1963	52.49	51.46	52.42	53.17	47.69	53.45
Difference	7.01	6.02	2.88	6.66	4.77	−1.03
(t)	(8.87 **)	(6.40 **)	(1.61 +)	(11.48 **)	(3.73 **)	(0.53 +)
Social Maturity						
1959	52.79	52.43	52.43	54.23	50.85	60.27
1963	62.31	61.54	64.80	63.87	56.89	64.93
Difference	9.52	9.11	12.37	9.64	6.04	4.66
(t)	(14.21 **)	(11.83 **)	(10.76 **)	(18.19 **)	(4.76 **)	(3.05 **)

+ p = not significant.
* p < .05.
** p < .01.

Table 44 (continued)

STANDARD MEAN NONAUTHORITARIANISM AND SOCIAL MATURITY SCORES OF COLLEGE PERSISTERS, 1959 AND 1963, BY TYPE OF COLLEGE ATTENDED IN 1963

Scales	Public	College Church-related	Private nonsectarian	Public	University Church-related	Private nonsectarian
Women						
(N)	(203)	(107)	(27)	(190)	(22)	(21)
Nonauthoritarianism						
1959	48.31	43.06	44.38	46.80	41.57	47.01
1963	52.60	51.21	53.49	53.88	46.12	57.01
Difference	9.29	8.15	9.11	7.08	4.55	10.00
(t)	(11.91 **)	(8.86 **)	(4.05 **)	(8.53 **)	(2.19 *)	(5.59 **)
Social Maturity						
1959	51.64	50.34	55.77	55.22	48.70	59.40
1963	62.50	59.12	65.98	66.57	56.96	69.63
Difference	10.86	8.78	10.21	11.35	8.26	10.23
(t)	(16.97 **)	(11.71 **)	(5.29 **)	(18.31 **)	(3.53 **)	(6.24 **)

+ p = not significant.
* p < .05.
** p < .01.

160

mean scores in a positive direction in 1963. The ranking of the group's 1959 mean scores were compared with the ranking of their change scores (from most to least change). The rho coefficient between rank on Nonauthoritarianism in 1959 and amount of increase on this scale in 1963 for the women grouped by college type was .53. For the men the rho coefficient was negative, but largely because the university men showed only a negligible change compared with the other student groups (in a negative direction on the Nonauthoritarianism scale). The coefficients comparing mean Social Maturity scores were comparable in pattern in all instances.

These patterns also generally held when high, middle, and low levels of ability and socioeconomic status were held constant. A coefficient of concordance (W) was computed comparing the ranking of the mean Nonauthoritarianism scores obtained in 1959 by the groups in toto and also by each ability and socioeconomic level.* For the men the W coefficient was .53 and for the women .43 when the scores were ranked by ability level. The corresponding W coefficients, taking into account ranks by socioeconomic level, were .87 for the men and .93 for the women. As has been found throughout the report, ability was apparently more related to differences in attitude than to socioeconomic status.

Analyses of variance confirmed that at both time periods the students grouped by the type of college they entered differed significantly overall in the scores they obtained on the two scales (see Appendix E), showing that there were significant differences among the rankings previously observed. However, it is also known from the *t* values in Table 44 that the students within each type of college changed significantly on the two autonomy scales between 1959 and 1963. The only exception to this was among the private college and university men and the denominational university women on the Nonauthoritarianism scale. The private nondenominational college and university men had the highest scores initially and failed to expand their scores in relation to the other student groups. The private denominational university women began with the lowest mean Nonauthoritarian-

---

* The coefficient of concordance quantifies the correlation among several ranked scores as the rho coefficient quantifies the correlation between two sets of ranked scores obtained by a distribution of groups or individuals.

ism score in 1959, obtained the lowest mean score in 1963, and changed the least of all the women between the two time periods. Among the nondenominational college men there is the possibility that a ceiling of measured autonomous disposition was reached relatively early. The denominational university women reflected little inclination toward growth in autonomy, and may have been attending institutions with environments not conducive to development of autonomy. This possibility is discussed in another publication which reports a study of groups and characteristics of sectarian college students (Trent, 1967), and pages 198–199 of the present study.

Analyses of variance of the change scores of the men and women attending different types of colleges were conducted to determine if there were significant differences between these changes. The computations in Appendix Table E-8 show a significant difference in the change in scores of men enrolled in different types of colleges, but not of women. It may be that the men's significant F ratio was occasioned by the extreme change scores, assisted by the little difference in scores obtained by the men in private universities. On the basis of Ψ values, no significant difference in change scores was observed among the men in the three types of institutions enrolling the most students—public colleges and universities and private denominational colleges. Among the women, both public college and university students changed significantly more than denominational college students on the Social Maturity scale (see Appendix Table E-1).

Indications are, then, that for men, degree and change of nonauthoritarian attitudes were more associated with the type of college chosen and with persistence in college than with any change that took place as a consequence of having attended a particular type of college. This condition also seemed to hold true for the women, although when they were classified by the type of college in which they persisted, there were some significant differences in their change scores.

Perhaps greater differences in personality development would have been found among students attending different types of colleges if the institutions could have been distinguished according to size, special programs, the training and quality of their faculty, and the ability distribution of their students. Also, many colleges may not have much impact on their students. If it were not for the relative lack of development found among the employed and the withdrawals, it might be argued that the attitude changes observed were a reflection of general maturation. Nevertheless, there is still reason to believe that the changes found result in large part from the combination of the students' readiness for growth and the college's subsequent facilitation of that growth.

Table 45

STANDARD MEAN NONAUTHORITARIANISM AND SOCIAL MATURITY SCORES,
1959 AND 1963, OF WOMEN COLLEGE PERSISTERS, WORKERS,
HOMEMAKERS, AND THOSE WHO COMBINED PURSUITS

Groups	(N)	Nonauthoritarianism [a]	Social Maturity [b]
College	(578)		
1959		44.52	52.85
1963		52.60	63.37
Difference		8.08	10.52
(t)		(18.29 **)	(23.07 **)
Employed	(478)		
1959		40.78	47.82
1963		40.46	51.16
Difference		−0.32	3.34
(t)		(0.60 +)	(7.85 **)
Homemaking	(216)		
1959		42.49	48.91
1963		41.07	52.04
Difference		−1.42	3.13
(t)		(1.88 +)	(5.45 **)
Combination	(1102)		
1959		42.24	49.79
1963		43.59	54.25
Difference		1.35	4.46
(t)		(4.15 **)	(17.25 **)

[a] Nonauthoritarianism: College vs. Employed—$\Psi = 8.40$ **; Employed vs. Homemakers—$\Psi = 1.10$ +; Homemakers vs. Combined—$\Psi = 2.77$ **; Employed vs. Combined—$\Psi = 1.03$ +.

[b] Social Maturity: College vs. Employed—$\Psi = 7.18$ **; Employed vs. Homemakers—$\Psi = .21$ +; Homemakers vs. Combined—$\Psi = 1.33$ *; Employed vs. Combined—$\Psi = 1.12$ *.

+ p = not significant.
* p = $< .05$.
** p = $< .01$.

Differences in change scores on the Nonauthoritarianism scale were more apparent among women who followed various post high school pursuits than among women in various types of colleges (Table 45). The college women were the only ones to increase appreciably in autonomy as measured by the Nonauthoritarianism scale. Highest in autonomy to start with, the women who persisted in college showed an increase of 8 standard points in their mean scores over the four years. The employed women showed a slight *decrease* in Nonauthoritarianism, and the homemakers who married before or immediately after high school graduation, without any further experience as either student or employee, showed a mean decrease in Nonauthoritarianism of nearly 1.5 standard points. In 1963, the combined standard mean Nonauthoritarianism score of both the employed women and homemakers was approximately 40; of women who combined pursuits, nearly 44; and of women who persisted in college, over 52. A statistically significant change in Nonauthoritarianism between 1959 and 1963 was made only by the college persisters and the group of women who had combined pursuits, including some college. The differences in mean Nonauthoritarian scores of the groups of women and the employed and college men may be compared in Figure 6.

Although all the groups of women changed significantly on the Social Maturity scale, they did so to considerably different degrees, as noted by the significant Ψ values in Appendix Table E-1. The homemakers increased their standard mean Social Maturity scores over the four years by a little over 3 points; the combined-pursuits group, by 4.5 points; and the persisters, by 10.5 points. The statistical analyses in Appendix Table E-1 confirm the obvious: Compared with the other women, women who persisted in college showed by far the greatest development in autonomy on both scales, and the homemakers by far the greatest constriction in autonomy. But the scores of the consistently employed women in many ways paralleled the scores of their classmates who became full-time housewives immediately after high school.

Differences in autonomy between the college and noncollege youth were indicated in ways other than measured attitudes (Table 46). Compared with their employed peers in 1963, the

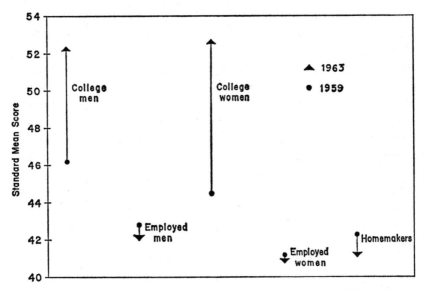

Figure 6. CHANGE ON NONAUTHORITARIANISM SCALE FROM 1959 TO 1963 BY POST HIGH SCHOOL PURSUIT.

Table 46

OPINIONS ABOUT INDIVIDUALITY EXPRESSED BY COLLEGE PERSISTERS AND THE CONSISTENTLY EMPLOYED, IN PERCENTAGES

	Men			*Women*		
Opinions	*College* *(N = 793)*	*Employed* *(N = 537)*	*Chi* *square* [a]	*College* *(N = 620)*	*Employed* *(N = 540)*	*Chi* *square* [a]
Viewed self as noncon- formist	26	16	19.40 **	18	11	9.34 **
Viewed self as common man	31	58	96.64 **	24	40	32.68 **
Reported most important issue facing society was loss of individuality	21	7	46.89 **	20	4	63.77 **

[a] Chi squares based on two by two tables—responding college and employed subjects to above items versus all others.

** $p < .01$.

college students tended more to view themselves as nonconformists and to express concern over the loss of personal individuality.

A majority of the employed men viewed themselves as the "common man," whereas less than one-third of the college men did so. What exactly these terms meant to the subjects is not known. On the surface, at least, proportionately more college students compared with their noncollege peers were seeking a personal identity of their own, distinct from the "common man" norm. Although many college students did not concern themselves over individual differences and autonomous self-expression, neither did they want to see themselves as common men. In both attitude and opinion, the college students appeared more likely than their working peers to approach life with more inner-directedness, and proportionately more college than noncollege youths stressed their uniqueness as individuals.

VALUES AND GOALS FOUR YEARS AFTER HIGH SCHOOL

In 1963, the graduates were asked an array of questions about their values—what they considered their source of greatest satisfaction and their views on marriage, politics, religion, and social issues. These items were not included in the 1959 survey and, thus, provided no direct information on the change of the graduates' values four years after high school. They did, however, serve as indicators of their general approach to life at the time they were assuming adult roles.

For both the college and employed samples of men and women, the factors ranked as most important to a satisfying life were first, marriage, and family, and second, jobs. Over 36 per cent of the men checked marriage and family as first or second in importance to a satisfying life; approximately 30 per cent said this about their jobs. Figures among the women were comparable. Other factors some graduates considered important to a satisfying life were: money, recreation, civic participation, religious, cultural, and scholarly activities. However, no more than 10 per cent of the graduates listed these activities as of prime importance, with the exception of the working women (19 per cent) who regarded religious activities as very important to a satisfying life.

Combining sexes, about 8 per cent of the college students checked cultural or scholarly activities as the first or second most important source of a satisfying life, compared with 2 per cent of their working peers. Conversely, in the assessment of the importance of money, approximately 8 per cent of the employed group and 2 per cent of the college group considered money of primary or secondary importance. Relatively few subjects considered participation in civic affairs of first or second importance (the highest proportion was 4 per cent of the college men, and the lowest, 1 per cent of the working men). The young adults in the sample, whether in college or out, did not view the life of the mind or spirit, or material wealth, as important as jobs and families.

The subjects interviewed were also asked to define a successful person. Their descriptions differed widely. They viewed as successful people who had acquired material goods, those who were stereotypes of the highly professional or respected, and those who had attained personal integrity and individuality. Typical comments were: "A successful person is one with lots of money . . . a person with position, money, a beautiful home, two cars in the garage, and a nice family . . ."; "Success just means to provide for your family—I guess some day I'd like to own my own business and be looked up to, but as long as I'm making money I won't complain . . ."; "Usually somebody with a big title such as president of a company . . . Someone with prestige in the community, someone who's looked up to and respected." Only rarely did a young person define a successful person as, "One who has fulfilled the aims and ideals he has set up for himself and contributed to his community and the world around him."

By far the most frequent definition of a successful person was, "Someone who is satisfied with what he is doing" (approximately 43 per cent of the men and 28 per cent of the women). Other relatively popular definitions were: "The person who is committed to what he is doing"; "The person who has accomplished or is accomplishing his goals"; "The person who is happy, whatever his status in life." Generally there was no marked difference between the patterns of responses of the two sexes or between the college and employed groups, but there were two exceptions: Significantly more men than women emphasized wealth and "getting ahead in life," and significantly more employed youths than college students stressed a good job and security (Respective Z ratios were: 2.75, $p < .01$; 1.98, $p < .05$).

When the entire 1963 sample was asked to note the first

and second most important factors leading to a happy marriage, 51 per cent of the college students and 41 per cent of their employed peers listed love, understanding, and respect as the first or second most important factor in a happy marriage. Other items deemed important by some were: communication and agreement on basic issues (14 per cent); having a common background (12 per cent); sharing common interests (11 per cent); romance and sexual compatibility (about 7 per cent); and security (1 per cent). Proportionately more college students than those employed emphasized love, understanding, and respect, and proportionately more working youths emphasized sex life (Respective Z ratios were: 7.85 and 4.03; $p < .01$). On the whole, most of the youths, at least in terms of gross responses of this kind, seemed to show a fairly mature and realistic awareness of several important factors of a happy marriage.

In the interviews, the high school graduates displayed more naïveté about politics than about marriage. Few could articulate anything in the way of a personal political philosophy; most appeared apathetic and unconcerned about the question of politics. Typical answers to the question, "What are your political beliefs?" were: "Most of the time I'm more liberal—as yet I haven't given politics much thought . . . I don't care too much about that"; "I can vote, but I don't want to"; "Politics have never interested me . . . I don't know what a liberal is—a conservative is smart"; "I haven't thought about it . . . I would tend toward the conservative politically—I don't really have time to go into the stuff."

Frequently the response was, "Oh, I guess I'm a Republican [or a Democrat] because my parents are," a statement representative of the entire sample in 1963. In their answers to the comprehensive survey questionnaire, which provided a comparison of the subjects' political affiliations with the affiliations they had reported for their fathers, 65 per cent of all of the responding high school graduates whose fathers had been Republicans in 1959 reported themselves as Republicans in 1963, and 68 per cent of those who checked that they were Democrats in 1963 had reported that their fathers belonged to this party in 1959.

In all, 35 per cent of the subjects in 1963 declared themselves Republicans, 35 per cent Democrats, 27 per cent Independents, and 3 per cent undecided. Ten students in the sample declared themselves Socialists. Characteristically, the subjects' party affiliations varied with their socioeconomic status and whether or not they had gone to college. There were some party variations by sex, but not systematically.

Combining sexes, 42 per cent of the college students were Republicans, 28 per cent Democrats, and 28 per cent Independent. Of the three political groups, the Republican party claimed the largest proportion of college students and the Democratic party the largest proportion of the working youths, a finding that corroborates previous research (Bone and Rarney, 1963; Greenstein, 1963). But a considerable proportion of the high school graduates (28 per cent, combining sample groups) did not subscribe to any particular party by 1963. From the interviews, it was apparent that a large number of these young people were not Independents, but rather hadn't bothered to register as voters, and that many were both uninformed and uninterested in the political aspects of American life. This was the case whether or not the subjects had attended college, although in 1959 only 17 per cent had reported having fathers who were neither Democrats nor Republicans.

Traditionally, the Republican party more than the Democratic party has drawn proportionately more members from the higher socioeconomic strata, or at least the higher income levels, and this was true of the young adults in the present sample. The proportion of Republicans at the high socioeconomic level was twice as great as that of the Democrats. Conversely, at the low socioeconomic level, the proportion of Democrats was more than twice as great as that of Republicans.

Since there is a relationship between party affiliation and socioeconomic status, and a relationship has been shown between college entrance and socioeconomic status, an important question remained. Are Republicans more likely to attend college than Democrats, or do they attend college in greater proportion only to the extent they come in greater proportion from a higher socioeconomic level? This question is examined statistically in Table 47. The Independents were omitted from the table so that the chi square analyses might refer exclusively to the differences in proportions of college persisters and employed at each socioeconomic level who claimed either one of the two major party affiliations.

Table 47

POLITICAL PREFERENCES OF COLLEGE PERSISTERS AND THE CONSISTENTLY EMPLOYED BY SOCIOECONOMIC STATUS, IN PERCENTAGES

Preference	High (N)	High College	High Employed	Middle (N)	Middle College	Middle Employed	Low (N)	Low College	Low Employed
Men									
Republican	(128)	91	9	(255)	71	29	(38)	45	55
Democrats	(45)	91	9	(235)	51	49	(105)	35	65
(Chi square)		(0.00 +)			(19.68 **)			(1.11 +)	
Women									
Republican	(111)	90	10	(237)	56	44	(44)	23	77
Democrats	(59)	81	19	(259)	42	58	(92)	23	77
(Chi square)		(2.66 +)			(9.69 **)			(0.00 +)	

Column grouping: High | Middle | Low (SES and Groups)

+ p = not significant.
** p = < .01.

Among the relatively few students at the high and low socioeconomic levels, there was no significant difference between the proportions of Democrats and Republicans who were college persisters. This was not true, however, for the middle socioeconomic level at which most of the youths were classified. A significantly larger proportion of Republicans than Democrats at this level attended college. Therefore, the conclusion is that the relationship between college attendance and political preference diminishes at the high and low socioeconomic levels, but is maintained at the middle level. It would be of great interest to delineate further socioeconomic variables that characterize the family backgrounds of the young adults grossly classified at this level, and to see if there are correlated values held by the families and the subjects that might account for the present finding.

Another area of values assumed important to the young adults was that of religion. But however important religion might be, the subjects were generally as vague about this as they were about politics. The interviewees were usually disconcerted when asked to describe their religious beliefs and frequently responded, "What do you mean by my religious beliefs?" When they did expand, after urging, they responded by stating a church affiliation. Pressed further, they typically said, "Well, I believe whatever the church teaches." Further inquiry seldom yielded more than rote and brief recitations of traditional Christian concepts of God, the commandments, and salvation. Current religious issues were rarely mentioned, nor was the function of religion in daily life, not even in terms of such basic issues as the Christian concept of charity and its relation to contemporary social problems. Most subjects interviewed said they held their religious beliefs because they had been held by their parents. The same explanation was usually given by those who said they had no religious beliefs.

Even though the subjects manifested a lack of knowledgeable commitment to religious belief and did not attend church regularly, most of them did profess some rudimentary religious beliefs, marked by a tolerance for others' beliefs. When the total sample in 1963 was asked to check which one of several religious items most represented their religious orientation, a majority of the subjects (53 per cent) felt theirs was the only faith acceptable to them, but that God could be revealed differently to others. Another large proportion of the youths (27 per cent) felt many faiths were correct. The rest of the youths either rejected all religious beliefs (9 per cent) or any religious belief other than their own (9 per cent). A few subjects failed to respond to the item.

Proportionately more college students than their employed peers rejected a religious faith (13 per cent versus 4 per cent respectively), and fewer college students than their employed peers considered their faith the only way to salvation (7 per cent versus 12 per cent). But these differences, though statistically significant, were not striking (Z ratios were 7.44 and 3.53, respectively).

Differences in religiosity between the young people in college and those in jobs were perhaps more clearly defined by their measured religious attitudes. Results of the 1963 administration of the Omnibus Personality Inventory's Religious Liberalism scale to the sample groups may be seen in Table 48. The higher the standard mean score, the greater the rejection of religion-oriented items. The lower the score, the more acceptance of traditional Judeo-Christian beliefs is indicated. Characteristic differences between sex groups as well as between career groups are immediately apparent. Men and women college students were significantly less religious in orientation than their working peers, and within both the college and employed samples, men were significantly less religiously oriented than women. The critical ratios in Table 48 indicate that the differences in religious orientation were greater between the college and employed groups than between the men and women.

At each ability level, mean differences in religiosity between the college and employed groups were found to be comparable to those seen in Table 48. No differences in religiosity scores were found, however, between the employed men and women of varying ability levels, and overlapping of scores was much more extensive than differences in scores, regardless of the group (see Appendix Table E-4).

Differences in the mean Religious Liberalism scores were more related to differences in socioeconomic status than to differences in ability level. On the basis of critical ratios of the mean differences, there were no significant differences in religious orientation between college and employed men of high socioeconomic status or between college and employed men and women of low socioeconomic status. College and employed groups differed at all

Table 48

STANDARD MEAN RELIGIOUS LIBERALISM SCORES OF COLLEGE
PERSISTERS AND THE CONSISTENTLY EMPLOYED, 1963

	College		Employed		Critical ratio
	(N)	Mean	(N)	Mean	(College vs. Employed)
Men	(723)	49.54	(444)	46.59	4.84 **
Women	(578)	47.31	(478)	41.36	9.60 **
Critical ratio—					
Men vs. women	(3.98 **)		(7.92 **)		

** p < .01.

other levels, as did men and women, except the college students
at the low socioeconomic level.

It is possible that the relatively few people at the high and
low socioeconomic levels repressed what would ordinarily have
amounted to significant differences between the college and employed groups at these levels, but in any event, differences between
men and women at each socioeconomic level were more consistent than differences between the college and employed groups.
Family or socioeconomic background and sex may sometimes be
more related to religious orientation than to college or work
experience, although this was not indicated for the sample at large
(Table 48).

Table 49

CHANGE IN VALUE PLACED ON RELIGION BY THE COLLEGE PERSISTERS
AND THE CONSISTENTLY EMPLOYED, IN PERCENTAGES

	(N)	Religion valued . . .		
		More	Same	Less
Men				
College	(793)	47	26	26
Employed	(537)	43	43	12
(Z ratio)		(1.52 +)	(6.44 **)	(6.25 **)
Women				
College	(620)	50	24	24
Employed	(540)	59	33	7
(Z ratio)		(3.18 **)	(3.46 **)	(7.53 **)

+ p = not significant.
** p < .01.

Since no instrument to assess religious orientation was administered to the sample in 1959, there are no scores for change in religious beliefs. However, the subjects were asked in 1963 to give their opinions as to whether they valued religion the same as they had in high school, or had come to value it more or less (Table 49). Sixty-eight per cent of the subjects reported some change, with 50 per cent reporting they valued religion more and 18 per cent reporting they valued religion less. Proportionately more of those in college (approximately 75 per cent) than those in jobs (62 per cent) reported a change in their religious values, and in both directions. Among the men a greater proportion of the college students compared with the workers reported valuing religion less (26 per cent and 12 per cent, respectively) and also valuing it more (47 per cent and 43 per cent respectively). Twenty-four per cent of the college women placed less value on religion, and 7 per cent of the employed women valued religion less, but proportionately more employed than college women valued religion more (59 per cent and 50 per cent, respectively).

College students' religious beliefs were less static than those of the employed, and although about 50 per cent of each group valued religion more after four years, 25 per cent of the students valued religion less, in contrast to 10 per cent of the employed. It cannot be said to what extent college contributed to the reported change in values, nor can the importance of these findings be judged conclusively; religion may have meant less to college students initially than to their noncollege peers. But since 75 per cent of those in college either didn't change their religious views or valued religion more, these data do not support the popular opinion that college greatly diminishes students' value for religion. Lehmann and Dressel (1962, 1963) also came to this conclusion on the basis of comparable data from their Michigan State University sample. However, in another study, Trent (1967) administered the Religious Liberalism scale and the correlated Religious Concepts Inventory to a group of students as freshmen and as seniors and concluded that except for those in Catholic colleges, college students in general became much more liberal in religious orientation.

The interviewed subjects were asked how they felt their values in general had changed since they graduated from high school. A great majority of the subjects, both college and non-college, either could not say or stated that they felt there was no change. However, a sizeable proportion of the interviewees believed their values had broadened and matured. By broadened values the young adults presumably meant a greater awareness of the meaning of their own and others' values. They explained their maturity generally in terms of being more adult and realistic about their values. Among the men, 19 per cent of the college students and 14 per cent of the employed in the sample felt their values had broadened, and 36 per cent of the college students and 41 per cent of the employed expressed the belief that they had matured in their values. Among the women, 22 per cent of the college students and 5 per cent of those with jobs felt their values had broadened, and 29 per cent of the college students and 23 per cent of the employed felt they had more mature values.

Ten per cent of the college students (sex differences were negligible) mentioned without specification that all their values had strengthened (that is, that they valued more what they had already valued in high school), whereas this occurred to none of the employed youths. On the other hand, over 12 per cent of the workers, compared with about 3 per cent of the college students, mentioned they felt they had become more practical, more respectful of education, and more interested in family life—all indicators of their encounters with and assumptions of adult roles. Some subjects mentioned they had become less self-centered and materialistic, valued religion more, and were more independent and tolerant of others, but rarely did more than 5 per cent of any of the sample groups volunteer these opinions, and usually not that many.

CONCLUSION

However vague and unarticulated their views, the youths in the sample expressed a variety of values and attitudes about important aspects of life. Some values, attitudes, and changes in values and attitudes clearly distinguished the groups under consideration; others did not. In either case, however, the patterns of differences were the same. Personality development, whether in terms of reported change of values or measured attitudes, took place most among the college persisters, followed by the withdrawals, then the employed youths, and least of all among the homemakers who experienced neither college nor employment the first four years after high school.

Degree of measured intellectual orientation distinguished the groups, but while many of the differences were statistically significant, they were by no means great, particularly when level of ability and socioeconomic status were held constant. Likewise, although a number of reported activities and interests, such as viewing art exhibits and preference for classical music, distinguished the groups, many activities did not distinguish them to the extent that might have been expected. As an example, college students showed the most interest in the world around them as evident from their increased interest in news magazines. But otherwise their reading habits did not appear especially intellectually oriented, nor especially different from the reading interests of the other youths. On the other hand the college persisters were far more esthetically oriented than the other youths.

What most distinguished the "experimental" group of college persisters from the "control" groups of withdrawals and especially nonattenders was the development of autonomy. Definitely there was a strong relationship between entrance to and length of stay in college and the growth of open-minded, flexible, and autonomous disposition, as measured by two scales designed to assess these traits. The fact that the carefully classified college withdrawals were more like the nonattenders than the persisters in their amount of manifest change indicates that the type of personality development measured continues to be associated with persistence in college beyond the early years. This held regardless of level of ability or socioeconomic status. On the basis of the Nonauthoritarianism scale there was a tendency for the experience of full-time employment and particularly early marriage combined with full-time homemaking to be associated with a constriction of flexibility and autonomy. Complexity scores of the full-time employed and early married indicated an even greater tendency toward constriction in intellectual curiosity, interest in new experiences, and tolerance for ambiguity. A central hypothesis is thereby substantiated.

Under the circumstances the evidence considered suggests that the work world is not conducive to that open, flexible disposition and spirit of inquiry that is so important to the attainment of identity, acceptance of others, understanding of the environment, and fullest realization of potentials. Yet the different effect college may have on personality development is not entirely clear. College students changed to about the same degree regardless of the type of college they entered. Colleges were classified only according to whether they were basically four-year institutions or universities, and whether they were private, public, or church-related. Liberal arts colleges and universities renowned for their academic excellence were not examined separately, and it is to be hoped this feature would make a difference. But, in general, it appears that college may provide the opportunity for students to grow, instead of making a conscious attempt to foster development. Moreover, even the college persisters showed a relative lack of development of intellectual interests as determined by the Thinking Introversion and Complexity scales. Evidently, the liberalization to be realized from higher education is limited in certain ways.

However, the fact that important changes take place in the attitudes and values of young adults, and the fact that these changes vary as much as they do by post high school pursuit makes it urgent to learn more about the specific factors underlying personality development. The data reviewed show that college experience is related to change, but it is also evident that change is related to family background and values. Although the causes attributed to change in personality are not discernible in the data, some of the conditions found to be related to personality development are explored further in the following chapter.

VIII

Conditions of Change

The young adults under study appeared to have changed their attitudes and values during the first four years following their high school graduation. Moreover, such changes varied by sex, ability, and family background as well as by post high school pursuits such as homemaking, work, and college. Changes were particularly apparent among college persisters, as determined by reliable attitudinal scales. This chapter reports further examination of the extent of measured change, searching out the factors that seem to bear on whether and how young people shift their points of view about certain fundamental issues as they go from high school into early adult experiences.

Three groups will be studied: those whose changes in scores on the Social Maturity scale of the Omnibus Personality Inventory were significantly above the average change score of the sample (exceptional changers); those who could not clearly be characterized as showing change significantly above or below the average change (average changers); and those who changed significantly from the average change in a negative direction (negative changers).

The trait of autonomy as measured by this scale was singled out for special analysis for two reasons. First, it was found to distinguish between the college persisters and withdrawals, and between the persisters and their employed peers, with respect to change of attitude, as much or more than any other variable examined. Second, as a reflection of objective, independent, flexible, and open-minded thinking, autonomy appears crucial to the satisfactory development and maturation of the age group under consideration.

The Autonomy scale itself would no doubt have been the best scale to distinguish degrees of change in autonomous attitudes since factorily it measures these attitudes more directly. However, since the Autonomy scale was not available for administration to the sample in 1959, the Social Maturity scale, a highly reliable scale which measures autonomous traits, was administered to the sample both in 1959 and 1963. Although it is not as discrete a measurement as the Autonomy scale, the correlation between the two scales, at .88, is very high (Center for the Study of Higher Education, 1962).

In addition to an analysis of the scores on the Social Maturity scale, the changes in scores will be related to factors which emerged from the answers to the questionnaires and personality inventories, and from the protocols of those in the three groups who were interviewed. Data from the interview sample provide a major supplement to the data obtained from the entire longitudinal sample. A majority of those who were interviewed also responded to the questionnaire and attitude inventories administered to the total sample both in 1959 and 1963 as well as to a special questionnaire and the Strong Vocational Interest Blank. This is important because the interview sample was considered representative of the original 1959 sample, and therefore may be somewhat more reflective of the change groups than the complete longitudinal sample.

Data in Chapter VII showed that noncollege women become more authoritarian than noncollege men after four years, but there was no clear basis for predicting that differences would obtain between the sexes in the amount of change on the other personality variables. It was assumed that the factor of ability, however, would be related to change among both the college and noncollege youths. In addition to ability and college attendance (as well as college curriculum), a variety of familial factors were expected to be related to an increase in autonomy among the subjects. Although socioeconomic status defined by father's occupation was not found to be highly related to attitude change, it seemed reasonable to suspect a relationship between parents' education and change, on the assumption that the higher the educational level of the parents, the greater the likelihood of objectivity, awareness of the environment, and critical thinking in the home. It was also assumed that students more ready for growth in autonomy would have parents who fostered autonomous thinking and relationships in the home and would therefore be characterized by their children as democratic in their interactions, liberal and independent in temperament, and intellectual. It was therefor hypothesized that those youths who grew most in autonomy after high school would also have been higher on the Social Maturity scale than the other students at the point of high school graduation since they would have been more disposed to growth on this dimension.

Several variables of personality were expected to be related to change on the Social Maturity scale: Intellectual disposition, as measured by Complexity and Thinking Introversion scales, was expected to be related since intellectuality requires objectivity of thought and interest and openness to the environment. Likewise, as indicated by the correlational analyses in Appendix C, it was expected that the generally greater degree of liberalness, tolerance, and flexibility presumed characteristic of the exceptional changers would be manifest in specific areas, such as religious orientation, measured by the Religious Liberalism scale. The flexible and unstereotypic thinking measured by the Social Maturity scale was expected to be reflected in the unihibited and imaginative thinking measured by the Impulse Expression scale.

It was not known whether the changers would differ in their overt orientation to other people as measured by the Social Introversion scale, and therefore this left an unknown dimension to explore. However, there was evidence from a previous report (Trent, 1967) that increase in autonomy was positively correlated with intellectual disposition, and that those subjects highest in intellectual disposition indicated more anxiety than others in the sample. Therefore it was expected that those who changed most positively on the Social Maturity scale would indicate the most anxiety on the Lack of Anxiety scale. It was argued that this would follow perhaps because of the greater tension that might result

from greater openness to the environment and increased awareness of the ambiguities that exist there. Finally, it was hypothesized that the subjects who changed most in a positive direction
would score highest on the idea-oriented Strong Vocational Interest
Blank occupational scales, such as the Author-Journalist scale, and
lowest on more authoritarian-oriented or applied scales such as
the Policeman and Accountant scales. This relationship would be
compatible with scores on the Social Maturity scale as it measures
autonomy, flexibility, and potential interest in ideas. For instance,
the Author-Journalist scale should indicate the interest in dealing
with ideas believed typical of high scorers on the Social Maturity
scale. Negative changers, scoring lower on the Social Maturity
scale after four years, should be more likely to score high on the
Accountant and Policeman scales, reflecting the practical and
authoritarian orientation more typical of people in these occupations.

The method used to determine three groups which manifested varying degrees of change on the Social Maturity scale will
be described. Then, the expectations about the conditions and
correlates of change will be explored in three ways: first, by comparing the groups on various background factors, including perception of parents, perception of the purpose of college, and
curriculum in college; second, by comparing various personality
scores obtained by the three groups; and third, by a summary of
characteristics indicated by the interview protocols of the group
that changed negatively on the Social Maturity scale after four
years, and the group that changed positively on the Social Maturity scale.

DETERMINATION OF DEGREES OF CHANGE

The first step in the identification process was to construct
frequency curves of the change scores of all of the subjects—shown
in Figure 7—and then to repeat this procedure for the two major
comparison groups, composed of those who persisted in college
and those who were employed for the four years—shown in Figure 8. (The curves were smoothed by averaging the points shown
adjacent to the curve.) The total sample changed an average of
four points. The difference scores of two-thirds of the sample fell
within a range of 14 points, but the total range of change scores

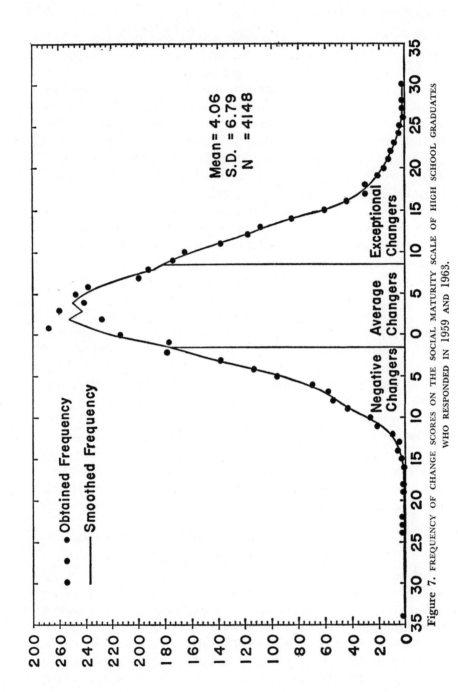

Figure 7. FREQUENCY OF CHANGE SCORES ON THE SOCIAL MATURITY SCALE OF HIGH SCHOOL GRADUATES WHO RESPONDED IN 1959 AND 1963.

182

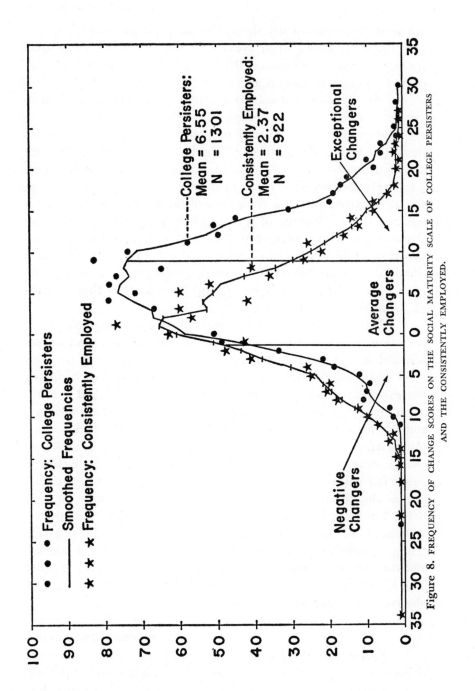

Figure 8. FREQUENCY OF CHANGE SCORES ON THE SOCIAL MATURITY SCALE OF COLLEGE PERSISTERS AND THE CONSISTENTLY EMPLOYED.

• • Frequency: College Persisters

—— Smoothed Frequencies

★ ★ ★ Frequency: Consistently Employed

College Persisters:
Mean = 6.55
N = 1301

Consistently Employed:
Mean = 2.37
N = 922

Exceptional Changers

Negative Changers

Average Changers

183

spanned 60 points, nearly the entire range of the scale. The college persisters changed an average of 6.5 points on the 67-item Social Maturity scale between 1959 and 1963; the consistently employed youths changed an average of 2.4 points.

The second step was to distinguish the exceptional, average, and negative change groups. The criterion used for selecting the change groups was plus or minus three-fourths of a standard deviation of the distribution of change scores from the average change score. In this way, we could distinguish groups which registered very distinct differences in degrees of change. The "exceptional" change group was comprised of those youths whose change scores fell three-fourths of a standard deviation or more above the average change score. The "average" change group was comprised of those whose change scores fell within three-fourths of a standard deviation above or below the average change score. The change scores of the "negative" groups were at least three-fourths of a standard deviation below the average.

When this criterion was applied to the change score distribution, three-fourths of a standard deviation was found to correspond to a value of 5. Since the average change score between 1959 and 1963 for the entire longitudinal sample was 4 points, the exceptional change group included youths who had a minimum change score of 9 (or 5 points above the average change), and the negative change group included youths who had a minimum change score of *minus* 1 point (or 5 points below the average change score of 4). This left a relatively large group whose change scores fell within plus or minus three-fourths of a standard deviation of the distribution of scores obtained by the sample, or well beyond the established limits of change scores which could be accounted for by chance alone. The exceptional and negative change groups each contained about 25 per cent of the sample, and the average group the remaining 50 per cent of the sample. The specific composition of the different groups by sex may be observed in Table 50.

BACKGROUND AND VALUES

Several factors found to be associated with amount of change on the Social Maturity scale are consistent with the findings discussed in the previous chapter, as may be seen in the fol-

Table 50

SUBJECTS CHARACTERIZED BY DIFFERENT DEGREES OF CHANGE IN
SCORES ON THE SOCIAL MATURITY SCALE

	Exceptional (N)	%	Average (N)	%	Negative (N)	%	Total (N)	%
Men	(518)	29	(855)	48	(402)	23	(1775)	100
Women	(521)	22	(1240)	52	(612)	26	(2373)	100
Total	(1039)	25	(2095)	51	(1014)	24	(4148)	100

Chi square: Men vs. Women = 28.64; $p < .01$.

lowing summary. These factors include sex, level of ability, father's occupation, parents' education, and college experience.

Table 51

ABILITY LEVEL OF SOCIAL MATURITY CHANGE
GROUPS, IN PERCENTAGES

	Change groups		
Ability level	Exceptional (N = 1012)	Average (N = 2027)	Negative (N = 975)
High	53	45	39
Middle	36	39	41
Low	11	16	20

Chi square = 54.08; $p < .01$.

It is evident that for the entire longitudinal sample, there were proportionately more men than women in the exceptional change group (Table 50). The data in Table 51 indicate an even greater difference between the groups when observed by level of ability. The greatest overrepresentation of youths at the high ability level was found among the exceptional changers.

In general, the exceptional changers reported a higher level of education and occupation for their parents than the negative and average changers (Tables 52 and 53). Without further testing, on the basis of chi square differences, father's education appeared to distinguish the three groups more than mother's education, and father's and mother's education more than father's occupation. Both of these indices of socioeconomic status appeared more associated with degree of change in Social Maturity than the youths'

Table 52

EDUCATION OF PARENTS OF CHANGE
GROUPS, IN PERCENTAGES

	Change groups		
Level of Education	Exceptional	Average	Negative
Father	(N = 970)	(N = 1946)	(N = 929)
Grade school or less	16	23	23
Some high school	18	23	24
Finished high school	28	27	28
Some college	16	13	14
Finished college, Postgraduate education	22	14	11
Chi square = 66.41 **			
Mother	(N = 992)	(N = 1990)	(N = 943)
Grade school or less	10	14	18
Some high school	17	21	25
Finished high school	43	40	37
Some college	15	13	10
Finished college, Postgraduate education	15	12	10
Chi square = 57.36 **.			

** p < .01.

level of ability. If it is assumed that differences in amount and kind of education are associated with differences in values, there is a suggestion here that the values of the better educated parents more than the aptitude of their children, may have influenced the degree of openness to change. It is yet to be known, however, exactly what these influences may be and how they operate to foster personality development.

Table 53

SOCIOECONOMIC LEVEL OF CHANGE
GROUPS, IN PERCENTAGES

	Change groups		
	Exceptional	Average	Negative
SES	(N = 965)	(N = 1944)	(N = 928)
High	24	16	13
Middle	60	64	65
Low	16	20	22

Chi square = 49.33; p < .01.

Although there was a greater proportion of men than women in the exceptional change group for the total sample, this was not true for the college students, who included a greater proportion of persisting women than men among the exceptional changers, and a greater proportion of persisting men than women among the negative changers (Table 54). These differences were not statistically significant, but the significant differences in amount of change in autonomy and intellectual disposition between the college persisters and withdrawals continued in the present context. For example, among the men, 37 per cent of the persisters changed exceptionally in a positive direction on the Social Maturity scale, compared with 26 per cent of the withdrawals. Corresponding figures for the women were 40 per cent versus 21 per cent.

Table 54

COLLEGE PERSISTERS AND WITHDRAWALS IN EACH CHANGE
GROUP, IN PERCENTAGES

| | | Change groups | | | Chi |
Pursuit groups	(N)	Exceptional	Average	Negative	square
Men					
Persisters	(723)	37	48	15	
					12.99 **
Withdrawals	(105)	26	47	27	
Women					
Persisters	(578)	40	48	12	
					44.33 **
Withdrawals	(195)	21	49	30	

Z ratios. College: Exceptional change men vs. women—.085 +. Negative change men vs. women—1.36 +. Exceptional change men: College vs. withdrawals—2.36 *. Exceptional change women: College vs. withdrawals—4.89 **.

+ p = not significant.
* p < .05.
** p < .01.

Still greater differences existed between the college persisters and their consistently employed peers (Table 55). Thirty-eight per cent of the persisters and 16 per cent of the employed youths were in the exceptional change group, and 14 per cent of the college youths and 31 per cent of the employed were in the negative change group. Whatever the conditions associated with college attendance that lead to growth in autonomy, they seem to have equal effect on men and women. In contrast, the inordinate decline of scores on the Social Maturity scale found among so many noncollege women—even when compared only with the noncollege men—may result from the very restrictive post high school experiences of a large number of these women, particularly those who did not enter employment.

Table 55

COLLEGE PERSISTERS AND THE CONSISTENTLY
EMPLOYED IN EACH CHANGE GROUP

	Change groups					
	Exceptional		Average		Negative	
Pursuit groups	(N)	Per cent	(N)	Per cent	(N)	Per cent	Chi square
Persisters	(500)	38	(624)	48	(176)	14	
							172.85 **
Consistently employed	(149)	16	(487)	53	(285)	31	
(Z ratio)	(9.94 **)		(2.27 *)		(11.38 **)		

* $p < .05$.
** $p < .01$.

The association shown between college experience and change in attitudes adds to the difficulty of interpreting another factor associated with amount of change. On the Social Maturity scale, the lower students scored on the scale in 1959, the more likely were their scores to change significantly in a postive direction in 1963. This phenomenon was demonstrated in different degrees in two ways. The mean Social Maturity scores of each change group in 1959 and 1963 were computed for the total longitudinal sample (Table 56). In 1959 the standard mean score of the negative changers was 55.3; of the average changers, 50.5; and of the exceptional changers, 47.8. The magnitude of the groups' means was reversed by 1963 and critical ratios confirm highly significant differences between the groups' scores at both time periods, particularly in 1963.

Table 56

STANDARD MEAN SOCIAL MATURITY SCORES OF CHANGE
GROUPS, 1959 AND 1963

	Change groups		
Year	Exceptional (N = 1039)	Average (N = 2095)	Negative (N = 1014)
1959	47.81	50.46	55.33
1963	66.82	56.21	48.67
Critical ratios		(1959)	(1963)
Exceptional vs. Average		6.2 **	23.5 **
Exceptional vs. Negative		20.8 **	46.4 **
Average vs. Negative		12.5 **	19.1 **

$** p < .01.$

This relationship was suggested (although not statistically confirmed) a second way when the interviewed sample was considered separately. The subjects whose Social Maturity scores in 1959 fell among the lowest 30 per cent of scores based on the sample's total distribution of scores on this scale were classified at the low level of Social Maturity; those whose scores fell in the middle 40 per cent of the distribution were classified at the middle level; and those whose scores fell in the upper 30 per cent were classified at the high level (Table 57). Of the negative changers, 17 per cent had been at the low level on the scale in 1959 and 31 per cent at the high level. Of the exceptional changers, 29 per cent had been at the low level of Social Maturity and 23 per cent at the high level. Although the overall chi square in Table 57 did not reach a level of statistical significance, the differences shown in the table follow the same pattern as that found for the entire longitudinal sample in Table 56.

The tendency these findings indicate was surprising. All college students, and particularly the college persisters, changed more on this dimension than the nonattenders, and in 1959 those who entered college scored some three standard points higher on the Social Maturity scale than those who entered employment (see Medsker and Trent, 1965). Yet of the whole sample, the exceptional change group had scored the lowest of all the groups in

Table 57

SOCIAL MATURITY LEVELS IN 1959 OF
CHANGE GROUPS, IN PERCENTAGES
(INTERVIEW SAMPLE)

Social Maturity level	Change groups		
	Exceptional (N = 72)	Average (N = 146)	Negative (N = 76)
High	33	34	43
Middle	36	38	40
Low	31	28	17

Chi square = 4.80; p = not significant.

1959. Further analyses are in order to see if this finding holds for both these groups when the relationship between initial level of Social Maturity and amount of change on this scale are examined separately for those who remained employed and those who persisted in college. It may be found that the most change on the Social Maturity scale was made by college persisters who had scored low on this scale in 1959.

Ideally, the base level of Social Maturity in 1959 should have been controlled when the change groups were examined. It is quite likely, for example, that a person who scored high initially on the Social Maturity scale and then changed significantly in either a negative or positive direction, would differ considerably in many traits from a person who initially scored low on the scale and then changed significantly in either direction. Even if this base level of Social Maturity had been controlled, however, the question would still arise as to what really constitutes exceptional, average, or negative change for those initially high, average, or low on Social Maturity. All these problems, as well as the great diversity of individual differences within the change groups, cloud insight into the exact nature of change and the way in which the human personality grows and develops.

Since a relationship between level of ability and amount of change on the Social Maturity scale was also found, there was a question about whether the relationship between initial level of Social Maturity and change would continue to exist when level of ability was held constant. When these variables were examined simultaneously for the interviewed subjects, a concomitant relationship was apparent between level of ability, level of Social Maturity, and amount of change. The largest proportion represented in the exceptional change group, regardless of level of ability, were those who began at the low level of Social Maturity. But at each level of the Social Maturity scale, there were proportionately more exceptional changers at the high level of ability than at the lower levels of ability. The largest representation in the exceptional change group was of young adults who in 1959 had been at the low level of Social Maturity but high level of ability. Forty-one per cent of these were among the exceptional changers, compared with 30 per cent of the high ability youths at the middle Social Maturity level, and 26 per cent of the able youths at the high Social Maturity level. However, just as was true for the longitudinal interview sample taken as a whole, none of these differences proved to be statistically significant on the basis of general chi square analyses.

Apart from such factors as ability or college attendance, it was hypothesized that a number of other variables would be associated with degrees of change in autonomy as measured by the Social Maturity scale. The list of variables, confined to the data gathered in the course of the study, included: 1) family characteristics; 2) orientation toward education and work; 3) self-concept and personal concerns; 4) religious orientation; and 5) measured intellectual interests and emotional disposition.

Previous research, such as that cited in Chapter VII, has shown that value formation and family environment are related. A relationship has already been observed between level of parents' education and change in score on the Social Maturity scale. Consequently, the expectations were, as noted previously, that the exceptional changers would come from family climates markedly different from those of the negative and average changers. For example, the assumption was that the parents of youths who had proved most open to change would be more open and liberal in attitude and more democratic in family management than the parents of the negative and average changers. It was also theorized that subjects who changed little or negatively would be more likely to come from rigid, authoritarian homes. However, on the basis of what could be assessed from paper-and-pencil questionnaire responses, the family characteristics of the three change groups were not discernibly different. The students' reports of their home atmospheres, parents' temperaments, and parents' reactions to their children's achievements, failed to distinguish the youths characterized by significantly different degrees of attitudinal change.

However, the questionnaire used was originally designed to obtain relatively general information on family background, and it may be that its items were not discriminating enough to make precise distinctions between variations in family patterns characterized by such factors as openness, training for independence, and orientation toward achievement. Although the importance of family climate was not statistically confirmed, family characteristics were shown to warrant continued consideration on the basis of information drawn from the interview protocols (to be described in later pages) which did indicate a relationship between family patterns and degree of change on the Social Maturity scale.

The variables examined which pertain to educational orientation and values showed a more consistent relationship to the change groups than did the family variables (Tables 58 and 59). However, the relationships were not extensive and seldom significant on the basis of chi square analyses. The exceptional changers tended most and the negative changers tended least to consider graduation from college very important, graduate work at least somewhat likely (college students only), and the most important purpose of college to be general rather than vocational education, but only in the latter instances were the differences statistically significant. Attitudes about the importance of college and graduate school distinguished the change groups more among the employed youths than the college students, and attitudes about the importance of general education distinguished the change groups more among the college students.

The major subject reported by the college students in 1963 also appeared to distinguish the change groups somewhat. The engineering, education, and natural science majors were least represented in the exceptional change group, and the social science and humanities majors most represented. The proportion of medical science and business majors in the exceptional change group

Table 58

EDUCATIONAL ORIENTATION OF COLLEGE PERSISTERS AND THE
CONSISTENTLY EMPLOYED OF EACH CHANGE
GROUP, IN PERCENTAGES

Pursuit groups and opinions	Change groups			Chi square
	Exceptional	Average	Negative	
College				
(N)	(500)	(624)	(176)	
Graduation from college very important	90	89	87	1.28 +
Attendance at graduate school likely	54	48	49	4.10 +
Most important purpose of education knowledge & ideas	47	40	35	9.40 **
Employed				
(N)	(149)	(487)	(285)	
Graduation from college very important	28	25	21	3.00 +
Attendance at graduate school likely	11	9	10	0.51 +
Most important purpose of education knowledge & ideas	15	22	15	7.39 *

+ p = not significant.
* p < .05.
** p < .01.

fell between the proportional representations of the other majors mentioned.

Involvement in the study of ideas and human systems is evidently related to development in social maturity, as defined by this scale. Therefore, it met expectations that the social science and humanities majors had the greatest representation among the exceptional changers and that, given the practical rather than intellectual focus of their curricula, the engineering and education majors had the least. In line with this reasoning, it had been anticipated that business majors also would be well represented among the negative and average changers, but this did not turn out to be the case.

Table 59

MAJORS OF THE COLLEGE CHANGE GROUPS, 1963,
IN PERCENTAGES

		College change groups		
Majors	(N)	Exceptional	Average	Negative
Applied				
Education	(305)	33	53	14
Engineering	(103)	34	50	16
Medical Science	(76)	41	46	13
Business	(132)	39	48	13
Forestry/Agriculture	(15)	13	60	27
Academic				
Natural Science	(165)	34	51	15
Social Science	(259)	44	43	13
Humanities/Arts	(234)	44	44	12

In any event, differences in proportions of the various majors in the three change groups were not very great; these varied roughly by 10 percentage points in the exceptional change group, and the chi square comparing the academic and applied majors by degree of change was not significant. Perhaps these differences, as well as others, were relatively small because the exceptional change group was not distinguished by level of Social Maturity, but only by large change in scores in a positive direction, regardless of actual score or corresponding attitudes and interests. In this context it must be borne in mind once again that although persistence in college is associated with growth in autonomy, a large number of students do go through college without changing.

Only one published study known to the authors includes analyses comparable to those in the present study.* To identify "changers," Lehmann and Payne (1963) used data obtained from Michigan State University freshmen at the beginning and end of the academic year 1958–1959. The scales used to measure change of attitudes and values were the Inventory of Beliefs designed to

* A developmental study of University of California and Stanford University students was completed by Katz and Associates (1968) as the present study was being readied for press. Levin's chapter in that publication also includes comparable and pertinent analyses of change data.

measure stereotypic thinking, and Prince's Differential Values Inventory, designed to measure "traditional" versus "emergent" values. Changers were classified as those students who scored 1.5 standard errors of estimate above or below their predicted post test scores on the two scales as determined by regression analysis. The positive and negative changers were asked in interviews to state whether experiences within 10 specified areas in college had had some impact, or little or no impact. The areas they were asked to assess were: instructors, courses, social activities, cultural activities, dormitory life, fraternity or sorority membership, conformity, rules and regulations, living away from home, and friends. There were 20 opportunities for the groups to be distinguished on the two scales. Among the men, only "rules and regulations" and "friends" distinguished the groups, and then on different scales. Among the women, only "course(s)" and "cultural activities" distinguished the change groups, but on just one scale.

In the present study, evaluative data of this kind were confined primarily to the comparisons made in the next chapter, between college persisters, withdrawals, and nonattenders. In both studies, there were only the subjective reports of young people, not always critically insightful, on which to base generalizations. Therefore, interpretations must be arrived at with caution, and judgment will have to be suspended on at least one conclusion drawn by Lehmann and Payne: "Although colleges assume that college instructors and courses will have some impact upon attitudes and values, our study does not bear this out [p. 407]." Obviously, more reliable information on this issue must be gained from further research, since in the present investigation there were distinct differences in kind and amount of change found between students in the different subject majors.

The specific impact of college on students remains unclear, and evidence advanced in this chapter and the previous one indicates that a second conclusion of Lehmann and Payne merits much further consideration. The authors wrote: "Possibly the most significant finding of this study was that for a selected group of individuals, the data suggests a reinforcement rather than a modification of prevailing values [p. 408]." Another and related interpretation, reached as a result of the findings in the previous chapter, seems just as plausible—that rather than effecting the changes, the college may facilitate change for many predisposed to it. But whether the process is facilitation or reinforcement, the specific catalysts for change have yet to be identified.

In the data at hand, a study of the subjects' vocational preferences, apart from their college curricula, also suggested that in some respects the exceptional changers' orientation, more than that of the other two change groups, was theoretical and ideological rather than applied and practical. Although differences by change group were not great, college students who were exceptional changers emphasized the theoretical over the practical contributions of scientists more than students who were negative and average changers. Both the college and employed exceptional changers in greatest proportion preferred challenging rather than secure occupations. Contrary to expectations, however, there were essentially no differences between the change groups in preference for business and technological occupations over occupations less applied in nature and very little difference in preference for professional occupations.

Table 60

SELF-DESCRIPTIONS OF SUBJECTS IN EACH OF THE
CHANGE GROUPS, IN PERCENTAGES

	Change groups			
Self-descriptions	Exceptional (N = 1039)	Average (N = 2095)	Negative (N = 1014)	Chi square
Intellectual	26	17	15	46.45 **
Nonconformist	22	16	17	14.15 **
Leader	16	12	10	17.13 **
Liberal	47	34	28	81.11 **
Common Man	33	40	43	24.34 **

** p < .01.

The self-descriptions of the young adults characterized by different degrees of change on the Social Maturity scale varied in ways that could be anticipated from the findings (Table 60). The exceptional changers in greatest proportion saw themselves as intellectuals, nonconformists, leaders, and, in particular, liberals. The greatest proportion of negative changers saw themselves as "a common man." These differences were significant beyond the

1 per cent level as determined by chi square analyses. The differences in self-description and much of the other data above consistently indicate that exceptional change on the Social Maturity scale bears a relationship to openness to ideas, tolerance of different points of view, and self-direction and may reflect the preponderant representation of college students in the exceptional change group.

Several religious factors were associated with degree of change. Compared with the exceptional changers, there was some tendency for the negative changers to attend church regularly in greater proportion (56 per cent versus 47 per cent, respectively) and an even more significant tendency for them to view their religion as the only correct one, or the only one acceptable to them (71 per cent and 56 per cent). This, again, may in part be a reflection of the different values held by the college and noncollege groups.

Table 61

STANDARD MEAN RELIGIOUS LIBERALISM
SCORES OF THE CHANGE GROUPS

| | Change groups | | |
	Exceptional	Average	Negative
Men (N)	(518)	(855)	(402)
Mean	50.35	48.29	46.02
Women (N)	(521)	(1240)	(612)
Mean	47.06	43.51	42.20

Critical ratios	
Men	
Exceptional vs. Average	3.8 **
Exceptional vs. Negative	6.6 **
Average vs. Negative	3.81 **
Women	
Exceptional vs. Average	7.71 **
Exceptional vs. Negative	9.47 **
Average vs. Negative	3.29 **

** $p < .01$.

Religious affiliation and attitude as measured by the Religious Liberalism scale was also related to personality change (Table 61): The mean score in 1963 of male exceptional changers was four standard points higher than that of negative changers, and the mean score of female exceptional changers was five standard points higher than that of negative changers.

These differences indicate that young adults who changed significantly in a positive direction were more liberal and skeptical in their attitude toward religion than the other youths in the sample. This finding is consistent both with the exceptional changers' greater tendency to describe themselves as liberal as well as with the signs they showed of the broadened outlook that is theoretically consonant with an increased score on the Social Maturity scale.

For the total longitudinal sample, it was observed in data not in table form that the few Jewish subjects included were underrepresented in the negative change group, and that there was a tendency for the Catholics to change negatively in greater proportion than the Protestants or Jews. The interviewed subjects, exclusive of the Jews, who were too few to be taken into statistical consideration, were questioned more closely for further evidence of this tendency (Table 62). In this analysis, Protestants whose denominations were considered fundamentalist because of their evangelistic and conservative orientation were distinguished from the others. (The fundamentalists included Nazarenes, Christian Reformed, Pentecostals, and the Evangelical United Brethren.) Only 14 per cent of the Catholics and 15 per cent of the Protestant fundamentalists changed toward exceptionally greater autonomy as measured by the Social Maturity scale, compared with 31 per cent of all other Protestants. Twenty-nine per cent of the Catholics changed significantly toward less autonomy, compared with 46 per cent of the fundamentalists and 19 per cent of the other Protestants.

This same phenomenon was observed for the Catholic college students in the total longitudinal sample (Table 63). When the college persisters in the change groups were observed according to the control of the college they were attending in 1963, the findings were that 41 per cent of the persisters in public colleges were in the exceptional change group, compared with 38 per cent of the students in nondenominational private colleges, 34 per cent in Protestant colleges, and 24 per cent in Catholic colleges.

Table 62

RELIGIOUS AFFILIATION OF THE CHANGE GROUPS
(INTERVIEW SAMPLE), IN PERCENTAGES

		Change groups		
Affiliations	*(N)*	*Exceptional*	*Average*	*Negative*
Catholics	(80)	14	57	29
Fundamentalists	(46)	15	39	46
Protestants	(129)	31	50	19
Others	(36)	36	45	19

Chi square $= 21.68$; $p < .01$.

Correspondingly, the Catholic college students also had the greatest representation in the negative change group, which had moved in the direction of greater authoritarianism rather than autonomy.

Table 63

TYPES OF COLLEGES ATTENDED BY CHANGE
GROUPS, IN PERCENTAGES

		Change groups		
College	*(N)*	*Exceptional*	*Average*	*Negative*
Public	(899)	41	46	13
Private	(118)	38	49	13
Protestant	(185)	34	53	13
Catholic	(99)	24	59	17

Chi square, college vs. Social Maturity change $= 13.00$; $p < .05$.

The evidence suggests that the lack of development shown on the Social Maturity scale is in part a function of religious subcultures inasmuch as this phenomenon has been found to be particularly marked among Catholics and fundamentalists. There is also evidence that this finding is not a peculiarity of any built-in bias in the Social Maturity scale. The lack of autonomy found within the Catholic subculture has been found, on the basis of a variety of criteria, to be a continuing, pervasive, albeit changing phenomenon which has resulted from a number of historical, doctrinal, and sociological elements. This story has been developed in another context (Trent, 1967).

A number of other personality and attitudinal characteristics distinguished the youths who manifested different degrees
of change on the Social Maturity scale (Table 64). This would be
expected for some of the scales, considering their intercorrelation
as noted in Appendix Table C-1. With very few exceptions, differences between the mean scores of the change groups were significant on each of the Omnibus Personality Inventory scales
administered to the sample in 1963 (Appendix Table E-11). Technical details of all the scales are described in detail in Appendix C.
Brief descriptions of the scales were also given in Chapters VI and
VII, with the exception of the three scales measuring manifest
anxiety, impulse expression, and social introversion. Descriptions
of the latter three scales follow:

> *Lack of Anxiety (LA)*; 20 items. These items were selected from
> the Taylor Manifest Anxiety scale. The scoring has been reversed,
> so that high scorers are those free from unusual amounts of
> anxiety. Low scorers tend to have a high degree of anxiety and
> are frequently neurotic or chronic complainers.
> *Impulse Expression (IE)*; 75 items. This scale assesses a general
> readiness to express impulses and to seek gratification in conscious
> thought or overt action. High scorers value sensations and have
> active imaginations, with feelings and fantasies which often
> dominate their thinking.
> *Social Introversion (SI)*; 54 items. The high scorers withdraw
> from social contacts and responsibilities. They display little in-
> terest in people or in socializing. The low scoreres are extroverts,
> seeking social contacts and gaining satisfaction from them.

Of all the groups, the exceptional changers showed by far
the greatest degree of independence, openness, flexibility, and
imaginative thinking, as measured by the Autonomy, Nonauthoritarianism, and Impulse Expression scales. They also had the highest intellectual and esthetic orientations, as measured by the
Thinking Introversion, Complexity, and Estheticism scales. Moreover, the data demonstrate that the comparatively extensive development of autonomous and intellectual attitudes shown by the
exceptional changers on the Social Maturity scale was not limited

Table 64

STANDARD MEAN OPI SCORES OF THE
CHANGE GROUPS, 1963

		Change groups	
OPI scales	Exceptional	Average	Negative
Men	(N = 518)	(N = 855)	(N = 402)
Thinking Introversion	51.69	47.68	45.91
Estheticism	47.27	45.12	43.77
Complexity	52.81	50.00	47.71
Autonomy	54.20	48.20	43.60
Nonauthoritarianism	51.70	46.94	43.63
Lack of Anxiety	53.99	50.97	50.69
Impulse Expression	54.05	43.92	51.98
Social Introversion	50.21	52.30	53.73
Women	(N = 521)	(N = 1240)	(N = 612)
Thinking Introversion	50.79	46.44	44.01
Estheticism	47.90	47.92	46.39
Complexity	51.27	45.93	44.06
Autonomy	52.82	44.83	39.65
Nonauthoritarianism	50.10	44.63	41.18
Lack of Anxiety	51.42	49.53	47.79
Impulse Expression	48.44	44.87	43.97
Social Introversion	49.89	50.88	53.75

to characteristics measured by that scale alone. This group also showed the most development on the Thinking Introversion, Complexity, and Nonauthoritarianism scales, which measure preference for abstract thought, tolerance for ambiguity, and lack of authoritarianism. This is indicated by the comparison of the differences between mean Omnibus Personality Inventory scores of the three groups in 1959 and 1963, including the t ratios showing the significance of these differences found in Table 65.

To this point, the differences observed between the three change groups on the Omnibus Personality Inventory scales were expected. The scores of the exceptional change group implied they had developed most in intellectual interests, autonomy, imagination, and flexibility, and this was consistent with the personality traits purportedly assessed by the Social Maturity scale and verified by statistical correlation to bear a relationship to one another and to social maturity.

Table 65

STANDARD MEAN OPI SCORES OF THE CHANGE GROUPS IN 1959 AND 1963

Sex and change groups	(N)	Thinking Introversion	Complexity	Nonauthoritarianism	Lack of Anxiety	Social Maturity
Men						
Exceptional	(518)					
1959		47.19	50.00	45.31	52.18	48.53
1963		51.69	52.81	51.70	53.99	67.30
Difference		4.50	2.81	6.39	1.81	18.77
t		11.68 **	6.91 **	13.53 **	4.35 **	84.56 **
Average	(855)					
1959		44.78	50.69	44.03	51.08	51.99
1963		47.68	50.00	46.94	50.97	57.66
Difference		2.90	0.69	2.91	0.11	5.67
t		10.15 **	−2.35 *	8.63 **	−0.34 +	44.71 **
Negative	(402)					
1959		44.65	53.29	45.41	50.83	57.46
1963		45.91	47.71	43.63	50.69	50.64
Difference		1.26	5.58	1.78	0.14	6.82
t		2.90 **	−10.66 **	−2.48 *	−0.24 +	−24.23 **

+ p = not significant.
* p < .05.
** p < .01.

202

Table 65 (continued)

STANDARD MEAN OPI SCORES OF THE CHANGE GROUPS IN 1959 AND 1963

Sex and change groups	(N)	Thinking Introversion	Complexity	Nonauthori-tarianism	Lack of Anxiety	Social Maturity
Women						
Exceptional	(521)					
1959		47.96	47.84	52.99	49.67	47.10
1963		50.79	51.27	50.10	51.42	66.34
Difference		2.83	3.43	7.11	1.75	19.24
t		7.28 **	7.95 **	15.15 **	3.95 **	76.45 **
Average	(1240)					
1959		46.24	48.08	42.18	49.94	49.41
1963		46.44	45.93	44.63	49.53	55.21
Difference		0.20	2.15	2.45	0.41	5.80
t		0.86 +	−9.15 **	8.83 **	−1.50 +	55.01 **
Negative	(612)					
1959		45.59	49.33	42.85	50.11	53.93
1963		44.01	44.06	41.18	47.79	47.38
Difference		1.58	5.27	1.67	2.32	6.55
t		−4.72 **	−14.63 **	−3.92 **	−6.05 **	−34.92 **

+ p = not significant.
* p < .05.
** p < .01.

There is no ready explanation, however, for the fact that the exceptional changers as a group had the lowest mean Social Maturity score in 1959 but did not differ at that time from the other groups on the Nonauthoritarianism scale, which extensively overlaps and is correlated with the Social Maturity scale (.71 for the OPI normative sample and .61 for the present longitudinal sample). It seems clear that in 1959, the exceptional changers responded to items on the Social Maturity scale differently from the way they did to the items which form the more specific Nonauthoritarianism scale. It is notably easier for young people to know what they are against than what they are for, and in the four years since they were first tested, the exceptional changers may have come to accept a more positive stance on the various issues concerning autonomy which are raised in the more complex Social Maturity scale. But any explanation of this finding must await, at the very least, some form of item or factor analysis.

Two other findings did not lend themselves easily to interpretation. In 1963, the exceptional changers manifested significantly less anxiety, as assessed by the Lack of Anxiety scale, than the other change groups, and also registered the greatest degree of interest in social contacts, as measured by the Social Introversion scale. Since the correlations of these scales with the Social Maturity scale are very low, the present findings cannot be dismissed as artifacts of the exceptional changers' Social Maturity scores.

Perhaps many people who have a great deal of the intellectual openness and autonomy measured by the Social Maturity scale are also more open to social interaction. Perhaps too, relatively greater freedom from anxiety helps to encourage—or at least to permit—the kind of openness and autonomy that are part of the construct of social maturity. It might also be argued, however, that those who develop intellectually, open themselves more to the complexities in life and experience increased anxiety temporarily as the result of these encounters. There is some evidence for this view (Trent, 1967). Yet those more disposed to develop in the traits measured by the Social Maturity scale may have larger thresholds for this kind of anxiety than those more afraid to venture out and explore life. On the basis of the present findings, the relationship between anxiety and autonomy remains obscure and needs to be clarified by further research.

Scores on the Omnibus Personality Inventory indicated that of the three groups, the exceptional changers had the greatest social interest in people. According to the Strong Vocational Interest Blank (SVIB), completed by most of the youths in the longitudinal sample who were interviewed, the exceptional changers also had the greatest altruistic interest in people. The SVIB is a long-standing and major personality inventory designed to assess patterns of vocational interest by comparing a subject's interests with those which have been found to distinguish people successful in different occupations. Ten scales illustrative of the 49 scales included in the SVIB were chosen for analysis (Table 66 and Appendix Table E-12). Three dissertation studies have explored the relationship of the Strong Vocational Interest Blank to the Omnibus Personality Inventory on dimensions of autonomy and intellectual disposition (Cummings, 1962; Weissman, 1958; and Williams, 1964). Discussion of the SVIB itself may be found in Strong (1943) and Layton (1960).

Table 66

STANDARD MEAN STRONG VOCATIONAL INTEREST BLANK (SVIB)
SCORES OF THE CHANGE GROUPS (INTERVIEW SAMPLE) [a]

| | Change groups | | |
SVIB scale	Exceptional (N = 63)	Average (N = 119)	Negative (N = 59)
Psychologist	46.4	42.5	39.9
Mathematician	36.7	38.2	38.8
Policeman	44.3	44.4	46.5
Social Worker	51.8	47.8	46.5
Accountant	41.6	45.0	46.6
Sales Manager	47.3	45.8	44.8
Author-Journalist	51.5	50.1	49.7
Interest Maturity	67.5	66.3	65.4
Occupational Level	69.6	68.1	66.5
Masculinity-Femininity	52.8	49.7	48.2

[a] Scores have been standardized on the standard deviation and mean of the total interview sample.

Of the three change groups, the exceptional changers had the highest mean scores on the Psychologist, Social Worker, and Sales Manager scales. High scores on these scales, taken together, reflect a correspondence with the interests of people whose occupations call primarily for observing, helping, or dealing with people—possibly further evidence that the subjects who changed most positively in social maturity were also most person-oriented. However, when the college persisters and consistently employed youths were observed separately, the Sales Manager scale distinguished the exceptional changers only among the noncollege youths (Table 67 and Appendix Table E-13).

The exceptional changers observed as a whole in Table 66 also made the highest scores on scales associated with occupations likely to be at a professional level and to deal with the world of ideas (the Occupational Level and Author-Journalist scales), a finding which corroborated the exceptional changers' higher level of intellectual disposition, as demonstrated on Omnibus Personality Inventory scales.

Table 67

STANDARD MEAN SVIB SCORES OF COLLEGE PERSISTERS AND THE
CONSISTENTLY EMPLOYED IN EACH CHANGE GROUP
(INTERVIEW SAMPLE) [a]

| | Change groups | | |
Pursuit groups and scale	Exceptional	Average	Negative
College	(N = 37)	(N = 48)	(N = 12)
Psychologist	48.4	43.4	42.9
Mathematician	37.8	38.7	34.5
Policeman	41.7	43.2	47.5
Social Worker	53.6	47.1	52.6
Accountant	38.8	42.7	46.0
Sales Manager	46.9	45.8	48.5
Author-Journalist	54.0	50.0	47.1
Interest Maturity	67.8	66.5	69.7
Occupational Level	72.0	70.4	68.8
Masculinity-Femininity	49.8	52.1	50.6
Employed	(N = 5)	(N = 29)	(N = 15)
Psychologist	39.5	39.9	34.2
Mathematician	31.0	35.9	37.6
Policeman	52.5	46.4	47.2
Social Worker	47.9	48.2	41.0
Accountant	49.0	48.8	49.5
Sales Manager	54.7	48.2	45.8
Author-Journalist	41.7	48.8	49.8
Interest Maturity	67.3	66.3	63.3
Occupational Level	63.8	66.2	65.2
Masculinity-Femininity	66.7	47.6	48.7

a Scores standardized by standard deviation and mean of total sample in Table 66.

When the total responding interview sample was considered, the exceptional changers also scored highest and the negative changers lowest on the Interest Maturity scale. However, this was not true for the college persisters, although it was still true for the employed sample. Perhaps for many youths the greater maturity of interests purportedly measured by the Interest Maturity scale (that is, interests which distinguish older men from high school students) is associated with increase in the objective and open-minded thinking that the Social Maturity scale intends to measure. Otherwise there is no obvious reason for a relationship between the two scales, nor any reason why the relationship would not hold for the college persisters when it existed for the other subjects.

Again exclusive of the college persisters, there was a relationship between masculinity of interests (as measured by the Masculinity-Feminity scale) and social maturity. This relationship is particularly difficult to interpret. In contrast to the more versatile and idea-oriented interests assessed by the Social Maturity scale, the Masculinity scale on the SVIB assesses the interests of men who are interested in the applied and practical things traditionally or culturally associated with masculine interests, and a negative correlation of —.26 has been found between the two scales on the basis of the scores of over 600 university freshmen men (Center for the Study of Higher Education, 1962). Whether the finding in the present study is extraneous to the assessment of the degree of change for the young adults who did not persist in college, or whether it represents some pertinent dynamic or personality development, is another consideration which at this point must be relegated to the interesting but unexplained.

In the total interview sample the exceptional changers scored lowest on the Mathematician, Policeman, and Accountant scales. This finding is more open to immediate interpretation. Items on these scales reflect relatively little involvement with humane, intellectual concerns, and in many ways reflect an authoritarian and practical outlook, traits incompatible with high scores on the Social Maturity scale. Perhaps the relationship of the interest scales to growth of social maturity is most clearly illustrated by the college students who were exceptional changers; they were particularly high on the Author-Journalist scale and particularly low on the Policeman scale.

However, it is to be noted in Appendix Tables E-12 and E-13 that in the majority of cases the differences between the change groups in SVIB scores were not statistically significant. This could be the result of the very small numbers included in some of the groups, or of a lack of relationship between vocational interests as measured by the SVIB and change in attitude as measured by the Social Maturity scale. These findings can only be regarded as suggestive until the present analyses are replicated with a larger sample. Moreover, while a study of the correlates of change may contribute to an understanding of the nature—or mystery—of personality change as here defined, the correlates do not necessarily delineate what fosters or precipitates change. For this reason the research staff studied the many interview protocols for any patterns that would provide clues to the conditions of change.

The general impressions gleaned from the protocols intensified the images of the characteristics of the different change groups, but added little new information about the possible sources of these characteristics. Individual case reports, however, suggested a great deal about the varieties of personal development and about important events in the lives of individuals who manifested radically different degrees of change in measured attitude. The general impressions gained from the interviews provide a good summary of characteristics found to be associated with change, and of individual aspects of personality change. Since the average changers consistently stood midway between the extremes of the traits exhibited by the exceptional and negative changers, the discussion will be limited to the latter two groups.

THE NEGATIVE CHANGER

In addition to the factors of ability and socioeconomic background, four other characteristics distinguished the young adults in the interview sample whose scores on the Social Maturity scale were lower four years after high school. These characteristics were: 1) a rather strict adherence to either Catholicism or some type of fundamentalistic Protestant religion; 2) an almost complete lack of concern with intellectual or cultural activities; 3) an overemphasis on a practical and materialistic orientation to life in general and education in particular; and 4) unusually close parental ties, whether single or married.

The situation found for the negative changer in the total longitudinal sample also existed for those interviewed: The negative changers constituted by far the greatest proportion of subjects of low ability and low socioeconomic level. It obviously followed that the educational level of the fathers of the negative changers was low; of those interviewed, 20 per cent of the negative changers reported fathers who had some college education, compared with 32 per cent of the average changers and 41 per cent of the exceptional changers.

Like their fathers, the negative changers showed little interest in pursuing higher education. One of the most striking facts about the members of this group was that so relatively few entered college, in contrast to those in the average and exceptional change groups. Fewer still persisted in college; those who did usually had majors in the applied fields of business, education, and engineering rather than in the humanities, social sciences, and sciences. Almost all of the negative changers who were interviewed had an exclusively practical, vocational orientation toward education; they saw a high school or college degree as having value mainly because it put them in a better job market.

Although the relationship between attitude and negative change was established in the discussions of education and religion, something more was learned from the interview sample about the relationship between change and attitudes toward religion. Virtually every negative changer was a religious believer, and for most of them religion was of great importance in their private lives. For a significant number, religion was central to and overshadowed all other activities. As examples: For one boy of below average ability, who was the only one of his family to graduate from high school and who was experiencing some difficulty in establishing a stable work identity, religion served as an all-encompassing frame of reference through which he maintained his entire sense of security and self-esteem. Another negative changer, a dedicated Jehovah's Witness, read the Bible constantly and had definite plans to go into the ministry. Still another boy felt religion motivated every act or plan he undertook, and he had structured his entire life around it.

These findings suggest that a strict adherence to a very conservative or dogmatic religion is not conducive to growth in autonomy, at least as measured by the Social Maturity scale. This might be expected, since the items in the scale measure authoritarianism in part by the extent of moralistic strictures expressed by the subject. The high commitment to conservative religious beliefs of so many negative changers may be explained by their having turned to overdependence on religious structure when they were faced with the ambiguities and uncertainties of young adult life.

In the interviews, few negative changers expressed flexibility and tolerance in their views toward life, which was expected in the light of their low Social Maturity scores. Some interviewees perceived their rigidity and dogmatism as a problem and expressed concern over their difficulties in tolerating others' points of view and maintaining good interpersonal relationships. Many, however, were not aware of their narrowness and restrictiveness. A minority were grossly intolerant. For example, one boy felt that "far out" religious sects should be banned because "the Jehovah's Witnesses have been proven to be the left arm of Communism." Almost all of this group were highly moralistic and judgmental in their attitudes toward premarital sex and other related problems of social behavior.

In contrast to the exceptional change group, none of the negative changers appeared to have undergone religious crises or doubt. Since the negative changers were marked by authoritarianism, which inhibits questioning the authority of accepted ideas, and so many in this group expressed highly conservative and fundamentalist religious beliefs, their lack of religious doubt was expected. Only one boy experienced difficulty with his religion and his problem was a unique one. He had been converted to Methodism after having been disturbed by his previous lack of religion. As he said, "I wanted to be religious, to join a church, but no one ever talked to me about it or encouraged me."

Women outnumbered men in the negative change group almost two to one. This finding, and the fact that many of these women had become housewives immediately after graduation from high school, helps explain the lack of intellectual and cultural interests in this group. Most of these women's interests centered almost exclusively on their husbands, children, and homes. Their great dependence on their home and family for a sense of identity and feeling of well being was best summed up by one woman when she was asked what were the most important things in life to her: "My husband and children. Without them, I'm nothing." The range of these women's interests outside the family was generally extremely limited and usually included television, gardening, and sometimes interest in a sport, most frequently bowling. Similarly, the men in this group were so involved with matters related to job security and advancement that they also had little interest in anything outside home and family, except for sports.

It is not to be assumed, of course, that a decline in Social Maturity score is an exclusive function of the housewife without experience outside the home. Some college students, too, yielded autonomy to authoritarianism. One college student was perplexed when asked anything about philosophical problems. He saw his biggest problem as, "learning to get along with others, learning to tolerate other people's points of view." And there was indication that his loneliness, his constricted interests, his stress on material values, his problems with interpersonal relations, and his apparent dependency upon his parents, would prohibit the boy from ever developing very much in the way of autonomy.

Most of the negative changers maintained very close ties with their immediate families, were unusually dependent upon them for advice and encouragement, and were in the habit of seeing them frequently if married, or lived at home if single. One young man visited his parents or called them at least once a day. He "didn't depend on them for anything . . . but advice." His parents advised him when his first child was born and helped him manage his money, and his wife's parents helped them buy groceries when they were first married. A young woman who lived at home and felt she was dependent and yet "not tied to mother's apron strings," remarked, "My family likes to do everything together. There is no running off after supper." Another young man and his wife lived in the same building as his parents. He married his girl friend because she became pregnant, and he claimed he was too young to handle the responsibility. At the time of the interview, he and his wife had not yet learned to face life together on their own; they continued to be dependent upon his indulgent mother when confronted with problems.

So many factors apparently prevent the negative changer from achieving autonomy that he eventually increases in authoritarianism. Limited ability, limited education, a constricted socioeconomic background, over-dependence on a dogmatic or fundamentalistic religion, and an unenlightened, unstimulating, and autocratic family background seem to be prominent factors associated with regression in social maturity. These factors were consistently observed in the interview protocols.

THE EXCEPTIONAL CHANGER

The richness, complexity, and diversity of the personality types found among many of the exceptional changers made them stand out, as a group, in striking contrast to both the negative and average changers. Characterized by relatively high intellectual and autonomy scores on the Omnibus Personality Inventory, and by a relatively high level of tested ability, they were more open to growth and willing to come to grips with the paradoxical elements of life. They did not bypass conflict situations; rather they sought them out, willing to test their values and face the possibility that some of their beliefs might be invalid. For the most part, the exceptional changers were comparatively thoughtful, concerned, striving young people who saw life broadly. They were generally relativists, feeling that values were neither black nor white, but shades of gray. They could best be characterized as having independence in thought and action.

That the exceptional changers seemed to be the brightest, most dynamic group, is partially explainable by the fact that 63 per cent of them were at the high ability level. It has been shown that they were also distinguished by their families' more advantageous educational and occupational backgrounds.

It has been noted that of the three groups, the exceptional changers had the highest rate of college attendance in 1959. Seventy-five per cent of the exceptional changers interviewed were attending college in 1959, as compared with 49 per cent of the average changers and 41 per cent of the negative changers. More of the exceptional changers persisted in college, their range of majors was broader, they majored more in the humanities and social sciences, and they seemed most concerned with the achievement of knowledge for its own sake. Narrow undergraduate specialization was uncommon in this group. Some reasons for choosing their majors were: "Sociology is a broad major with a number of possibilities. It leaves room for a changing mind. It is a vital new field"; "English seems to me the most vital study, related to issues, where you can see patterns of man's thought." Many of the men planned to work for a Ph.D. or other higher degrees.

The women in this group differed from the women in other groups in several ways. Many were dedicated to a field of study, had definite plans for continuing their education past their baccalaureate degree, and hoped to combine a career with marriage.

Even those of the exceptional changers interviewed who were withdrawals, nonattenders, and military service enlistees were notably different from the rest of the sample. Most of the withdrawals expected to return to college and felt that their experience away from school was enriching and educational. Several girls had recognized that they had emotional problems, had seen psychiatrists, and were steadily growing in independence and self-acceptance. Others had gone to Europe, traveled through the United States, or worked. One young man of very high potential, confused about the direction in which he had been heading, withdrew from engineering school and traveled. He felt the experience helped him mature and he intended to return to college in a major more compatible with his interests. One young woman had dropped out of college because lack of funds had forced her to return to her parents while going to school. Feeling that staying at home was emotionally disturbing, she decided to earn the money she needed to finance her schooling away from home and she planned to re-enroll as soon as it was financially feasible.

Military service served as a period of thought and goal orientation for some. For example, one young man in this change group said of the Navy: "It broadened my views. You get to know people all over the world, and how they live, and what they actually think about things. It's an education." The noncollege exceptional changers generally had had more varied and enriching experiences and were more independent of their families than those in the other two groups, and some had done particularly well. One man, as thoughtful and aware as most college students in the sample, held a highly responsible job in a prominent department store.

In their evaluations of the purpose of education, the exceptional changers were the least vocationally oriented, demonstrating their greater tolerance for ambiguity and conflict. One boy said the purpose of education was, ". . . to shake up thinking, particularly in regard to what one believes." Another said, "The thing I value most is the searching mind, and the level of achievement will follow." Many of these young people stressed that education was a process of opening up the mind and letting in new ideas. This same feeling of expanding horizons and broadening understanding was particularly revealed in their views about religion.

One of the greatest differences between the three change groups was evidenced in their views toward religion and morality. The few avowed agnostics in the sample were almost evenly divided between the average and exceptional change groups; there were none in the negative change group. The significance of the immense overrepresentation of Catholics and fundamentalists in the negative change group and their corresponding underrepresentation in the exceptional change group, considered earlier, bears some further discussion here. Those young adults who became more authoritarian were inordinately affiliated with religions characterized by authoritarian administrative systems and creeds. The exceptional changers, considerably less aligned with the more conservative religions, were also more flexible and tolerant and less judgmental.

The attitude of those exceptional changers who did belong to conservative sects was marked by emphasis on individualism and questioning. One such exceptional changer said that the individual must decide moral and ethical beliefs for himself. Another claimed, "Belief in a God is all that matters." In general, the views of those exceptional changers belonging to Catholic or fundamentalist Protestant churches were qualitatively different from their fellow church members in the negative and average change groups.

Many of the exceptional changers, agnostics and religious believers alike, had experienced severe religious conflicts and questioning. One exceptional changer, who had been a Methodist all his life before becoming an agnostic, said, "It didn't happen overnight. About four years ago I decided I didn't know enough about my religion. I was going to become a minister and studied every religion I could. I found common fallacies, common rituals which are baseless. I saw holes I couldn't fill. . . ." Another agnostic, rather antagonistic toward organized religion, said, "anything that represses the human spirit, tries to force it into a mold, ought to be done away with. . . . Christianity is a negative religion. It says 'no' to life. All good things on earth are to be used, not prohibited." And one young man in this group who still described himself as a nondenominational believer concluded that he believed only in "purpose in life and reverence for life."

Most of the exceptional changers seemed to be moral relativists. Responding to the question on premarital sexual relations, one exceptional changer answered, "If that was all we had to deal with we'd have little to worry about. These are just issues which cover up things. Alcoholism and unmarried mothers are symptoms; something else is causing these rather than immorality. To me hard and fast rules are ridiculous; it is all relative when you look at the situation. So many moral issues are strictly a matter of yourself. This is the height of morality—your own moral reactions." Another stated, "I believe that a person can do what he wants as long as it doesn't hurt anyone else."

The exceptional changers were characteristically more complex and questioning individuals. And just as many of them questioned their religious values, they also questioned other values they, as well as their parents, had cherished. Ideological and emotional conflict figured in their lives. One young woman had been extremely distressed by the religious doubt provoked by a philosophy professor and by the tension generated between her religious spirituality and her tendency toward materialism. Another young woman had also gone through a religious upheaval which had caused her to convert from Catholicism to Lutheranism because, "I didn't believe in confession or the emphasis on Mary." Several attributed certain aspects of their behavior to reaction against parents they viewed as overly restrictive. Some "went beat," some severed family ties, and some incurred psychosomatic illnesses.

In one way or another, most of the exceptional changers showed evidence of groping with ambivalences, trying to choose between the material versus the spiritual, the ideal versus the real, independence versus security. Many of the young people were introspective, trying to find out who they were and what they believed. Tolerance of others and awareness of self were outstanding qualities of the exceptional changers as a group. Even those who tended toward authoritarianism were in most cases conscious of the tendency and were trying to improve upon what they considered an undesirable trait.

Thus individualism, intellectual orientation, introspection, involvement in conflict situations, complex, flexible, and objective thinking, and a relativistic view of the world set the exceptional changers apart from the other two groups. They also had higher ability than the negative and average changers, were less oriented toward religion, and came from better educated families. In contrast to the accepting and parentally dependent negative changers, many of the exceptional changers interviewed reported conflict with their parents' values.

The interview data revealed one other important finding not discernible in the data obtained from the larger sample: the unique and different personal characteristics and circumstances of school and family background reported by the different individuals who manifested the same degree of change in Social Maturity. Many of the exceptional changers had outgoing personalities, but many did not. A majority of them were at a high level of ability and attended college, but many were not exceptional in tested ability and many did not enter college. A good number of the exceptional changers came from advantaged, supportive, permissive, and democratic family backgrounds, but many did not. Like many of the youths who had great obstacles to overcome in life, so, too, did many of those who changed exceptionally in Social Maturity. This serves as a reminder that what may be considered as a condition of change for a group may not function for a given individual. Sanford (1964) arrived at a similar conclusion as a result of his case study of two Vassar women whose scores on an early version of the Impulse Expression scale increased radically after four years in college, but who exhibited very different qualities in the process of this change:

> When we say, on the basis of mass testing, that impulse expression increases during the college years, we are saying quite a lot. But we are also leaving much to obscurity, for we know

that two students who obtain the same or similar scores on the IE scale may differ very much both in the quality of their impulse expression and in the broader system of personality within which it occurs [p. 36].

This situation also leaves a question in great part as yet unanswered: What does lead to change in attitude or personality, as here defined?

CONCLUSION

Out of the variety of background data examined from questionnaire responses, only three factors clearly distinguished the three change groups: parents' education, the youths' level of academic aptitude, and their religious orientation. Compared with the other groups, the exceptional changers as a group were favored by the most ability, had parents with the greatest amount of education, and had the most liberal religious beliefs. It had been expected that the exceptional changers, more than the other change groups, would come from families characterized by autonomous patterns of interaction among members, liberal attitudes, intellectual interests, and shared enriching experiences. This hypothesis was supported by the interview protocols but not by the questionnaire data returned by the larger sample.

Data in Chapter VII led to the expectation that persistence in college would be closely associated with exceptional change, and this was found to be true. Still, the particular college experiences related to increase in Social Maturity scores have not been isolated in this research or in that of Lehmann and Payne (1963). Even the students' major fields of study were not nearly so related to change of attitude as expected.

The exceptional changers, compared with the other young adults, perceived themselves as more individualistic, independent, and liberal. They were more interested in idea-oriented occupations, more intellectual in disposition, and more open to the world around them. They also manifested less anxiety. Here again, however, not all correlates of change were remarkable.

From a sociological viewpoint, many of the more circumscribed characteristics of the negative changers have been found to be typical of a great many lower class, lower ability subjects investigated in other studies, such as Lipset's (1962) on "Working Class Authoritarianism." The question is, of course, how much native ability and societal factors influence learned personality traits, dispositions, and attitudes. Certainly it appears that below average ability, a limited educational background, an autocratic and unstimulating family life, restricted economic opportunities, and an authoritarian religious subculture may have served as forces constricting growth of social maturity for a great many negative changers. Regression on this personality dimension may actually be prompted by such a contextual framework, particularly in social milieus in which independence, autonomy, and tolerance are not viewed as desirable traits.

This is not to say that low native endowment and restricted social advantages are necessarily the major factors which determine the development of social maturity. Some people with this kind of background can and sometimes do show positive growth in this direction. In some cases, it is also true that people of high ability and from advantaged backgrounds can be low on Social Maturity. Nevertheless, optimal development of the kind of autonomy and intellectual disposition measured by the Social Maturity scale is apparently less likely to occur under the conditions which had been met by many negative changers in the sample.

Evaluation of Family, School, and Environment

Graduation from high school marks a major point at which decisions must be made that may have a profound effect on a way of life and permanently shape a future career. Decision-making is, of course, an ongoing process. It does not start nor end at any specific point, but it is at the end of high school that young people must begin to implement decisions in ways not heretofore necessary. They must then put aside much of the fantasy and vicarious thinking about adult roles and begin to test reality by choosing a vocation, seeking a marriage partner, entering college and electing a major, and carrying out numerous other adult roles.

Indications from the interviews were that many students submit passively to the educational process until suddenly, on the threshold of young adulthood, they find themselves called upon to evaluate their education in the light of life goals. These goals and the students' perceptions of the purpose of education have been colored to some extent by their high school experience, and no doubt to a greater extent by values drawn from their home backgrounds. It is therefore educational experience and family environment—elements that enter so critically into decisions

219

about college, occupational directions, and other personal choices
—which bear examination.

The data examined to this point have provided wide-
ranging information about the postgraduate pursuits of a large
sample of high school graduates and significant factors associated
with those pursuits. This chapter presents the graduates' opinions
about important aspects of their lives and indicates some of the
influences which figured critically in their major decisions.

The material analyzed in the present chapter was drawn
primarily from responses to the questionnaires submitted to the
subjects in 1963 and from the protocols of the representative
interview sample first described in Chapter III. Thus, opinions
of the high school graduates were elicited as they looked back
on their early adult lives, nearly four years after high school.

In order to distinguish between the views and experiences
of young people who made different decisions about their post
high school education and careers, the sample was divided into
three groups: those who persisted in college over the four years
covered by the study (persisters); those who entered college but
withdrew without a baccalaureate degree (withdrawals); and those
who had no college experience (nonattenders).

A central purpose of this report has been to examine how
formal education, as a critical intervening process, contributes to
maturation—the complex process of human development that
evolves from the interaction of education, personal potential,
family background, environment, opportunity, and chance. An
attempt was made, and reported in this chapter, to assess the role
of education in this process through examination of the subjects'
retrospective evaluations of: 1) their families; 2) the meaning of
education; 3) counseling and other student personnel services;
4) their work experiences; 5) their current status in life.

Expectations were that the three post high school pursuit
groups would be characterized by differences in family climate,
or by what is also referred to as family "ascription" (see Cicourel
and Kitsuse, 1963; Clark, 1964; Coleman, 1961). Students who
persisted in college were expected to have received the greatest
encouragement to do so from parents who valued education
highly, and more support in terms of parental interest, interaction, and temperament. It would follow that the more motivated

students would put a greater premium on high school and college, derive more satisfaction from school, become more involved in education, make more use of opportunities such as counseling services, and view education as having goals beyond the pragmatic and vocational.

Whether or not schools and colleges would be found to compensate for lack of parental support among able youths remained an open question, although the poor record of college attendance among cultural minorities suggested that the brighter students among these subcultures have not been sufficiently encouraged to further their education—a problem which has been highlighted in the 1960's. By the same token, it was expected that college persisters, presumably better able to realize their potentials, would express the greatest satisfaction with their education and personal status. The noncollege students and withdrawals who were frustrated in their plans or by their job choices were expected to be the most dissatisfied with their status.

FAMILY LIFE

A strong association was found between family values and the behavior and career choices of youths, and 64 per cent of the sample reported parental influence in their decisions about either education or career. However, evidence of a failure of perception was also apparent in the subjects' views of their families' characteristics. Although the interviewers who made home visits were struck by many unique familial features, such as immense show of solidarity, overt hostility and jealousy, great cultural deprivation, unusual ease of relationships, marked refinement of surroundings and demeanor, and evidence of personal and physical chaos, when the young people were asked how their families differed from other families, they typically responded, "Oh, it's no different from any other family; just average." Many of those interviewed also found it difficult to describe their parents' characteristics and temperaments, although this task was met better in 1963, when most of the responding sample checked one or more of a choice of adjectives to describe their parents (Table 68).

A majority of the youths considered at least one of their parents "loving." At least 37 per cent of them considered their parents "energetic," "ambitious," "orderly," "easygoing," and in

Table 68

PARENTAL CHARACTERISTICS DESCRIBED BY THE
PURSUIT GROUPS, IN PERCENTAGES

Parents' temperament	Persisters (N = 1300)	Withdrawals (N = 1187)	Nonattenders (N = 1654)	Chi square
		Pursuit Groups		
Ambitious	55	51	43	47.57 **
Easygoing	63	69	70	18.27 **
Quick-tempered	42	41	48	17.34 **
Excitable	52	50	37	80.81 **
Energetic	57	53	39	106.93 **
Intellectual	31	29	19	61.37 **
Loving	74	69	59	74.02 **
Orderly	55	50	42	49.54 **

** $p < .01$.

the more negative terms of "quick-tempered," and "excitable."
Less than 33 per cent considered their parents "strict" or "moody,"
and less than 13 per cent considered them "nagging" or "domineer-
ing," terms not noted in Table 68. Twenty-six per cent thought
of their parents as "intellectual." *

The different groups in the sample described their parents
by most of the above traits in varying proportions. The college
persisters in greatest proportion and the nonattenders in least
proportion described their parents as loving, energetic, ambitious,
orderly, excitable, and intellectual. The nonattenders in greatest
proportion considered their parents easygoing and quick-tempered, and although the differences in the use of some of the terms
do not appear noteworthy, all the descriptions used distinguished
the groups at a level of statistical significance beyond the 1 per
cent level. These data, however, must be considered in light of
the large samples involved.

It was expected that those youths with the traits necessary
to persist in college would have patterned themselves after parents
they could characterize as intellectual, ambitious, active, and or-

* Recalled and subjective data of the kind reported in this chapter
may lack reliability and validity or may be drawn from responses given within
a frame of reference not intended by the authors. Such data provided by the
subjects could not, of course, be examined for accuracy.

derly. That a greater proportion of persisters also saw their parents as "loving" is consistent with the finding that compared with the nonattenders, they also perceived their parents as more ready with praise and more interested in their achievements. (The relationship between parental attitudes and the graduates' post high school pursuits has been discussed in some detail by Trent and Ruyle [1965].)

It seems evident that as a group the young adults who persisted in college came from different family climates than did the withdrawals and nonattenders. Nearly 70 per cent of the high school seniors who became college persisters reported while still in high school that their parents definitely wanted them to attend college, compared with less than 50 per cent of the withdrawals and less than 10 per cent of the nonattenders. Even among those nonattenders who had the ability to attend college, only about 15 per cent reported that their parents encouraged them to do so. A similar finding has been reported by Little (1959) in a statewide study of a class of Wisconsin high school seniors.

Table 69

HIGH ENCOURAGEMENT FROM PARENTS TO ATTEND COLLEGE, AS
REPORTED IN 1959 BY SUBSEQUENT PERSISTERS AND
WITHDRAWALS, IN PERCENTAGES

Source of encouragement	Men			Women		
	Per-sisters (N = 793)	With-drawals (N = 658)	Z ratio	Per-sisters (N = 620)	With-drawals (N = 706)	Z ratio
Father	69	48	7.0 **	60	44	5.3 **
Mother	73	54	6.7 **	65	48	5.9 **

** $p < .01$.

The relationship between parental encouragement and persistence in college is examined more specifically in Table 69, which shows for each sex the proportions of persisters and withdrawals who reported being highly encouraged to attend college by their mothers and fathers separately. Whether referring to men or women or encouragement from their mothers or fathers, approximately 20 per cent more persisters than withdrawals reported while still seniors in high school that their parents definitely wanted them to attend college. When students who obtained their degrees after four years were compared separately with the withdrawals, the difference between group responses on the variable increased to 30 per cent. Although differences were smaller than those found between the withdrawals and persisters, proportionately more men than women reported parental encouragement, and more mothers than fathers were reported as the source of encouragement. In 1963, a related question to the earlier one about parental encouragement was asked, and drew responses which showed even greater differences between the two groups. When asked how important it was to their parents that they graduate from college, approximately three-fourths of the persisters but only about one-third of the withdrawals reported it was very important.

These significant differences existed regardless of sex, ability, or socioeconomic level. However, the lower the students' socioeconomic level, the less they reported parental encouragement, whether or not they persisted in college. Among the men, 91 per cent of the persisters at the high socioeconomic level reported that it was very important to their fathers that they graduate from college, compared with 58 per cent of the withdrawals. At the low socioeconomic level, 70 per cent of the persisting men reported college graduation as very important to their fathers, compared with 32 per cent of the withdrawals. Only 20 per cent of the women withdrawals at the low socioeconomic level reported that it was very important to their fathers that they graduate from college. Considering the marked relationship between parental encouragement and enrollment and persistence in college, it is reasonable to conjecture that parental characteristics have a great deal to do with the differences in academic motivation that distinguished the college persisters from the withdrawals (see Chapter VI).

The differences in amount of parental encouragement given to attend college led to the expectation that the college attenders would also report discussing college more often with their parents (Table 70). This hypothesis was supported by the data. Among the men, 71 per cent of the persisters had discussed college "quite a lot" with their parents by the time they were graduating seniors in high school, compared with 61 per cent of the college withdrawals and 28 per cent of the nonattenders. Persisters also constituted the greatest proportion of students who sought advice from their parents about their future careers as well as about matters in general.

Table 70

KINDS OF PARENTAL ADVICE SOUGHT BY THE
PURSUIT GROUPS, IN PERCENTAGES

		Groups		
Parental advice	*Per-sisters*	*With-drawals*	*Nonattenders*	*Chi square*
Men	(N = 793)	(N = 658)	(N = 602)	
Frequent discussion of college	71	61	28	265.56 **
Advice about occupation	69	65	55	28.95 **
Frequent advice in general	28	24	18	18.46 **
Women	(N = 620)	(N = 706)	(N = 1294)	
Frequent discussion of college	82	72	39	392.78 **
Advice about occupation	81	78	75	11.24 **
Frequent advice in general	42	31	28	36.77 **

** $p < .01$.

The differences observed between the groups on questions of how much general and occupational advice was sought were not as great as the differences between the groups on how much they had discussed college, but the pattern of differences held constant. Sixty-nine per cent of the persisting college men stated that they sought occupational advice, compared with 55 per cent of those who did not attend college, and 28 per cent of the persisting men compared with 18 per cent of the nonattenders stated that they frequently sought advice on matters in general. On each variable, and for each group categorized by amount of post high school education, women sought more help from their parents than men. However, the variables distinguished the two groups of women in the same way as they did the men, and overall chi squares distinguished significant differences between the three pursuit groups on all variables for both sexes.

Although a majority of the young adults, regardless of sex

or post high school pursuit, did not report "resentment" of their parents, but rather a feeling of closeness and understanding, a sizeable proportion did express differences with them. Thirty-nine per cent of the subjects would have liked to have had a better understanding of one or both of their parents; 37 per cent would have liked to have felt closer to them; 29 per cent would have liked to have been on better terms with them; and 20 per cent expressed some feeling of resentment.

There were only nominal sex differences apparent in the youths' reaction to both their parents, but there did appear to be a tendency for proportionately more men than women to report some friction. Proportionately more men also tended to express differences with their fathers and proportionately more women than men differed with their mothers, although both sexes reported more differences with fathers than with mothers. Twenty per cent of the men compared with 14 per cent of the women reported they would like to be on better terms with their fathers; 7 per cent of the men and 10 per cent of the women reported they would like to be on better terms with their mothers. (Another 4 per cent of both the men and women would have liked to have been on better terms with both parents.) Differences between pursuit groups were slight, but on the basis of overall chi squares there was a significant tendency for the college persisters in greatest proportion to report themselves as being on good terms with their parents and having a good understanding of them.

Clearly, then, although the larger portion of the young adults regarded their families in a positive manner, a great many did not. And although most of the youths saw themselves as independent of their families and not influenced by them to any great extent, it has been shown that the kind of interaction that occurred in these families and the degree of encouragement offered by them were highly related to the subsequent pursuits of the youths in the sample.

THE MEANING OF EDUCATION

As noted in Table 71, the majority of graduates, whatever their pursuits after high school, considered the most important purpose of education to be either vocational training or general education (the gaining of knowledge, an understanding of community and world problems, and appreciation of ideas). Approximately 20 per cent of the men and 16 per cent of the women thought the most important purpose of education was related to the development of talents and creative abilities, personal development (including character formation) and the ability to get along with others, or preparation for marriage and family life. Close to 10 per cent of the sample—mostly those who did not go to college —did not check any of the prime purposes of education listed.

The main, and most striking, difference between the three groups analyzed for both sexes has already been noted in Chapter VI. Those with the most exposure to college emphasized general education as the most important purpose of education; those who withdrew placed more importance on vocational training than did those who persisted in college; and those with no college experience stressed vocational training the most. Overall chi squares were highly significant.

In analyses not included in Table 71, the young adults at the high ability level were found to emphasize general education somewhat more, and those at the lower levels inclined toward vocational training more, but the relationship of perceived purpose of education to ability was not nearly as great as it was to post high school experience. (The respective chi squares were 101.01 versus 203.15.) Although socioeconomic status was earlier established as closely associated with entering college, in this analysis emphasis on general or vocational education was more related to ability level than to socioeconomic level. Respective chi squares were 100.01 versus 72.93. By 1963, their views about the purpose of education had shifted; now these views seemed to be less related to ability or family background than to what they had seen, learned, and experienced in the past four years.

The high school graduates in the longitudinal sample were also asked to specify the most important goals to be attained by attending college. The response pattern followed that of the responses to the broader question about the general purpose of education. In this context, however, a larger proportion of all groups than in the previous instance considered practical training the main goal, and only 3 per cent of the nonattenders considered the purpose of college as general education.

Many college persisters, of course, viewed college as a way

Table 71

MOST IMPORTANT PURPOSE OF EDUCATION, AS REPORTED BY THE PURSUIT GROUPS, IN PERCENTAGES

Purpose of education	Men			Women		
	Persisters (N = 793)	Withdrawals (N = 658)	Nonattenders (N = 602)	Persisters (N = 620)	Withdrawals (N = 706)	Nonattenders (N = 1294)
Vocational training	28	41	47	26	38	46
General education	44	28	20	52	39	25
Development of talent & creative abilities	11	10	7	5	4	3
Personal development	9	12	13	11	11	13
No answer	8	9	13	6	8	13
(Chi square)		(125.26 **)			(163.92 **)	

** p < .01.

to attain occupational skills, but a much larger proportion thought the principal purpose of college was to get a general education. This latter group remained generalists throughout. Four years after entering college, 43 per cent of the persisters still considered the gaining knowledge and appreciation of ideas as the main goal of college; only 11 per cent indicated a primary interest in more specific areas such as community and world problems, science, humanities and the arts, or scholarly pursuits.

Regardless of the youths' pursuits, most considered college at least "somewhat" important (men—92 per cent and women—69 per cent). Seventy-eight per cent of the men who did not go to college nevertheless felt college was important to them; 63 per cent of the men and 85 per cent of the women felt college was also important for a woman. However, the three groups analyzed were clearly differentiated by sex, the degree of importance attached to a college education in general, and the extent to which college was considered very important personally.

More women than men considered college very important for men generally, although most men, whatever their pursuit, shared this opinion—83 per cent of the persisters (who differed little in this respect from the withdrawals) and 77 per cent of the nonattenders. Comparable figures for the women persisters and nonattenders were 94 per cent and 89 per cent respectively. But fewer of the subjects viewed a college education for women as equally important. A slight majority of women who persisted in college (51 per cent) considered college very important for women, but otherwise only 21 per cent of the subjects shared this view. Only 7 per cent of the women nonattenders and 27 per cent of the women withdrawals felt college was very important for women. Although men who persisted in college might be expected to considered education important for women, they too took a more traditional viewpoint, less than one-fourth of them considering college for women "very important."

Perpetuating a long prevalent attitude, the majority of young adults apparently believed higher education more important for a man than a woman. It would be interesting to observe how those who considered general education as the prime purpose of college viewed the question of college for women. The data were not broken down to answer this question, but our speculation is that a vocational orientation toward college is probably often linked with the belief that higher education is more important for men than for women.

Despite the general high regard for college, however, many of the men nonattenders divorced themselves entirely from the pursuit they reported to be important for men generally. Seventy-seven per cent of this group reported they felt college was very important for men, but only 42 per cent felt college was equally important for them personally. For many of these men this response doubtless constituted a rationalization for lack of ability, opportunity, or interest. Less than 10 per cent of the women who did not attend college felt that a college education was of any great importance to them personally.

EVALUATION OF HIGH SCHOOL AND COLLEGE

Most of the youths in the sample reported in 1959 that they had liked high school at least somewhat. But there were significant differences between the three pursuit groups in proportions of youths who had reported at the end of high school that they had "liked high school very much" (chi square = 137.81; p < .01). Sixty per cent of those who entered college and 43 per cent of those who did not reported as high school seniors that they liked high school very much. The greatest proportion (67 per cent) of seniors who reported liking high school very much were those who continued their education four years beyond high school, although most of them made suggestions for changes, and had some criticisms to make both about their own high school activities as well as the programs and services offered by their schools.

Table 72 shows the proportion of graduates who in 1963 reported various programs they wished had been emphasized more in high school. A sizeable proportion (over 10 per cent) mentioned teaching procedures, courses, and several areas subsumed under "personal development" that they felt needed greater emphasis. Small classes, classes for the gifted, and classes for slow learners were frequently urged. Smaller classes were recommended by approximately 40 to 50 per cent of the graduates, regardless of their sex or later education. Forty-two per cent of the college persisters, but only 23 per cent of the noncollege men,

Table 72

HIGH SCHOOL PROGRAMS IN NEED OF GREATER EMPHASIS, AS
APPRAISED BY THE PURSUIT GROUPS, IN PERCENTAGES

Areas	Per-sisters	With-drawals	Non-attenders	Chi square
Men	(N = 793)	(N = 658)	(N = 602)	
Teaching procedures				
Small classes	42	45	41	1.81 +
Classes for gifted	42	32	23	47.37 **
Classes for slow				
learners	17	24	35	51.77 **
Course Work				
Math. & Science	26	35	51	79.04 **
English &				
Communication	52	45	35	33.44 **
Vocational training	12	26	35	92.65 **
Personal development				
Counseling	44	37	30	24.36 **
Discipline	12	18	21	18.71 **
Study assignments	13	10	11	3.00 +
Women	(N = 620)	(N = 706)	(N = 1294)	
Teaching procedures				
Small classes	51	49	46	4.21 +
Classes for gifted	45	37	25	75.89 **
Classes for slow				
learners	23	31	40	30.04 **
Course Work				
Math. & Science	16	24	34	67.40 **
English &				
Communication	50	43	37	27.19 **
Vocational training	16	27	36	77.07 **
Personal development				
Counseling	48	41	34	32.64 **
Discipline	9	18	22	44.33 **
Study assignments	12	14	8	17.05 **

+ p = not significant.
** $p < .01$.

advocated more emphasis on classes for the gifted, and 35 per cent of the noncollege students, as against 17 per cent of the persisters, advocated classes for slow learners.

English (or Communicative Arts), mathematics, and science were the subject areas the largest proportion of youths felt needed more emphasis. Men nonattenders in particular were more inclined than the college students to feel that science and mathematics should be stressed (51 per cent versus 26 per cent), and the college students showed more interest in improved English and communication courses (52 per cent versus 35 per cent)—perhaps reflecting their different needs on the job and in the college classroom. Differences for the women were similar in pattern but less marked. English was mentioned by the interviewees more often than any other subject as the one most needed but most poorly taught, and was the subject singled out most by the sample at large as needing greater emphasis.

Over 35 per cent of the nonattenders felt vocational courses should be emphasized more, compared with less than 15 per cent of the college persisters. However, subsequent analyses showed that few of the high school graduates, whether they entered college or employment, had found vocational courses most useful or thought they would take them if they were back in high school.

Despite the evidence that the noncollege students could have used at least as much counseling in high school as the college persisters, a greater proportion of persisters thought counseling should have been emphasized more (45 per cent versus 33 per cent). At the same time, over 20 per cent of the noncollege group felt more emphasis should have been placed on discipline, compared with 10 per cent of the college persisters. This is a curious fact and suggests, among other possibilities, that the youths who chose not to go to college would have liked to have been guided and controlled more. It will be seen that many of them regretted not having studied harder and not having entered college, and data observed in an earlier chapter also suggested that this group was less autonomous than the college students, a further indication perhaps of a greater need for imposed structure on their lives.

Greater emphasis on study assignments was suggested by just over 10 per cent of the sample, least of all by the noncollege sample, but not markedly so. Although this finding does not appear in Table 72, nearly 12 per cent of the youths felt less emphasis should be placed on electives, the only area so many students thought should be de-emphasized. On the basis of chi square analyses, all differences between the three pursuit groups were significant beyond the 1 per cent level, with the exception of the men on the subject of study assignments, and both men and women on the subject of smaller classes.

Some sex differences are noticeable in Table 72. Women more than men felt the need for smaller classes, classes for slow learners, and counseling. Men more than women felt that science and mathematics classes should have had greater emphasis. Generally, the group of men and women who withdrew from college fell between the college persisters and the employed in proportion of respondents to any given item.

Judging from the absence of volunteered comments, the subjects registered almost no concern about other matters that would seem pertinent to the education of young adults, such as the need for original and better teaching, the inclusion of more academic courses and extracurricular activities, and the development of ethics, morals, and responsibility. The lack of concern over emphasis on responsibility may be of special interest since it was only two years after the questionnaire was administered that manifestation of what has been taken to be massive student unrest reached a point of national attention. Much of the student disturbances such as those which took place at the University of California between 1965 and 1967 centered in issues of educational policy and self-responsibility in terms of student and faculty academic freedom and political advocacy. However, the evidence in the present report and in research such as that of Heist (1965) and Peterson (1966) indicate that these concerns were shared by very few students. Trent and Craise (1967), among others, have also argued that current student activist movements are not reflective of the majority of college students and that most students continue to reflect the relatively apathetic and conforming traits which have characterized students of previous years.

It is not surprising that the courses the youths felt should be emphasized more were also those they reported most useful. Asked to nominate the two high school subjects which had proved most useful, 58 per cent of the responding sample chose English, including over 46 per cent of those who did not go to college. Second on the list of importance were mathematics and algebra for the men (52 per cent) and business and typing for the women who did not enter or persist in college (66 per cent compared with 23 per cent of the women who persisted in college). Twenty per cent of the noncollege men felt a shop course had been one of their two most useful subjects, and an equal proportion of men who persisted in college stated that a physical science course fit this category. A home economics or marriage course figured importantly for 24 per cent of the noncollege women.

Although most of the youths reported a school subject which had been most useful to them, they were less confident that any one person had been a great source of help, as may be seen in Table 73. Nearly one-half of the responding sample explicitly stated that no one had been a great source of help during high school. Nevertheless, the overall chi squares continued to indicate significant differences between the three pursuit groups categorized by differences in post high school education. The source of help reported most was parents and relatives, perceived as such in greatest proportion by the persisters and least by the nonattenders. After family came teachers of academic subjects, mentioned by 15 per cent of the college persisters and 8 per cent of the nonattenders. Teachers of vocational subjects, physical education teachers, coaches, and such "other" persons as high school principals and ministers were mentioned as a source of help by a total of 10 per cent of the subjects. High school counselors and deans, as a group, were mentioned by 7 per cent.

Friends were considered a source of "help" in frequency only after family, academic teachers, and counselors, which raises a question about the importance of peer influence. Certainly it is not congruent with the popular belief that adolescents are influenced above all by their peers. This judgment is based on the assumption that in contemporary adolescent culture friends who are perceived as being helpful are also influential. This relationship between helpfulness and influence cannot be demonstrated with the data at hand, however, and it may very well be that perceived helpfulness is entirely distinct from perceived influence.

In the interviews, parents more than friends were indicated as the greatest source of influence upon the lives of the young adults. Parents were singled out as more influential than any event or other person. This report is not the first to find a relationship between family values or parental encouragement and the personality and pursuits of youths (see Bloom, 1964; Levenson, 1965;

Table 73

GREATEST SOURCE OF HELP DURING HIGH SCHOOL, AS PERCEIVED
BY THE PURSUIT GROUPS, IN PERCENTAGES

| | Groups | | | |
Sources of help	Per-sisters	With-drawals	Non-attenders	Chi square
Men	(N = 793)	(N = 658)	(N = 602)	85.31 **
No one	45	48	50	
Parents & relatives [a]	21	17	11	
Academic teacher [b]	15	13	9	
Counselor or dean	5	7	9	
Friends	5	4	5	
Vocational teacher	2	3	8	
Coach	3	5	2	
Other	4	4	3	
Women	(N = 620)	(N = 706)	(N = 1294)	78.84 **
No one	39	47	49	
Parents & relatives [a]	28	21	19	
Academic teacher [b]	14	10	8	
Counselor or dean	7	10	7	
Friends	6	7	7	
Vocational teacher	1	3	6	
Coach	0	0	0	
Other	4	2	6	

[a] Z ratio of college vs. noncollege, sexes combined: 5.47 **.
[b] Z ratio of college vs. noncollege, sexes combined: 5.91 **.
** $p < .01$.

Slocum, 1956). But the relative impact of parents versus peers on young adults apparently has yet to be determined. Moreover, sources of influence are complex; they go beyond family and friends.

McDill and Coleman (1965) concluded that high school status (such as recognition and rewards for extracurricular activities, popularity, and achievement), as well as the plans of peers, had greater influence on students' college plans than either interest in learning or parents' education. Bordua (1960) found that sex, religious affiliation, and occupational level of parents were related to college plans in addition to parental emphasis on education. Bell (1963) found that the aspiration level of students was influenced by that of their parents, that authoritarian and conforming students followed the motivational directives of their parents more than other students, and that students who interacted more with high school reference groups developed higher aspiration levels than other students. Simpson (1962) found that parents and peers together formed the greatest influence on the aspirations of middle class and working class boys. Solomon (1961) found that the impulses and values of the youths themselves influenced "selected decision situations" more than peers and particularly more than parents. Finally, Brittain (1963) found that the relative impact of peer versus parental influence over youths depended upon the specific situation.

The research cited all centered on high school adolescents. The young adults interviewed in the present study had been out of high school for about three years. By this time many of them had gained independence from their parents and, no doubt, from their peers. Perhaps they were more objective in retrospect and recognized the influence of their parents more than they had a few years earlier. Perhaps, too, parental influence is greatest before adolescence. Family values may inculcate a tendency for youths to choose certain friends, goals, and modes of behavior in high school which become influential and seem more influential than parents at the time. Parsons' (1962) thesis noted in Chapter I may be pertinent here. It may be that in a complex world which neither parent nor child sufficiently understands, parents cease to be adequate models for adolescents and peers are then substituted as models. Still, the parental model may heavily influence choices of subseqeunt models for behavior, and therefore actually constitutes the greatest influence.

In any event, young adults do not readily admit being influenced or helped by anyone. Help is evident, however, and, as may be noted in Table 74, among the areas in which the young people most reported receiving help, three stand out: in their attitudes towards college, with personal problems, and with school work (including class work and choice of subjects). Less than one-fourth of both the persisters and withdrawals in the sample reported help in their choice of college, but the persisters in greatest proportion reported help in attitudes toward college. Nine per cent of the sample reported having gotten most help with financial problems, and 11 per cent got most help in selecting jobs.

Table 74

AREAS IN WHICH GREATEST HELP WAS RECEIVED DURING HIGH SCHOOL,
AS REPORTED BY THE PURSUIT GROUPS, IN PERCENTAGES

| | Groups | | | |
Areas of help	Per-sisters	With-drawals	Non-attenders	Chi square
Men	(N = 793)	(N = 658)	(N = 602)	206.92 **
School work	21	23	31	
Attitude toward college	34	30	8	
Choice of college	19	11	2	
Personal problems	23	25	22	
Family problems	7	8	6	
Job selection	9	7	13	
Financial problems	10	11	6	
Women	(N = 620)	(N = 706)	(N = 1294)	388.46 **
School work	20	24	29	
Attitude toward college	36	27	6	
Choice of college	24	14	3	
Personal problems	33	30	29	
Family problems	9	9	12	
Job selection	9	9	15	
Financial problems	11	10	7	

** $p < .01$.

Differences between the sexes in reported sources of help observed in Table 73 were nominal, with the exception that women in greater proportion than men mentioned their parents and relatives as the greatest source of help in high school. Previous data have shown that women also reported themselves closer to their parents than did the men, and more ready to go to them for advice. The only impressive sex differences regarding kind of help apparent in Table 74 exist with respect to the handling of personal problems. Over 20 per cent of the men and more than 30 per cent of the women, in college or out, reported receiving help with personal problems, a difference significant at the 1 per cent level. There is no evidence to explain the difference between the men and women in the amount of help reported. It may be that the women had more personal problems or that they found it easier to seek or acknowledge help.

That a greater proportion of young people who went to college should report having gotten help with questions and attitudes related to college is no surprise. What heightens interest in the finding was the consistent relationship found between college attendance and how much help with decisions about college was reported. Regardless of ability, help in this area was reported in greatest proportion by the persisters, in next proportion by the withdrawals, and in least proportion by the nonattenders.

Despite the young adults' pragmatic, vocational orientation toward education, they reported having gotten relatively little assistance in choosing a vocation. Perhaps it is more remarkable that this was also true of the many who did not go to college, most of whom entered employment after graduation from high school.

The interviewed youths were asked how adequately their high school education had prepared them for three major functions in their lives: work, college, and marriage. Most of the subjects expressed neither blanket approval nor disapproval. Thirty-one per cent felt that high school had prepared them adequately for work, compared with 30 per cent who felt their preparation was inadequate. The remainder felt that judgment of adequacy depended on the particular student, high school, occupation, or skill involved. College persisters in least proportion (16 per cent) felt high school had provided them with adequate preparation for work, compared with 30 per cent of the withdrawals and 43 per cent of the nonattenders. Of course, many of the college students were interested in professional occupations which called for training beyond what they could have gotten in high school.

More important in the case of the college students may be whether they felt they had been adequately prepared for college work. A majority (59 per cent) felt they had been. Only for college did a majority of any group feel adequately prepared, but as many as 21 per cent of the college students felt their high school training had been inadequate. Another 16 per cent felt that the question of suitability of preparation could most properly be judged in relation to the individual student, school, or college.

Preparation for marriage given them by their high schools fell under heaviest criticism by a majority of both sexes across all groups (53 per cent). This was the case even for 57 per cent of the noncollege men, a majority of whom were married in 1963, and

40 per cent of the noncollege women, most of whom also were married by this time. These figures include 18 per cent of the men and 15 per cent of the women who considered their high school education had been irrelevant to their marriage.

If the youths were reserved about giving approbation to their high school education, those who entered college gave more to their college experiences. A considerable majority of the men and women who attended college expressed a general satisfaction with important aspects of their college life, including the intellectual challenge, training for their careers, leisure activities, and social contacts.

Although the majority of the college withdrawals also reported themselves satisfied with their college experiences, they consistently did so in less proportion than the persisters. For example, approximately 90 per cent of the persisters felt satisfied with their intellectual growth as a result of college, compared with about 70 per cent of the withdrawals. Over 85 per cent of both the men and women who persisted in college were satisfied with their training for their future careers (albeit before having had a chance to test this training) compared with 53 per cent of the men and 60 per cent of the women who withdrew. Thirty-four per cent of the men withdrawals and 14 per cent of the persisters were expressly dissatisfied with their vocational training. Corresponding figures for the women were 27 per cent and 13 per cent.

The college students' responses to specific items relating to faculty, administration, and regulations showed less unanimity of opinion than existed about the college experiences in general (Table 75). The record of responses is interesting, particularly in view of the current apprehension about the student activism and revolt mentioned earlier.

The majority of college students considered their faculty intellectually stimulating (67 per cent, combining all figures), the rules and regulations governing student behavior sensible and necessary (72 per cent), and the faculty and administration "quite successful" in developing responsibility in students (57 per cent). There was a tendency for proportionately more persisters to consider their faculty intellectually stimulating, and for more withdrawals to consider existing rules necessary.

Almost one-half of the persisters and a little more than

Table 75

COMPARISON OF PERSISTERS' AND WITHDRAWALS' AGREEMENT WITH STATEMENTS ABOUT
COLLEGE FACULTY, ADMINISTRATION, AND REGULATIONS, IN PERCENTAGES

Statements	Men			Women		
	Per-sisters (N = 793)	With-drawals (N = 658)	Z ratio	Per-sisters (N = 620)	With-drawals (N = 706)	Z ratio
Most of the faculty are intellectually stimulating	70	64	2.71**	69	65	1.39 +
Existing rules and regulations regarding student behavior are sensible and necessary	67	76	3.72**	69	75	2.76**
The faculty and administration are quite successful in developing responsibility among the students	56	59	0.46 +	55	59	1.43 +
Students are too much bound by course work and not free to pursue interests of their own	49	37	4.54**	52	33	6.91**
Rules and regulations should definitely be more permissive	49	35	5.13**	37	25	4.63**
The administration and faculty generally treat students more like children than adults	33	21	4.83**	31	22	3.64**

+ p = not significant.
** p < .01.

one-third of the withdrawals felt that students were so bound by course work they had no time or affect left for exploring interests of their own. A minority of all students thought that rules should be more permissive or that the administration and faculty treated students more like children than adults. A considerably smaller proportion of withdrawals than persisters felt that course work was restricting, that rules should be more permissive, or that they were not treated like adults. Withdrawals evidently preferred more control in their lives than did the persisters, again reflecting the differences in autonomy between these two groups (see Chapters VI and VII). The persisters differed significantly from the withdrawals on all issues noted in Table 75 with the exception of both the men's and women's opinions on development of responsibility and women's opinions about the intellectual stimulation afforded by the faculty.

Some students felt the need for more independence, responsibility, and intellectual challenge, but this feeling did not represent the consensus. On the basis of these findings, there is no case to be made for the existence of any prevailing stand of student nonconformity or dissent. Katz (1968 [Ch. 1]) reached a similar conclusion on the basis of his survey of opinions of University of California and Stanford University students, even though his study took place during a time of visible unrest on the two campuses. His finding was that most of the students would have liked improvements in their education, but were basically satisfied with the rules on their campuses.

EVALUATION OF STUDENT PERSONNEL SERVICES

Many of the young adults felt more emphasis should be put on counseling services in high school; few noted they had gotten good counseling. College students also expressed less satisfaction with student personnel services than with any other aspect of their college life, a majority rating them either fair or poor.

At the same time, student personnel services, perhaps more than any other function of the school and college, can serve to take the place of parents by assisting youth in their educational, vocational, and personal development. It is therefore important to assess what counseling help was given the youths who entered college and those who did not, and how this related both to their family situation and to their various pursuits after high school.

In high school, help with course scheduling was the only counseling service reportedly received with any frequency, that is, at least once a semester. And, at that, only 51 per cent of the youths who entered college and 38 per cent of the nonattenders reported getting help of this kind. Information about college was received by 22 per cent of those who subsequently enrolled in college and 9 per cent of those who never attended. Fifteen per cent were given aptitude tests and 10 per cent vocational tests on a regular basis, regardless of their subsequent pursuits. Job information and help with disciplinary or personal problems was received on a semester or yearly basis by less than 8 per cent. Sex differences were nominal in the amount and kind of counseling received.

The quantity of counseling was also nominal. Members of the research team repeatedly found, in their visits to the schools which participated in the survey, that because of heavy case loads and administrative duties, counselors generally could spend only 15 minutes a semester with each student at best, and a little longer with those who presented particular problems. Thirty-seven per cent of the subjects did rate as good the help they got with course scheduling, but all other counseling services were rated as good by no more than an average of 17 per cent of the students.

The personnel service evidently used most in college was faculty advice on such matters as course and major requirements; 37 per cent of the college persisters and 23 per cent of the withdrawals reported receiving such advice regularly. Regular use of health services was reported by the next largest proportions—15 per cent of the persisters and 7 per cent of the withdrawals.

Financial and housing assistance, vocational guidance, and occupational placement were used by still smaller proportions of students, but consistently more by persisters than withdrawals. Less than 5 per cent reported regular use of counseling and only 1 per cent reported using psychiatric services. Four per cent more men withdrawals than persisters used counseling or writing and reading clinics. Five per cent of each group of women reported receiving counseling. Considering how helpful services like these could be to a student's career, it is remarkable that so little use was made of them. The lack of use of **personal and vocational** counseling is particularly noteworthy on the part of the withdrawals, many of whom, one could argue, were evidently in special need of these services. Most vocationally oriented and least satisfied with their vocational training in college, the withdrawals nevertheless made the least use of vocational guidance services.

These findings suggested the importance of inquiring into the kind of person who makes the greatest use of educational opportunities. Throughout this study certain factors—ability, socioeconomic status, intellectual disposition, and particularly parental encouragement—were consistently found to be related to student development and academic progress. It therefore seemed important to distinguish how these separate and interrelated factors affected the development of students.

Specifically, we wondered if, after holding the factors of ability and socioeconomic status constant, the same relationship already observed would be found between parental encouragement and progress in college, and also if high school and college personnel compensated for any lack of parental encouragement reported by the able but less motivated and intellectually oriented students.

Consequently, all graduates were selected who placed in the upper 30 per cent of the sample's distribution of ability scores; of these, students who reported a great deal of parental encouragement to attend college were distinguished from those who did not report this kind of encouragement. The two groups were then additionally divided into persisters, withdrawals, and nonattenders. Thus, those of equally high ability who reported different family climates and differed in patterns of post high school education, could be compared on a number of the variables already studied in reference to the larger sample.

It was found that even when they shared the same high level of ability, the graduates grouped by different college patterns reported markedly different amounts of parental encouragement while seniors in high school, just as was observed for all persisters and withdrawals in Table 69. Eighty per cent of the persisters of high ability reported in 1959 that their parents definitely wanted them to attend college, compared with approximately 63 per cent of the highly able withdrawals, and 22 per cent of the highly able nonattenders. The relationship between persistence in college and parental encouragement of bright high school graduates also existed regardless of level of socioeconomic status (Table 76).

Table 76

PARENTAL ENCOURAGEMENT AS REPORTED BY SUBJECTS OF
HIGH ACADEMIC APTITUDE, BY SOCIOECONOMIC
STATUS (SES), IN PERCENTAGES

SES and encouragement	(N)	Persisters	Withdrawals	Nonattenders	Chi square
High					
Strong					
encouragement	(295)	80	16	4	67.70 **
Other	(73)	41	26	33	
Middle					
Strong	(606)	61	27	12	247.70 **
Other	(436)	23	20	57	
Low					
Strong	(101)	50	28	22	67.56 **
Other	(132)	8	21	71	

**$p < .01$.

The differences at the high socioeconomic level set the key for the remainder of the table; among the students at this level who reported a great deal of encouragement from their parents, 80 per cent were persisters, 16 per cent withdrawals, and only 4 per cent nonattenders. However, where strong parental encouragement was not reported at the high socioeconomic level, only 41 per cent of the highly able students persisted in college, while 26 per cent entered but withdrew, and 33 per cent never entered. At the low socioeconomic level, when no strong parental encouragement was reported, 71 per cent of the bright youths did not enter college.

Similar relationships were found to exist on the other variables examined: when the decision was made to attend college; the amount of importance given to graduating from college; and level of intellectual disposition (Trent, Athey, and Craise, 1965). The decision to attend college was made even before high school by 70 per cent of those who became persisters and who reported having been highly encouraged by their parents to attend college. Conversely, nearly 75 per cent of the many bright nonattenders who were not encouraged by their parents reported no decision at all; over one-fourth of these students said they had not even discussed college with their teachers while in high school.

Regardless of post high school pursuit, advice about attending college from high school teachers and counselors was reported proportionately more by students who also reported strong encouragement from their parents. The largest proportion of students who reported having gotten such advice was among the future persisters whose parents urged college attendance (over 50 per cent); the smallest proportion was among the nonattenders who had not been highly encouraged by their parents (about 30 per cent).

Proportionately more persisters sought advice from counselors than from teachers, whereas the bright nonattenders reported seeking advice somewhat more from teachers than from counselors. This finding suggests that since teachers are in direct contact with their students, they may be better able than counselors to recognize or at least to work with students who are not realizing their potential. Counselors, on the other hand, may be fully occupied by the task of assisting students already directed toward college goals. In any event, of students at the high ability level, 76 per cent of the persisters and 61 per cent of the withdrawals who had had parental encouragement reported having been highly encouraged to attend college by their high schools, a difference significant beyond the 1 per cent level ($Z = 3.85$). Of the academically able students who were not encouraged by their parents to attend college, 61 per cent of the persisters and 54 per cent of the withdrawals reported they were not encouraged by their high schools, a difference, however, that was not statistically significant ($Z = 1.36$). Persisters consistently more than withdrawals reported parental encouragement, but what remains even more significant satistically is that both the persisters and withdrawals who reported less parental encouragement than their more highly encouraged classmates also reported receiving less encouragement from their high schools ($Z = 4.67$; $p < .01$).

These differences in reports may in part result from a lack of perception on the part of the students. Students with no interest in college, even if they are bright, may not recognize guidance when it is given; nevertheless, formal counseling for these students was limited almost entirely to the routinely offered once-a-semester session of course-scheduling.

One case, doubtless exceptional because it was so extreme, nevertheless points to the general kind of failure in communication still possible in counselor-teacher-student relationships. A troubled teacher reported finding a former student, whom she knew to have high ability, in a class for the retarded. At one time, emotional and family problems had radically affected the student's grades, but with the help of teachers and special tutoring aids, he had come to show exceptional promise. Nevertheless, he had been pigeonholed as a student of low ability by a counselor who, disregarding other pertinent information about the student and his work, had depended solely on grade records.

As was true of all the other students, the brighter students also reported that faculty advice was the student personnel service they used most. But faculty advice was sought regularly only by a minority of the bright students, and more by persisters than withdrawals (39 per cent versus 22 per cent). Of those bright withdrawals who had not been strongly encouraged to attend college by their parents, only 18 per cent made use of faculty advice.

These findings are not singular. Gibson (1962) polled the opinions of 904 seniors from 12 high schools in three states about counseling services. Most of the students felt that counseling added to the value of their schools, but nearly half could not say they had been assisted personally. One-half were not sure of the nature of the guidance program and approximately one-third said it had not been explained to them. A majority had not had access to their cumulative records or had them explained, although without exception they wished this had been done. Most thought they knew their strengths and weaknesses, but a majority reported they did not understand themselves well enough. Again, a majority thought they had enough opportunity to learn about their occupational interests (66 per cent), but an even greater proportion (76 per cent) had serious doubts about their tentative occupational choices. Only 24 per cent had had an opportunity to discuss training problems and job opportunities with people already in the field and only 8 per cent had participated in field trips of an occupational or educational nature, even though these experiences were considered most valuable. A majority of the students had a pressing problem and nearly half some personal problem they would have liked to have discussed with a teacher or counselor, but in most cases they felt it would not be possible, mostly because the counselor lacked enough time.

Lack of sufficient and systematic guidance was also found by Cicourel and Kitsuse (1963) among a small sample of students in a high school relatively outstanding in the quality of its programs, its guidance program, and the generally high socioeconomic status of its students. The researchers learned that this apparently advantageous situation did not have a positive effect on the counseling process. They found that: 1) Although students whose parents expected them to attend college took these plans for granted, the parents were uninformed about college requirements and for the most part did not attend conferences designed to give this information; 2) a majority of students were unaware that they had been assigned to a college preparatory curriculum; 3) a majority of college preparatory students were not informed about specific college entrance requirements; and 4) counselors' assignments of students to the college preparatory curriculum were often based on questionable subjective criteria.

From their interviews of counselors, Cicourel and Kitsuse arrived at other relevant conclusions: 1) There was a widespread resentment of professional counselors by teachers; 2) in large high schools with professional, full-time counselors there was more interaction between counselors and students and more awareness of pupils' problems than there was in small settings with teacher-counselors; 3) professional counselors sought out students with problems whereas teacher-counselors tended only to see the better students who came to them; 4) professional counselors were able to elicit more cooperation from teachers and administrators; and 5) students' choices with respect to curricula were curbed and channeled by the counselors who themselves were misinformed about the meaning of such factors as socioeconomic status and college characteristics and requirements, so that equal educational opportunities were not assured for all students of equal ability.

Cicourel and Kitsuse's samples were too small and isolated to permit conclusive generalizations—especially with reference to social class. The related findings in the present study, however, suggest that the findings cited above would probably hold for a much wider sample than the few schools and counselors surveyed. The evidence once again suggests that academic involvement is closely associated with a supportive family climate and is developed early. When an encouraging home climate does not exist, however, the schools evidently do little to compensate for the lack. And although we know that changes in values can take place, students who presumably could have profited from student personnel services most were least exposed to them in high school and college. These students evidently did not actively seek out these services; but for whatever reasons, neither did the schools and colleges seek out the students. Of course, much traditional "faculty advice" and guidance in general, like college itself, may be irrelevant to the needs of many who withdraw from college. Schools and colleges earnestly attempting to learn more about the causes and consequences of attrition might well seek the counsel of their withdrawals in addition to pursuing other sources that could contribute information related to attrition.

ATTITUDES TOWARDS JOBS

As indicated in Chapter VII, next to marriage and family the young adults in the sample felt that jobs and careers were the most important sources of life satisfaction. And although something was learned from the data in Chapter IV about the patterns of employment during the four years after high school, questions remain about the young people's evaluation of their work experiences, including what they knew about the world of work and what they hoped to find in their jobs.

For the college persisters, particularly those who obtained their baccalaureate degrees by 1963, the most important element of a satisfying job was their liking for the work involved in it. This was also important to the withdrawals and noncollege students, but to a far less degree, especially among the men. For example, 39 per cent of the college persisters felt liking their work was most important, compared with 22 per cent of the noncollege men. But 26 per cent of the noncollege men and only 6 per cent of the persisters felt that steadiness of employment contributed most to a satisfying job. Being able to take pride in one's work and having the chance to use one's talents were considered the principal factors in a good job by 21 per cent of the persisters, 19 per cent of the withdrawals, and 19 per cent of the noncollege

men. Good pay and opportunities for advancement were important to 15 per cent of the persisters, 18 per cent of the withdrawals,
and 16 per cent of the noncollege men.

Of relatively little importance to the men were such mat-
ers as working with people rather than things, the opportunity
to be helpful, and working conditions. They were least interested
in fringe benefits and responsibility. Nearly 8 per cent of the men
listed no conditions as important for a satisfying job. College
women (not noncollege women) were more interested than men
in working with others and being helpful, and less interested in
good pay; otherwise they shared the men's views about what they
considered to be the most important requisites of satisfying jobs.

The data permitted examination of the young people's
opinions about the relevance of their high school and college training to their subsequent vocations. Without yet having tested their
training, 86 per cent of the college persisters in the sample were
satisfied in 1963 that college had adequately trained them for their
future careers. This was the case for only 53 per cent of the men
and 60 per cent of the women who withdrew from college, most
of whom were actually working in 1963.

In Chapter IV, comparative analyses were made of the
California men in the sample who attended junior college two
years or less with those who had never entered college, in order
to examine the relationship between amount of sub-baccalaureate
post high school education and subsequent occupational patterns.
Additional analyses of those groups are presented in the present
context.

Of the California men in the sample who had attended
junior college two years or less and were employed, less than half
(47 per cent) expressed satisfaction with their college's contribution to their job training. Thirty-seven per cent expressed dissatisfaction, and the remaining 16 per cent were noncommittal.

As had been true of the rest of the high school graduate
sample, both the junior college and noncollege samples of California men reported having received most of their occupational
training on the job. Only 36 per cent of the junior college men
reported having received training through some form of post high
school education, and only 16 per cent mentioned getting their
training in college. Also, as was true of the larger sample, many
California men found it difficult to get the jobs they wanted (55

per cent of the junior college men and 42 per cent of the non-college men). In 1963 less than one-fourth of them unqualifiedly reported that their jobs were offering them the opportunities they wanted (28 per cent of the noncollege and 16 per cent of the junior college men). More former junior college students (45 per cent) than noncollege men (30 per cent) expressed disappointment in the opportunities offered by their jobs.

Repeating the pattern of the total sample, by 1963 only a minority of the California youth were working either at the type or level of occupation they had expressed as their choice in 1959—which might be expected for young adults only four years beyond high school. Fifty per cent of both the California sample and the total sample thought what they missed most in their jobs were good pay, security, and the chance for advancement.

An effort was also made to learn how the young men re-garded the kind of skilled occupations they would be most likely to encounter—those of factory foreman and draftsman. Respond-ing to questionnaire items, the youths reported how much they knew about each occupation, the amount of education they felt the occupations required, and how appealing they were.

A majority of the men, particularly those who did not enter college, felt they did not know much about either occupation. Less than 10 per cent of the men reported having a "great amount of knowledge" about the occupations and 36 per cent reported having a "fair amount" of knowledge. A majority of the non-college men felt a foreman needed at least a fair amount of edu-cation, but only 39 per cent of the former junior college students thought this. The youths felt that a draftsman needed considerably more education than a foreman: 45 per cent of the noncollege men felt a draftsman needed a great amount of education, com-pared with 18 per cent of the junior college men, 65 per cent of whom, however, felt a draftsman needed a "fair amount" of education. Few found the job of foreman "of great appeal," and only 20 per cent found it "fairly appealing," although a majority found the job of draftsman at least "fairly appealing." However, even the job of draftsman had "great appeal" for only 15 per cent. The noncollege and junior college men did not differ markedly with respect to the amount of appeal the two occupations had for them, although over 12 per cent more of the noncollege than former college men found the jobs of foreman and draftsman at least fairly appealing.

The kind of item reported on here is general, and therefore open to a variety of interpretations. What a "fair amount" of education meant to the subjects, for instance, is not clear. Even so, answers to the item do suggest that the young adults perceived quite common occupations vaguely, and differently, according to the amount of education they had had. It may be only realistic to acknowledge that few youths would know very much about occupations unfamiliar to them. But many who had been employed four years reported knowing very little about the quite common occupations of foreman and draftsman. Important questions raised by this finding are: When do young adults learn about common occupations? When should they learn about them? What is the relationship between information about occupations and their appeal? As between the skilled "white collar" occupation of draftsman and the often equally skilled but "blue collar" occupation of foreman, what constituted the greater appeal of the former? Are students' opinions to be relied upon when they claim to know about job opportunities and their own potentials?

It was observed in Chapter IV that military service was no salvo for most of the men in the sample. There were numerous other examples of young adults in the sample who were still naïve in 1963 about the world of work and the many complex problems modern, automated society will entail for their generation. Too much of young people's vocational development is still being left to hit-and-miss environmental circumstances. This stiuation may prove to be increasingly unsatisfying as the years go by if potentials remain unrealized.

An unfavorable prognosis can also be made about the college careers of students who lacked educational commitment before entering college. Forty per cent of the students who entered college after 1959 were undecided or unspecific, while seniors in high school, about their field of interest, compared with 9 per cent of the students who entered college in 1959 and persisted through 1963, and 17 per cent of the students who entered in 1959, and withdrew. Some of these students, however, may not have answered this part of the questionnaire in 1959 if they were still unsure of their plans.

Perhaps in part related to this situation, most of the youths expressed some worry about their lives. The greatest worries reported by the noncollege men were, in order: about finances and debts, marriage and children, and jobs. The former junior college men shared these worries, but the worry expressed by the greatest proportion of them was whether they would be able to complete their college education.

CHANGES THE GRADUATES WOULD HAVE MADE

Answers to a series of items designed to elicit retrospective evaluations showed that close to 90 per cent of the total sample felt they would have made some change in high school, and a majority reported that, given the chance, there were other choices they would have made since high school.

In one way or another, the young adults expressed disappointment that they hadn't gotten more out of high school, both academically and in their extracurricular activities. A majority said that, given it to do over again, they would study more diligently and take school more seriously; included were 49 per cent of the male college persisters, 70 per cent of the withdrawals, and 75 per cent of the nonattenders. Fewer women shared this view, perhaps because they had taken high school more seriously.

Over 40 per cent of the youths would have engaged in more extracurricular activities, and only about 3 per cent would have engaged in less of these activities. Few were concerned about whether or not they had defined goals while in high school, but over 25 per cent stated they would have learned more about job possibilities. This was more the case for the noncollege men considered separately (31 per cent). Nearly 20 per cent would also have sought more help from teachers and counselors for personal problems, and some 10 per cent said they would have chosen a different circle of friends. In general, those at the lowest ability level expressed a desire for change in greatest proportion, but the differences noted between the various groups existed regardless of ability.

A large proportion of the youths also reported that they would have made a major change in their lives in the four years since their graduation from high school; this was reported most by the working men who had not attended college. Approximately

70 per cent of these men would have made some change since high school, compared with 50 per cent of the men persisters. Fifty-two per cent of the working women and 42 per cent of the college women would have made a change and, as previously, women reported more satisfaction with the status quo than did the men. Former college students of both sexes were more satisfied with their lives than were the workers.

The major changes mentioned by college students involved the choice of a different college or major (in nearly equal proportions). The change mentioned by fully half of the working men was that they would have gone to college, and 20 per cent would have taken a different job or gone into military service. Another 20 per cent of the working men would have made a change by not marrying, postponing marriage, or waiting to have children. The patterns of the employed women's responses were similar to those of the working men, but in smaller proportions.

CONCLUSION

The youths who persisted in college, withdrew, or never attended differed greatly in their descriptions of their families. College persisters were much more likely to report that even before they entered college, their parents had highly encouraged them to attend. They interacted with their parents the most, and somewhat more of them reported being closer to their parents.

The three groups differed considerably in their attitudes towards high school, college, and the value and purpose of education. The persisters were more interested and involved in their education before and after entering college, and were much less likely to perceive its purpose as solely within the confines of vocational training. They were also more satisfied with the results of their education. While the young people generally approved of their education, they also had criticisms. The noncollege youths and college withdrawals particularly felt a lack of preparation for work and marriage. Counseling services appeared to have been insufficient for most of them, and they also indicated a lack of knowledge and understanding of the various vocations open to them. Many felt that they had not worked enough in school and were lacking in basic skills such as English and mathematics.

The students' personal and vocational development was

obviously affected by the interaction of individual and environmental factors. Certainly the schools figured largely. But to consider the high schools and colleges as necessary contributing agents to individual development is to return to the ethical questions raised in Chapter VII about the extent to which schools should be involved in students' personal development. These are not questions which can be dealt with in this context, but what cannot be ignored here is the finding that lack of family support with respect to higher education is related to a forfeiting of educational opportunities, and that schools compensate little for missing parental interest. The need for some solution to this problem becomes compelling when young adults who did not enter college, those who withdrew, and those who persisted reported such different degrees of satisfaction with their high school experiences and their lives.

X

Education for Adulthood: Some Conclusions

Questions persist about the nature of the vocational and personal development of young adults and about the factors that influence their development and change as they begin to assume adult roles after high school. Certainly society's prevailing values, its economic system, and schools are important influencing determinants, but value systems and modes of living must inevitably be modified in order to adapt to a world in flux. Many occupations, for instance, are being eliminated or are changing in kind and requirements, and technology is now so dominant in our society that it must be dealt with consistently and creatively by educational and other agencies of society.

The schools are largely responsible for making it possible for young people to earn a living and to achieve "self-actualization" by facilitating their personal and vocational development and helping them toward the identification and realization of their best potential. In this function, the influence of formal education is second only to the family. Therefore, schools and colleges cannot be satisfied with providing only such fundamentals as communication and computational skills, citizenship training, and vocational education. They must also make it possible for youths to acquire principles that will prove sound as they try to shape a satisfying and contributive life. Whether technology becomes a dominating factor or not, human potential needs to be developed so that man can control his environment by making informed and humane decisions when technological advancement affects his way of life.

As a result, what is needed is that awareness of the complexities of life which results from open, autonomous, objective and flexible thinking, an interest in ideas and social issues, and greater general understanding of the nature of society and of the world of work. Consequently, the educator needs to know as much as possible about how the necessary disposition towards learning, understanding, and realization of human potential is developed.

This report follows the patterns of employment and college attendance of a group of young adults during their first four years after their high school graduation. It presents in particular a study of aspects of the vocational and personal development of young adults, including a study of the impact of the schools and colleges. The report proceeded from the hypotheses, derived from theoretical and empirical bases, that there would be a relationship between entrance and length of persistence in college and degree and type of personality development; that much development of college students could be ascribed more to a predisposition to change than to the direct influence of college; and that those in the noncollege group would find their jobs lacking in opportunities for occupational choice, self-understanding, and the personal development considered important for many of this age group.

The data and their implications will be summarized as they relate to the following topics: 1) patterns of employment of youths who either did not enter college or entered and did not persist; 2) patterns of college attendance; 3) the development of autonomy and intellectual disposition; 4) widely held theories of personal and vocational development and their relationship to the evidence presented by the young people in this study; and 5) the role of education in the development of the young adults studied.

OCCUPATIONAL ATTAINMENT

Neither in 1959 nor in 1963 did the high school graduates who did not enter college indicate much knowledge about common occupational fields. It was also evident that occupational choice was as limited as occupational knowledge. Most of the noncollege men took jobs in factories, those classified by the occupational indexes as "technological." Their interview responses indicated that they usually took whatever jobs they could find. Not many held their jobs from preference, but very few, by 1963, had been able to change their type of job. Most of them found skilled work of little appeal, preferring instead jobs of a professional nature for which they did not have the necessary education or, in many cases, the demonstrated ability. Most of the women were employed in business-detail work during the four years of the study. Their attrition from paid employment was high—a majority of the noncollege women were full-time housewives by 1963. Also, many of the women who continued to work would have preferred other types of jobs.

Most of the employed youths entered and remained in semiskilled and skilled occupations. Relatively few had unskilled or semiprofessional jobs either in 1959 or 1963. Little change in occupational pattern or advancement of a major order was apparent over the years of the study. Rate of unemployment was never high at any one time, but over the four-year period it affected over 22 per cent of the employed men and women, including the college withdrawals, and 34 per cent of the noncollege men.

Unemployment was particularly prevalent among the youths of relatively low ability. Of the noncollege men whose academic aptitude scores were among the lowest 30 per cent of the sample's distribution, 40 per cent were unemployed at some time during the first four years after their high school graduation. Such a picture of unemployment among the low-ability groups is bleak enough today, but if in the future there is a demand for skills which youths with low ability cannot master, the problem of unemployment for this group will become even greater.

Most of the young adults, whether or not they attended college for a limited period, reported that what job training they had was not formal occupational training, but received "on the job." Only a nominal proportion of junior college men completed a terminal vocational program. Further, most of the youths employed in 1963, including the college withdrawals, felt that their high school and partial college training had not adequately prepared them for work. Many of the nonattenders regretted that they had not entered college, and the withdrawals were concerned, above all, about returning to college. Few of the employed would have taken vocational courses if they had high school to do over again, and generally their responses agreed that greater emphasis should be given to courses in communication arts, science, and mathematics. This study did not extend into an inquiry into the work experience of the college persisters, but at the point of graduation from college these young people felt they were adequately prepared for employment. It should be noted, however, that since they had not yet embarked upon their careers, they had not had an opportunity to test their adequacy.

These findings probably can be variously interpreted and certainly should be closely examined in subsequent research. But to this point, several possibilities are strongly suggested which bear on issues raised from the outset of this report. The high school graduates entered the work world with little understanding of it, and often with too little preparation. These conditions, together with the limited ability of many, may have been responsible in part for the lack of choice so many of them had about the kind of jobs they found. Under the circumstances, it is regrettable that at least the college withdrawals did not make more use than they reported of the vocational guidance and occupational information presumably available to many of them. But the problem suggested by the findings goes beyond the question of guidance and touches on the entire nature of adult development and the role of the school and college towards this development.

PATTERNS OF COLLEGE ATTENDANCE

Because of the effect—direct or indirect—that college may have on vocational and human development, it is important to know the patterns of entrance and flow through college and as much as possible about the factors which influence these patterns.

Forty per cent of the high school graduates in this study entered college full time. As has been typical of the college student population over the last four decades, slightly over half of the entrants persisted in college for four years and only half of the persisters graduated in four years. Currently an estimated 52 per cent of high school graduates enter college, and attrition is high.

Factors of background, general environment, and educational opportunity and experience have been found to be related to entering and remaining in college. No doubt many of these factors also contribute to what has been hypothesized as a predisposition essential to growth of intellectual disposition and autonomy.

Level of ability was related to entrance into college but there was a closer relationship between socioeconomic status (defined by father's occupation) and college entrance. Relatively few students at the high socioeconomic level failed to attend college, regardless of ability, but a disproportionate number of students at the low socioeconomic level failed to attend even if they possessed high academic aptitude. Ability and socioeconomic status were more related to entrance into college, however, than to persistence in college.

In the final analysis, it was not lack of finances that appeared to be primarily related to failure to attend college, but lack of interest. Apart from ability, the values of the youths and their parents seemed to figure more than finances in the relationship between socioeconomic status and college attendance. These values appeared to be major contributors to motivational differences. Specifically, responses to three items on the questionnaire administered to the students when they were high school seniors proved to be most predictive of persistence: 1) It was very important for them to graduate from college; 2) their parents had definitely wanted them to attend college; 3) they had either always assumed they would go to college or had decided to attend no later than their second year in high school. Other factors that considerably distinguished the college persisters from the withdrawals included: great liking for high school; interest in general rather than vocational education; willingness to study regardless of amount of part-time work; emphasis on the need for more permissive campus rules and self-responsibility; and—at least by 1963—a higher level of intellectual orientation and particularly a much higher level of autonomy as measured by the instruments used.

Availability of college was highly related to rate of entrance into college, but not to rate of completion. High school graduates in cities with two-year community colleges had the highest rate of college entrance; in cities with no colleges or with two-year extension centers, which are generally relatively selective in curriculum and costly in tuition, they had the lowest. But the two-year college students, even after transferring to four-year colleges and universities, were found to have a higher rate of attrition than native students, and a much lower rate of attainment of baccalaureate degrees within four years.

Most high school graduates who entered college enrolled in full time programs immediately after high school; only a nominal proportion that did not enroll in 1959 entered during the subsequent four years. There were no signs that a dormant interest in college was awakened after a period of work or military service, and the vast majority of students who did not enter college immediately after high school withdrew before 1963.

In a variety of ways the data indicate that, aside from adequate intelligence, the factor most related to entrance and persistence in college is motivation. The signs are also that this motivation is formed early in life, probably largely in response to parental influences and early school experiences.

The causes of attrition and the consequences of withdrawal have yet to be isolated and sufficiently examined. Withdrawal may be a salutary and temporary experience for many students. The student who consciously or unconsciously needs to seek self-understanding and developmental experiences on his own may be well-advised to leave college to travel, work, or study independently for a time. A number of students may also leave college because of a feeling that it does not provide them with the challenging, creative atmosphere conducive to the development of intellectualism and autonomy. It has been suggested earlier that the withdrawals themselves might serve as one of the best sources of information about the causes and nature of attrition.

While there may be multiple reasons for nonattendance and withdrawal, on the basis of this study it was evident that most of the able students became nonattenders or withdrawals out of lack of academic orientation and motivation. Their stress on the importance of rules and regulations and their relatively low scores on the autonomy scales indicated how much more than the persisters they sought outside control over their lives. Although these young people expressed most interest in vocational training, a great majority did not complete any such training and were not intellectually open to the idea that theoretical ideas had value for good vocational training.

There is evidence that basic values and attitudes, including attitudes toward education, are formed very early in life, largely before elementary school, and certainly before high school. Nevertheless, attitudes can and do change in late adolescence and early adulthood. During the four years subsequent to their high school graduation the young adults studied were found to change considerably on reliable measures of intellectual disposition, and especially on measures of autonomy. The amount and direction of change, however, varied greatly according to post high school experiences.

As high school seniors in 1959, those high school graduates who eventually persisted in college did not differ widely from their classmates on the various personality scales used in the assessment. But by 1963 they were more intellectual and far more autonomous, as these traits were measured by the Thinking Introversion, Complexity, Nonauthoritarianism, and Social Maturity scales. Students who went to college but withdrew within three years changed in attitude more than the high school graduates who did not enter college at all, but they did not develop in intellectual and autonomous orientation nearly as much as the college persisters. Nonattenders, particularly the women who became full-time housewives immediately after high school, regressed in intellectual interests and autonomy as measured by the Complexity and Nonauthoritarianism scales. As determined by their scores on these attitudinal scales, the high school graduates who immediately became employed did not become more interested in exploring ideas important to society, but rather more closed-minded. Further, they knew and cared less about such matters as international relations, social justice, and reasoned formations of political beliefs.

One inference to be drawn from these findings is that college seems to foster, or at least facilitate, the growth of autonomy and intellectual disposition, whereas early employment and marriage seem to retard and even suppress development of these traits. It may be said that college students, even the withdrawals, have a period beyond high school during which they can learn more about themselves, their potential, and their desires, and at the same time gain a greater awareness of their environment as well as a greater openness to it. But the high school graduate who does not enter college must immediately plunge into adult life, often knowing little about the world of work or the broad social issues and forces which confront him. Since society outside of college apparently does not encourage autonomy or intellectuality, either the burden of nurturing the potential of at least half of the nation's young adults must be carried by the high school or other noncollegiate agencies, or college must extend its influence in ways that have not traditionally been considered its function.

Of course, the exact extent of the influence of college is not known, nor are there any clear guidelines for determining the degree of autonomy and intellectual interest necessary for the full realization of human potential. It is known only that students who persisted in college increased in intellectual disposition and especially autonomy more than all other youths studied, although even the college students could not be regarded as possessing a high degree of intellectuality and autonomy. Their personality scores, after four years of college, were high only in comparison with those of their peers who had less college or none at all. And on the basis of responses to a variety of questionnaire and interview items, they could be judged to be largely apathetic to intellectual inquiry and social issues.

The finding that a large number decreased in autonomy after four years of college can be matched with the evidence from the interview protocols that the youths who grew in autonomy the most came, as a group, from relatively more autonomous and educationally oriented families. It may be, therefore, that the college students who increased most in autonomy and intellectual disposition were predisposed to make use of those opportunities in college that were most likely to encourage these traits. Although at the point of high school graduation they did not appear to differ very much from their classmates in attitudes as measured by the scales, they may have been more motivated to change than their peers with less favorable backgrounds.

THEORIES OF PERSONAL AND VOCATIONAL DEVELOPMENT
AND THE EVIDENCE FROM THE STUDY

Although this study was not designed to evaluate theories, such as those advanced by Erikson, Maslow, Ginzberg, and Super, which attempt to account for the personal and vocational development of the particular age group under study, its findings do suggest possible qualifications to certain theories.

It was noted in Chapter I that the period immediately following high school might be regarded as an exploratory period during which the adolescent seeks out his identity so that he may assume adult roles compatible with his concepts of himself and his needs. Erikson considers this period a moratorium during which the development of identity, so crucial to that full realization of human potential implied by Maslow's term, "self-actualization," takes place. The development of autonomy is very important to ego development as manifested in the formation of identity or achievement of self-actualization.

Vocationally, in the moratorium period of late adolescence and early adulthood, youths take steps towards self-realization through a trial process during which they attempt to make choices about jobs and careers that will be congruent with their self-concepts. As Super sees it, after a period of fantasy and vicarious role-playing, reality is tested; occupational roles are explored so that intelligent decisions can be made which will lead to satisfying adult status. Work experience represents the final test of whether the young adult has found an occupation compatible with his needs and concepts of himself. Ginzberg, among others, sees in this process elements of compromise and irreversibility; the desired goal must be matched both against ability and availability.

The elements of compromise and the possible limiting effects of basic decisions mentioned by Ginzberg correspond with general theories of adult development. The applicability of the theories is not without some demonstration. Measurements of self-actualization have been devised, such as that of Shostrom (1964). There is also some evidence of a significant relationship between development of ego identity and "concept attainment," and between excessive dependence on parents and lack of realistic goals and a high degree of authoritarianism (Marcia, 1966). The conclusions of two studies of students (Bronson, 1959; Howard, 1960) indicate some substantiation of Erikson's theory regarding the struggle between identity achievement and identity diffusion. Difficulties in the area of identity achievement have been perceived clinically to bear on difficulties involved in vocational decisions (Galinsky and Fast, 1966). Forer (1953) has found per-

sonality to be reflected in job choice, and Bohn (1966) has uncovered evidence indicating that vocational maturity is related
to development of personality, a sense of realism, and autonomy.
Super and his associates (1963) have tested Super's theories empir-
ically with results that at least warrant their continued consideration.

Much research is yet needed, however, to demonstrate that
personality and vocational theories are widely applicable, as both
Ginzberg (1952) and Super (1963) have themselves asserted. The
limitations of current research have been many, including the
reliance upon unvalidated instruments, use of questionable criteria for concepts of identity and vocational development, and
almost exclusive confinement to high school and particularly
college samples without systematic and longitudinal follow-ups
of the personality and vocational development of young adults
after they leave high school and college. The research to date
indicates that the different theories remain unverified assumptions
and that the development of vocational theory and also related
counseling theory must depend upon more refined personality
theory.

Subsequent to her review of theory and research on personality structure and occupational behavior, Roe (1964) concluded that:

> . . . [many studies] have confirmed the assumption that some
> personality characteristics are somehow and to some extent in-
> volved in occupational choice behavior. But the detailed nature
> of the relationship remains unknown. The lack of any general
> consensus on personality theory is a considerable drawback.
> Although Segal [1961] and Nachmann [1960] have demonstrated
> the fruitfulness of some aspects of analytic theory in the develop-
> ment of specific hypotheses, and some use has been made of
> Maslow's theory [see Centers, 1948; Roe, 1956] in developing
> quite different approaches, there is no personality theory which
> effectively spans the life cycle from the cradle to the grave. Vo-
> cational development theory can hardly advance beyond its
> present very early stage, without further advance in general
> personality theory [p. 201].

Similarly, Bordin and Wrenn (1954) have urged that the
specific evaluation of counseling depends upon the further de-

velopment of personality theory, a position Fishman (1962) has
taken about the prerequisites for the development of higher education in general. In the meantime, Carkhuff (1966) has argued
that there is little "comprehensive, integrative approach to research and theorizing" in counseling which can be translated into
human benefits.

Holland (1964), writing in the same volume as Roe, takes
note of more positive evaluations of research and theory, but then
goes on to state:

> The writer's view is that our theory-building efforts have out-
> run the little research we do, and that we have generally failed
> to write confirmable theories. We have sometimes become so
> enamored of theory that we have lost sight of the ultimate goal
> of theory—to provide something of value to society. Theory is
> interesting, but it is only an academic exercise unless we show
> that it is or is not useful in research and practice [p. 278].

From both a theoretical and practical point of view, the
data here reported do not fully substantiate the theories about
post adolescent development outlined in Chapter I. For a good
many of the youths studied, there was no manifest post adolescent
quest for self-identity. For most, self-identity appeared to be more
a matter of family identity; they followed their parents' religious
and political beliefs uncritically, described their families as being
like all other families, and saw themselves as a "common man,"
without indicating any desire for a unique identity. Indeed, a
great many of the youths appeared to have been affected by an
early identity foreclosure. Their lack of complexity and autonomy
indicated an authoritarianism, conformity, and lack of interest that
precludes any belief that they engaged in very much introspection.

Important factors, such as the decision to attend college
and the academic motivation to remain in college, were rooted in
early familial environment, even before the period of early adolescent fantasy, let alone the period of role-testing. For most youths—
at least for those who did not complete college—there seemed to
be little in the way of a trial period. As high school seniors, and
even four years later, the subjects had only vague notions about
the nature of occupations. They took the jobs they could get,
which for the men were almost exclusively factory jobs, and for

the women, clerical jobs before marriage. Interest centered on personal family life and the security of jobs rather than on the meaning of work.

In many ways the high school graduates appeared to make their choices out of predisposition rather than reasoned contemplation. They seemed to enter adulthood with a prefabricated outlook, limited in view and passive in nature. They accepted what was available for security and satisfaction of basic needs, but were not actively open to gaining greater awareness of the world, testing it, or becoming committed or involved in it. The theories assume a degree of self-understanding, spirit of inquiry, logical testing, and freedom of choice; in reality these seemed to be restricted by prior environmental experience, ability, lack of introspective qualities, and available opportunity.

The development of the individual, whether vocational or personal, is a transactional process at each stage with parents, family, physical and emotional environment, quality of education, close friends, and special influential events. Ability, opportunity, and chance are critical factors in the process, as are the values, attitudes, perceptions, and desires that are fostered by all these variables. Predisposition, potential, environment, and opportunity are interlocking elements which form a regulator for many of the directions the young adult takes.

Identity-seeking and corresponding role-testing and decision-making in early adulthood comprise elements of reasonable theories. If they are not clearly substantiated in the present report, it may be because the subjects' exploration of themselves and their environment and their tests of reality were too subtle to be discerned by the data at hand—and, apparently, by the data of most other research. It is also possible that the theories apply more to college graduates, because they may have greater opportunity during college to engage in a moratorium. Super (1957) has said as much about his own theories, and has suggested that personal development and satisfaction for lower class and noncollege youths may have to come from activities entirely outside of work or those related to post high school education. But these qualifications do not reduce the importance of factors which contribute to adult development, and certainly one of these factors that deserves continuous consideration is formal education.

Although basic values, attitudes, habits of learning, self-concepts, and even world-views begin with early environmental and familial experiences, it is clear now that they are not exclusively determined by these early experiences. Since change in attitudes and values has been found to be associated with college experience, several proposals can be made about the role of education in the formation of values.

Because of the philosophical and ethical issues involved, there is need for further study of the function of the school in value formation. In 1965 Dressel argued that the college should foster the change of certain values for some students. But who is to decide which values and which students? Certainly no agency has the right to impose its values on the individual, and the individual has the right to his own beliefs and attitudes, even if they do not represent widely respected or accepted ones, so long as they do not injure himself or others. But values are, of course, promulgated by any number of agencies in society. Thus, American society indoctrinates principles of citizenship through various required courses in its schools, and churches and political activists systematically urge their views by means of various media.

Some interest in ideas and disposition toward objective, open thinking are necessary before the individual can assess the values he must confront or before he can understand crucial elements of society. If the individual is not helped to become aware of the nature of his environment and if he is not encouraged to regard his environment with attitudes of flexibility and openness, then he will not become aware of the personal and vocational alternatives open to him. Without having developed the capacity for making the complex decisions demanded by a complex society, his freedom to regulate his life and realize his best potential will be diminished. Consequently, when schools fail to broaden their students' intellectual horizons and do not help to develop autonomous attitudes in students lacking these traits, they forfeit the opportunity to contribute to the freedom of individuals.

How the schools are to determine the values and traits which different kinds of individuals need in order to live effectively, and how these values are to be fostered without resorting to social engineering, are major problems. But the fact that they are problems does not relieve the schools of the responsibility for doing all that they can to promote self-development. As a matter of precedence, there is some evidence that the development or reduction of autonomy can be experimentally influenced (Tippett, 1966). One case has been reported of a group of gifted students who were helped toward self-actualization through counseling (Drews, 1965) and there is some indication that the "identity image" of college students may vary by college environment (Murray, 1964), which suggests that certain college environments may positively influence the development of identity.

This is not to suggest that vocational training should be preempted by the schools. Although certain essential occupational skills can only be gained through formal education at the collegiate or subcollegiate level, nevertheless a vocational training narrowly conceived may be more hindrance than help if the individual only learns to accomplish very specific tasks which may soon be out-dated. It may be wise to place greater emphasis on the understanding of the nature of various occupational areas and on teaching the principles of skilled work so that they might be re-applied in each new working situation. This, of course, has been urged for many years by educational generalists.

In seeking to fulfill their responsibilities, schools need to engage in a great deal of self-evaluation. The nature of the school —its purposes and how it is to operate—increasingly needs re-examination, as does the assessment of the effectiveness of specific curricula, teachers, and courses. Innovation and experimentation should be included with this evaluation from the start. Society has changed much more in the last century than has the educational system. In light of the data in this report, questions may be raised about the appropriateness of many aspects of the schools and colleges, even the whole notion of college as it has traditionally been regarded, ignored, or rejected. Experimentation should have as its purpose the improvement of the established patterns of education so as to make it relevant, in whatever form, to all those in need of it. Simultaneous evaluation will be necessary to make sure the experimentation is an improvement.

Other possibilities for experimentation, some already suggested or initiated by various educators, include: 1) a collaboration of college, high school, elementary school teachers and counseling personnel in special courses and programs at all grade levels; 2) the establishment, from the junior year of high school through the sophomore year of college, of "moratorium" intermediate colleges to explore the meaning and achievements of society, and the values, characteristics, occupations, and activities of its members and groups; and 3) a greater use of tutorials, seminars, and electronic teaching aids, with more reliance on learning resources such as field work in which complex subject matter could be observed in addition to being read about. College admissions officers could be encouraged to make frequent visits to elementary and secondary schools to explain the meaning and worth of higher education in general and their college in particular. More colleges might include a core course in which students are stimulated to think critically about their assumptions, prejudices, and goals.

Improved and expanded counseling and teaching (especially in the elementary schools) are very important. Cicourel and Kitsuse (1963) have stated:

> We are concerned . . . that the organizational emphasis upon talent and the pursuit of narrow specialties virtually ignores the significance of adolescence as a period during which individuals may explore the alternatives of personal style, interests, and identity. With the diffusion of specialized educational programs from the graduate school through colleges into the lower school systems, the adolescent is forced to make decisions and declare choices from a range of alternatives he can hardly be expected to know [p. 146].

However, there were indications from the Cicourel-Kitsuse research, as well as evidence in the study reported in this volume, that it was the students who were most academically motivated and most encouraged by their parents who reported the most use of counseling services in high school and college. At best, however, most counseling was very limited. More and better counselors are needed who can consistently collaborate with teachers and administrators in assisting towards self-discovery from a student's early school years through college.

Many of the students who did not attend college or who withdrew, evidently were not sufficiently disposed in attitude, interests, or study habits to meet expectations in college. It is also evident, however, that their needs and expectations were not met by the schools and colleges. Without doubt this problem could be dealt with in part through the efforts of stimulating teachers and counseling services designed to promote self-understanding. As examples, Alden (1963) cites a special program which stimulated so much interest in science among teachers who had disdained the field, that the teachers, in turn, stimulated an interest in science in their students; as noted earlier, Drews (1965) showed that counseling can assist youths toward self-actualization; and Rose has shown that counseling can effectively prevent college withdrawal. Ford and Urban (1965) write of the possible gains to be achieved by restructuring approaches to college dropouts, including the serious consideration that experiences other than college may be more helpful to the development of many who withdraw.

However, data referred to previously (Trent, Athey, and Craise, 1965), which will be discussed in detail in a subsequent report, suggest that many teachers lack the intellectuality to stimulate students in this direction. Data in this report and elsewhere also indicate that counselors are often poorly trained "inductees" rather than professionals with graduate training and proven talent for their jobs. Whatever their training, counselors are generally in such short supply that there is little time for assisting capable but academically disadvantaged students toward self-understanding, appreciation of their capabilities, and awareness of the complex world around them.

To be effective, counseling must go beyond routine programming of students' courses and the handling of "problem" cases. This report joins others in urging a re-examination, revision, and revitalization of the education and training of counselors and current counseling programs.

It has been observed that the teacher in many ways is also a counselor because in his teaching role, the teacher very often is the one best able to help the student discover his potential. It is also known that imaginative, stimulating teaching is too seldom found in the schools.

What has been said in this chapter about the nature of adult development and the role of education in this development is surely not unique to this report. The problems and possibilities raised here, however, do gain in significance from the implications of the data presented. The research indicates the need for additional investigation and for increased efforts to resolve a number of problems uncovered by it.

Although the steps urged here may be deemed excessively idealistic, the ideal might at least be realized as far as possible. As a start, the issue might be raised whether a society capable of immense technological development can at the same time be incapable of a corresponding development in education. The establishment and maintenance of consistently superior educational programs would, of course, be expensive. But if our affluent society were to reduce its need to spend such staggering sums on national defense, money might be released for the development of unprecedented educational excellence in the nation. And then the schools would be able to turn to their task of fostering the traits necessary for the full realization of human potential in a democratic, complex society.

Erikson (1963) bases his "charting" of the development of the human personality on the assumption that "society, in principle, tends to be so constituted as to meet and invite a succession of potentialities for interaction and attempts to safeguard and to encourage the proper rate and the proper sequence of their enfolding. This is the 'maintenance of the human world' [p. 270]." Questions must persist about how well society is maintaining the "human world." Ideals can be postulated as answers to these questions. But more than rhetoric is needed. Answers to these questions are urgent, and to be of greatest value, they must be answers put into suitable action.

Appendix A

Selection of the
Communities

The study reported here is based upon a sample which was originally drawn primarily to investigate relationship between college attendance and the type of college available in a community. In order to eliminate community factors other than types of colleges which might affect college attendance, communities roughly comparable in major demographic and industrial characteristics were chosen to participate in the survey.

The communities fell within certain industrial, economic, and ethnic limits: Each had some diversity of industrial and business enterprises, with no more than approximately 50 per cent of its population classified as belonging to the white-collar class; an adult population with neither an unusually high nor an unusually low level of education; no private colleges, which might compete with neighboring public colleges for local enrollments; and no other public colleges within commuting distance.

Approximately 50 communities were originally investigated. The final selection was narrowed to 16 communities, all roughly comparable (except the one metropolitan area included for comparative purposes) according to the criteria described below, and each possessing one of the types of colleges under consid-

272

eration, with the exception of the communities containing no college. The community characteristics were ascertained from the *Market Guide* of the Editor and Publisher Company (1957) and documents of the United States Bureau of the Census (1952, 1957). Following are the characteristics on which the selection was finally based:

1. *Population.* For the 15 "basic" communities the population range according to the 1950 census was 22,467 to 115,911, with a median of 40,517. The population of the metropolitan community was 775,357.

2. *Percentage engaged in white-collar occupations.* The percentage of the population engaged in white-collar occupations ranged from 31 to 50 per cent, with a median of 44 per cent. In the metropolitan community, the percentage was 53.

3. *Percentage of population engaged in manufacturing.* With the exception of Freeport, Illinois, for which information was not available because its population fell below 25,000, the range in the percentages of the population engaged in manufacturing was 6.9 to 56.2, with a median of 34.3. (County data indicated that in and around Freeport 25 per cent of the population was engaged in manufacturing.) In the metropolitan community, the percentage of those engaged in manufacturing was 16.9.

4. *Percentage of population engaged in trade.* The percentage of the population engaged in trade, primarily in sales and retail, again with the exception of the one community for which no information was available, ranged from 15.1 to 34.5, with a median of 21.6. In the metropolitan community, 25.5 per cent of the population was engaged in trade. The breakdown of the percentage of the population engaged in manufacturing and trade, as defined by the U.S. Bureau of the Census, was considered a sufficient index of the economic composition of each community since the remainder of the labor force in all communities would be principally engaged in white-collar occupations as indicated above, or in peripheral service and clerical occupations.

5. *Types of principal industries.* The median number of types of principal industries for the 15 communities was 5, with a range of 4 through 9. The one large metropolitan community had 8 such industries.

6. *Median salary.* The median salary for all the communi-

ties, based on the median within each city, was $3,335. The median salary in the communities ranged from $2,600 to $4,374, including the metropolitan community.

7. *Median grade of education completed by those 25 years or over.* The median grade level of education completed by those 25 years or over for all of these communities combined was 10 years; the range of grades completed for this group among the communities was between 9.2 and 11.5 years. In the case of the metropolitan community, the median grade was 11.7.

8. *Ethnicity.* The percentage of foreign-born white, both male and female, ranged from 1 to 15, with a median of 4. The metropolitan community had the largest percentage of foreign-born white, namely 16 per cent. In two communities no Negro population was reported. The range of the Negro population in the remaining communities extended from 2 to 8 per cent, with a median of 4 per cent. Six per cent of the population was reported Negro in the large metropolitan community.

A list of the participating communities and a summary of their characteristics may be found in Table A-1.

Table A-1

CHARACTERISTICS OF PARTICIPATING COMMUNITIES

Community	Type of local college	Number of participating high schools	Population	Per cent white-collar	Per cent manufacturing	Per cent trade	Number of types of principal industries	Median salary	Median grade completed	Per cent foreign-born white	Per cent Negro
Altoona, Pennsylvania	Extension center	2	77,177	35	11.0	21.5	8	$2,907	9.5	5	0
Bakersfield, California	Junior college	3	34,784	33	6.9	27.6	4	4,374	11.5	6	4
Danville, Illinois	Junior college	1	37,863	44	24.6	24.6	5	3,292	9.2	2	8
Eau Claire, Wisconsin	State college	2	36,058	44	34.3	23.6	5	3,670	10.8	4	0
Freeport, Illinois [a]	None	1	22,467	46	25.0 [a]	— [a]	3	3,064	9.4	4	3
Hutchinson, Kansas	Junior college	1	33,575	47	16.5	30.9	7	3,147	11.0	2	3
Joplin, Missouri	Junior college	1	38,711	50	16.0	34.5	5	2,600	9.9	1	2
Kalamazoo, Michigan	State college	4	57,704	44	39.1	19.8	4	3,593	10.7	7	4
Lorain, Ohio	None	1	51,202	31	56.2	15.1	4	3,681	9.5	15	5
Muncie, Indiana	State college	3	58,479	37	44.4	20.3	4	3,335	10.0	1	8
Port Huron, Michigan [b]	Junior college	1	35,725	44	34.7	21.6	4	3,472	10.1	10	3
Racine, Wisconsin	Extension center	4	71,193	39	55.2	16.7	5	4,051	9.5	12	4
San Francisco, Calif.	Variety of colleges	3	775,357	53	16.9	25.5	8	3,923	11.7	16	6
South Bend, Indiana	Extension center	5	115,911	47	50.8	18.0	5	4,349	10.1	8	7
Springfield, Missouri	State college	3	66,731	49	13.9	30.4	9	2,819	10.6	1	3
Zanesville, Ohio	Extension center	2	40,517	44	40.2	22.8	4	3,064	9.2	2	6

[a] No information could be found regarding the percentage of the community population engaged in trade; manufacturing was determined on a county-wide basis.

[b] Information on types of principal industries was available for this community only on the basis of classification of industries employed by The Editor and Publisher Market Guide (1957).

Appendix B

Conversion of High School Aptitude Test Scores to a Common Measure

Aptitude scores were available from all the 37 participating high schools, although the scores represented 18 forms of 11 different tests administered at various times between the ninth and twelfth grades.

In order to derive a common measure which would indicate the relative scholastic aptitudes of the 10,000 subjects, the School and College Ability Test, Form 1A (SCAT) was selected as the measure to which all other tests would be equated. There were two reasons for this choice: 1) the SCAT was most commonly used in the 37 high schools studied, and 2) it was considered to be among the tests most familiar to those in education and related fields.

Two methods of equating test scores were originally considered. The first was the maximum likelihood method, described by Lord (1950). It involves equating the means and standard deviations of two tests, x and y, administered to two different random samples of the same population, to a third test, w, admin-

276

istered to both samples. It requires that the distributions of the two samples have the same shape, and that the anchor test, w, correlate at least .50 with x and y. In the present study, the 20-item Verbal Section of the Thorndike CAVD test, administered to the entire sample, served as the anchor test. However, Lord's method of equating tests was rejected because the correlations of the other aptitude tests with the CAVD ranged from .23 to .65, with many coefficients in the .40s. Moreover, since the SCAT distribution had greater spread than the other tests, the distributions for the two tests were not the same, and this requirement for equating the two tests could not be satisfied.

A second method of test conversion is to equate tests through common percentiles (see Karon, 1955). This method is not based upon an assumption difficult to demonstrate, such as that required by the maximum likelihood method. Furthermore, it had a precedent, since it was used to equate earlier versions of the ACE Psychological Examination to the SCAT when the latter test was published in 1955. For these reasons this method was adopted for use in the present study.

In the present instance, scores on the SCAT were available for 1,033 subjects in four high schools in one community. Percentile ranks were computed for the SCAT, based on the scores of these 1,033 subjects. Similarly, percentile ranks were computed for each of the other tests used, based on all subjects for whom scores on the tests at each grade level were available. In order to equate each test to the SCAT, its scores were plotted on one axis and the SCAT scores on the other. Points were then plotted where scores of the two tests had the same percentile rank. A smooth curve was drawn through the points, and equivalent scores for the two tests were assumed to fall on the curve. Tables of equivalent scores were then constructed for each test from the appropriate curve.

The range of SCAT scores falling within each decile as a result of this procedure compares favorably with the range of scores on the national norms as reported in the manual. The derived scores cannot, of course, be as accurate as scores from a single test would have been, but they represent a reasonable approximation to that ideal.

Appendix C

Construction and Validation of the Omnibus Personality Inventory

The Omnibus Personality Inventory is an attitudinal inventory whose scales are designed to measure intellectual, emotional, and dispositional personality traits. It was developed at the Center for Research and Development in Higher Education at the University of California, Berkeley, and in format resembles the Minnesota Multiphasic Personality Inventory and the California Psychological Inventory. The Omnibus Personality Inventory was devised primarily for research on college students and has demonstrated an impressive capability for distinguishing differences in intellectual and emotional attitudes and behavior in a variety of student groups.

The ensuing discussion applies to selected scales in Forms C and D of the Omnibus Personality Inventory which were administered to the sample in 1959 and 1963. The inventory has since been further revised and refined and a new manual is under preparation. The final Form F of the Omnibus Personality Inventory and the corresponding manual is scheduled to be available for circulation by the Psychological Corporation in 1968.

Validity and reliability data summarized for each scale are drawn from the OPI manual (Center for the Study of Higher Education, 1962) in all cases not otherwise specified. Considerable validation data are based on correlations with other known, functional scales, such as those in the Minnesota Multiphasic Personality Inventory (MMPI), California Psychological Inventory (CPI), Allport-Vernon-Lindzey Study of Values (AVL), the Kuder Preference Record, the Myers-Briggs Type Indicator (MBTI), the Stern Activities Index, the Strong Vocational Interest Blank (SVIB), and the Opinion, Attitude, and Interest Survey (OAIS). Among the references which discuss the various published instruments cited as possessing a validating correlation with the Omnibus Personality Inventory are the following: Allport, Vernon, and Lindzey (1951); Dahlstrom and Welsh (1960); Kuder (1957); Fricke (1963); Gough (1964); Hathaway and McKinley (1951); Myers and Briggs (1962); Stern (1958); Strong (1959); Weissman (1958); Williams (1964). Other validation data are based upon various ratings and recognized performances, such as prize-winning artistic endeavor.

Five major factors have been identified as comprising the Omnibus Personality Inventory on the basis of Quartimax and Varimax rotated factor analyses: 1) tolerance and autonomy, or ideological openmindedness and nonauthoritarianism; 2) psychological adjustment, including manifestation of anxiety as measured by the Lack of Anxiety scale; 3) scholarly orientation; 4) masculine-feminine interests; 5) social introversion. Several of the scales are intercorrelated, but each possesses its own unique variance, with the exceptions to be noted for the three autonomy scales. The intercorrelations of the scales used in the present study appear in Table C-1 for the college and noncollege students combined, who responded both in 1959 and 1963.

Only brief descriptions of the scales will be included here, in each case followed by a general summary of the validity data.

Autonomy (Au): This scale measures nonauthoritarian thinking and a need for independence. It correlates with the Intuition and Perception scales in the Myers-Briggs Type Indicator (MBTI) related to nonauthoritarianism, and, as noted in the revised manual, it is also highly correlated (approximately .45–.60) with esthetic and creative inclinations, independence of thinking, and flexibility and intellectual quality as measured by a number of AVL, CPI, and OAIS scales. It is significantly related to measures of objectivity and (negatively) to measures of deference and abasement. It is negatively related to the SVIB Policeman scale and most business-oriented scales, and positively related to such scales as Psychologist, Author-Journalist, Minister, Artist, Musician, and Social Worker. Students who consider the main satisfaction of employment to be the opportunity to be creative and original obtain a significantly higher score on Autonomy compared with other students who view job satisfaction in such terms as opportunity for advancement, security, and working with others. Students planning to attend graduate school score significantly higher on the scale than those who plan to attend professional school or report no plans for postgraduate education. The Autonomy scale correlates with instructors' ratings of "oral assignment presentation," "written performance," and "overall evaluation." (See also: Social Maturity in this appendix.) Reliability: .80 (KR 21); .88 (test-retest, Form Fx). (40 items.)

Complexity (Co): This scale measures orientation towards an experimental, inquisitive viewing of experience and tolerance for ambiguities. The scale correlates with the AVL Theoretical and Aesthetic measures, which distinguish creative individuals, and with the Myers-Briggs Intuition and Perception scales, designed to measure a person's tendency to approach his environment with an open, receptive mind. In data to be published in the revised manual, this variable correlates highly with critical thinking and the flexibility necessary for problem solving, with the variety of perspectives with which one views a limited range of concepts, with measures of creativeness of personality, intellectual quality, and (negatively) with a need for order. Reliability: .71 (KR 21); .83 (test-retest). (27 items.)

Estheticism (Es): This scale measures diverse interests in artistic matters. The scale correlates highly with the AVL Aesthetic and the Kuder Literary scales. Data in the new manual show moderate correlations (approximately .35) between the Estheticism scale and creative disposition, the SVIB Artist scale, and the Kuder Musical scale (but not the Kuder Artistic scale).

It significantly distinguishes art and humanities majors, and students elected to an honors program. Reliability: .80 (KR 21); .90 (test-retest). (24 items.)

Impulse Expression (IE): This scale measures the extent to which a person tends to express his impulses in overt action or conscious feeling and attitude. High scores indicate proneness towards imaginative work and freedom of thought. It correlates negatively with CPI Responsibility, Socialization, and Self-control scales, presumably measurements of social conformity, and correlates positively with the CPI Flexibility scale. It distinguishes students highly rated by instructors for "oral assignment presentation," "written performance," and "overall evaluation," and distinguishes graduate students and prize-winning artists. In data to be published in the revised manual, this variable correlates significantly, although not highly (approximately .21), with measures of ability to comprehend and solve complex or unique problems. It correlates with scales indicating emotional disturbance and also correlates highly (and negatively) with measures of restrictiveness. Reliability: .91 (KR 21); .94 (test-retest). (75 items.)

Lack of Anxiety (LA): This scale measures freedom from unusual amounts of anxiety. The scale correlates negatively with schizoid tendencies; persons scoring high in Lack of Anxiety tend to score low in Schizoid Functioning. There is a moderate correlation with Impulse Expression and Social Introversion. Reliability: Reliability is unavailable in the OPI's preliminary Research Manual. The internal consistency coefficient computed on the normative sample in the revised manual is .82. Test-retest reliability coefficients obtained separately by the authors and reported for two other samples in the revised manual range from .79 to .93. (20 items.)

Nonauthoritarianism (Na): This scale, a refinement of the original California F scale, measures independence and freedom from authoritarianism and opinionated thinking (see Christie and Associates, 1958). The scale correlates highly with CPI measures which distinguish achievement through independence, intellectual efficiency, and flexibility, with interest in occupations involving ideas. It correlates negatively with the SVIB business occupations and significantly distinguishes professional social scientists and graduate students. The Nonauthoritarianism scale correlates highly with the Omnibus Personality Inventory Social Maturity and Autonomy scales (see Table C-1). Its highest loading is on the first factor of the Omnibus Personality Inventory (autonomy and tolerance)—.64 to .60 compared with the Autonomy scale loading of .77 to .71 on the basis of unrotated two-factor analysis. (See also: the description of the Social Maturity scale in this appendix.) Reliability: Information is unavailable in the manual. The coefficient computed separately on the college students considered here is .51 (KR 21). The coefficient computed for a random sample of students in four colleges is .62 (Center for the Study of Higher Education, 1960). The internal consistency reliability coefficient is relatively low, probably because of the small number and heterogeneous nature of the items composing the scale. Test-retest data with a three week interval obtained separately by the authors from a freshman psychology class at San Francisco State College in the spring of 1967 yielded a highly acceptable reliability coefficient of .92. (20 items.)

Religious Liberalism (RL): This scale measures tendency towards skepticism or rejection of religious beliefs and practices. The scale correlates highly and negatively with the AVL Religious scale and the CPI Sense of Well-being, Self-control, Good Impression, and Responsibility scales. It significantly distinguishes groups of known religious orientation and degree of religious commitment and correlates with Trent's (1967) Religious Concepts Inventory (RCI) and Religious Practices Index (RPI). Reliability: .84 (KR 21); .93 (test-retest). (29 items.)

Social Introversion (SI): This scale reflects more a style of relating to people than an expression of avoidance of people stemming from feelings of alienation or pathological suspicion. It correlates highest with Affiliation (-.57), Exhibition (-.47), and Nurturance (-.43) in the *Activities Index*. It has an equally high correlation with the CPI dimensions of Sociability, Dominance, Self-acceptance and Social Presence, all correlations being in the expected negative direction. Correlations between the scales in the SVIB and the Social Introversion scale clearly reflect the same general social orientation as the CPI scales. The highest of these correlates are: YMCA Physical Director (—.43), Personnel Director (—.41), YMCA Secretary (—.41), Sales Manager (—.43), and Life Insurance Salesman (—.41). In a junior college sample, student leaders had the lowest mean score (extroversion) of the three distinct subgroups on the Social Introversion scale. This is supported by the mean scores for people involved in student government on other campuses. Among university students specifying ideal job requirements, those indicating a preference for the "opportunity to work with people" and a "stable, secure future" obtain the lowest mean scores. Reliability: .85 (KR 21); .91 (test-retest). (54 items.)

Social Maturity (SM): This scale, a 67-item abridgement of the 144-item Form C version, measures different dimensions of autonomy, openness, and flexibility, as well as some cultural interests. Because of the importance of the autonomy measures used in the present study and because of the importance of understanding the nature and interrelationship of the Autonomy, Nonauthoritarianism, and Social Maturity scales, several relevant sections of the Research Manual are quoted:

> Over a decade ago, Adorno *et al* (1950) reported some research on anti-Semitism, ethnocentrism, and anti-democratic political attitudes which indicated that these characteristics are functionally related within the 'authoritarian' personality. Since then it has been found that related measures of authoritarianism also correlate with a great variety of social behavior. The Social Maturity scale was first developed in research on Vassar women as a measure of (non) authoritarianism that was relatively insensitive to political and religious ideology (Webster, Sanford, and Freedman, 1955). For inclusion in the OPI, the SM scale underwent subsequent revision in an attempt to improve reliability, to reduce the correlation with measures of response set, and to increase the relevance of the content for subjects of both sexes attending a variety of colleges. The present revised form contains more items which reflect intraception, intellectual skepticism, and freedom of thought than was true of the SM scale contained in the VC *Attitude Inventory*. . . .
>
> A shorter version of the Social Maturity (SM) dimension was obtained also as a result of the general attempt to construct scales that were more independent, experimentally, by reducing item-overlap and similarity of content among several scales. Despite lower reliability, the correlation of these 40 items with SM remains amazingly high. At the same time, however, by comparison with SM, the Au items focus more upon the need for intellectual

and social autonomy and upon the desire for independence and freedom from restraint as imposed by social institutions.

In constructing the Au scale, more so than in the other revised short-form scales, major attention was given initially to removing selected items, especially those which also served in the following scales: TI, TO, Es, Co, and RL. The content of a large percentage of the remaining items warranted a final item analysis to determine which items functioned at the .01 level or better. Both the reliability (.80) of the 40 discriminating items and function of the scale across various groups were basic to the decision to use Au as a distinct scale. . . .

[Social Maturity] correlates highest with the Change scale (.45) in the *Activities Index*. In terms of CPI correlates, it correlates highest with Capacity for Status (.47) and Social Presence (.42) for men, and with Achievement via Independence (.49), Capacity for Status (.44), and Intellectual Efficiency (.43) for women. This measure polarizes several scales on the Strong Interest Blank: Psychologist (.60), Social Worker (.43), vs. Mortician (–.42), Purchasing Agent (—.47) and Banker (—.48). After correction for attenuation, SM was indistinguishable from Na in several college samples (Center for the Study of Higher Education, 1962).

Also, graduate students in all fields have consistently been found to score significantly higher on the Social Maturity scale than college students not attending graduate school. Reliability: .80 (KR 21, 67-item version); .79 (test-retest, Form C). (67 items.)

Thinking Introversion (TI): This scale measures liking for abstract, reflective thought and an interest in a variety of areas such as literature, art, and music. The scale correlates highly with the Literary score in the Kuder Preference Schedule, the AVL Aesthetic and (negatively) Economic scales, the Guilford-Zimmerman Thoughtfulness scale, the Understanding score in the Stern Activities Index, and with occupations in the Strong Vocational Interest Blank emphasizing ideas and interpersonal relations rather than those dealing with business and other practical concerns. It significantly distinguishes graduate students rated highly by their instructors for their "power of assimilation and logic" and "written performance." Reliability: .85 (KR 21); .94 (test-retest). (60 items.)

Table C-1

INTERCORRELATIONS AND RELIABILITY COEFFICIENTS OF
OMNIBUS PERSONALITY INVENTORY SCALES [a]

Scales	TI	Es	Co	SM	Au	Na	RL	LA	IE	SI
TI	(.87)									
Es	.69	(.80)								
Co	.51	.47	(.71)							
SM	.44	.32	.49	(.80)						
Au	.48	.37	.51	.82	(.82)					
Na	.44	.38	.45	.61	.70	(.51)				
RL	.18	.14	.35	.47	.53	.48	(.80)			
LA	.11	—.14	—.12	.24	.06	.02	—.02	(.82)		
IE	.16	.26	.59	.28	.39	.32	.47	—.32	(.87)	
SI	—.33	—.23	—.10	—.19	—.10	—.07	.06	—.36	—.05	(.85)

[a] N = 4,313, which includes all high school graduates in the simple (college and noncollege) who were tested in 1959 and 1963. Reliability coefficients (KR 21) are in the diagonal parentheses. All reliability coefficients are those listed by the Omnibus Personality Inventory manual with the exception of the Social Maturity and Nonauthoritarianism scales which are computed on the sample under consideration. Test-retest reliability coefficients are noted in the text of this appendix.

Appendix D

Comparison of 1959 Characteristics of 1963 Respondents and Nonrespondents

Table D-1

ABILITY LEVEL IN 1959 OF 1963 RESPONDENTS AND NONRESPONDENTS

| | Ability Level | | | | | | | | |
| | High | | Middle | | Low | | No score | | Chi |
Pursuit group	(N)	%	(N)	%	(N)	%	(N)	%	square
College									
Respondent	(1489)	53	(951)	34	(294)	10	(75)	3	123.98 **
Nonrespondent	(755)	39	(728)	37	(386)	20	(82)	4	
Noncollege									
Respondent	(503)	27	(794)	43	(492)	26	(74)	4	128.24 **
Nonrespondent	(501)	16	(1255)	39	(1231)	39	(179)	6	

** p < .01.

Table D-2

SOCIOECONOMIC LEVEL IN 1959 OF 1963
RESPONDENTS AND NONRESPONDENTS

Socioeconomic Level

Pursuit group	High (N)	%	Middle (N)	%	Low (N)	%	No information (N)	%	Chi square
College									
Respondent	(620)	22	(1640)	58	(362)	13	(187)	7	9.02 *
Nonrespondent	(375)	19	(1106)	57	(297)	15	(173)	9	
Noncollege									
Respondent	(109)	6	(1094)	59	(482)	26	(178)	9	2.42 +
Nonrespondent	(168)	5	(1688)	54	(827)	26	(483)	15	

+ p = not significant.
* p < .05.

Table D-3

STANDARD MEAN OPI SCORES IN 1959 OF 1963
RESPONDENTS AND NONRESPONDENTS

Pursuit group	Thinking Introversion	Complexity	Nonauthoritarianism [a]	Lack of Anxiety
College				
Respondents	47.89	50.20	44.66	51.29
Nonrespondents	46.48	51.10	44.45	50.65
(Critical ratio)	(4.98 **)	(2.57 +)	(.63 +)	(2.20 *)
Noncollege				
Respondents	42.91	48.50	41.56	49.35
Nonrespondents	42.75	49.83	42.49	49.03
(Critical ratio)	(.57 +)	(5.97 +)	(2.96 +)	(1.98 *)

[a] Scores were not computed for the correlated Social Maturity scale in these analyses.
+ p = not significant.
* p < .05.
** p < .01.

Appendix E

Statistical Analyses of Mean Differences and Change Scores

1. *Significance of Differences Between Correlated Means*

To determine the significance between correlated means (or, as in the present study, the difference in mean scores obtained by the same group of students at different time periods), the standard error of the difference between the correlated means must first be determined (see McNemar, 1955, p. 83). The expression for σM_D may be expressed:

$$\sigma M_D = \sqrt{\sigma\bar{X}_1{}^2 + \sigma\bar{X}_2{}^2 - {}^{2r}12\,\sigma\bar{X}_1\,\sigma\bar{X}_2}$$

where $\bar{X}_1$ = the mean of the group's pretest, $\bar{X}_2$ = its post-test mean, and N = the number of subjects in the group. Confidence limits are then expressed in terms of this standard error:

$$\left(\bar{X}_1 - \bar{X}_2\right) + t_{\frac{1}{2}\alpha}\sigma M_D \sqrt{1/N};\ \ \left(\bar{X}_1 - \bar{X}_2\right) - t_{\frac{1}{2}\alpha}\sigma M_D \sqrt{1/N}.$$

The t values above are determined for a desired level of significance from a t table using $(N - 1)$ degrees or freedom (see Dixon

288

and Massey, 1957, p. 128). The probability is $(1 - \alpha)$ that the true difference, $\overline{X}_1 - \overline{X}_2$, lies within the interval specified by the limits. When the two limits are of opposite sign, we accept the assumption that the difference is zero; thus the difference between the two means is not significant. If, however, both limits have the same sign, then the value zero does not fall between these limits, indicating that there is a difference between the means. The null hypothesis that there is no difference can thus be rejected at a specific level of significance according to the value chosen for t.

2. *Significance of Differences Between the Change Scores*

In testing the significance of differences in mean changes in Omnibus Personality Inventory scores obtained by the groups under study (Table E-1) as noted in Chapter VII, formulas were combined from several sources.

Let $\overline{X}_1 =$ mean of pretest for group 1
$\overline{Y}_1 =$ mean of post test for group 1
$\overline{X}_2 =$ mean of pretest for group 2
$\overline{Y}_2 =$ mean of post test for group 2
$n_1 =$ number of subjects in group 1
$n_2 =$ number of subjects in group 2

Let $\Psi = (\overline{Y}_1 - \overline{X}_1) - (\overline{Y}_2 - \overline{X}_2)$ \hfill (1)

The formula (see Garrett, 1958, p. 214) for the variance of the difference between these two means is:

$$\text{var } (\Psi) = \text{var } (\overline{Y}_1 - \overline{X}_1) + \text{var } (\overline{Y}_2 - \overline{X}_2) \tag{2}$$

The variance, however, of $(Y_1 - X_1)$, and similarly of $(Y_2 - X_2)$, involves the variance of the difference of correlated means. This formula (see Garrett, 1958, p. 226) is:

$$\text{var } (\overline{Y}_i - \overline{X}_i) = \text{var } (\overline{Y}_i) + \text{var } (\overline{X}_i) - 2 \text{ cov } (\overline{Y}_i, \overline{X}_i)$$

$$= \frac{s\overline{Y}_i^2}{n_i} + \frac{s\overline{X}_i^2}{n_i} - 2r_i \frac{s\overline{Y}_i s\overline{X}_i}{n_i} \tag{3}$$

Substituting (3) in equation (2) and using number subscripts, we obtain:

$$\text{var } (\Psi) = \left(\frac{{}^s\overline{Y}_1{}^2}{n_1} + \frac{{}^s\overline{X}_1{}^2}{n_1} - 2r_1 \frac{{}^s\overline{Y}_1{}^s\overline{X}_1}{n_1} \right) +$$

$$\left(\frac{{}^s\overline{Y}_2{}^2}{n_2} + \frac{{}^s\overline{X}_2{}^2}{n_2} - 2r_2 \frac{{}^s\overline{Y}_2{}^s\overline{X}_2}{n_2} \right)$$

Confidence levels (see Hays, 1963, pp. 314–22) for with $n_1 + n_2$ — 2 degrees of freedom are:

$$\Psi - t_{(\alpha/2, \text{ dt})} \sqrt{\text{var } (\Psi)} \text{ and } \Psi + t_{(\alpha/2, \text{ dt})} \sqrt{\text{var } (\Psi)}$$

When these two confidence limits are the same in sign, the value zero which would indicate no difference between the means of the change scores for the two groups does not fall between these limits, and we can thus reject the hypothesis of no difference at the level of significance chosen for t. When these limits are opposite in sign, we fail to reject the hypothesis that the difference between means of the change scores is zero, in other words, observed difference is not significant.

The above derivation of the analysis of the significance of differences between change scores is the work of Dr. Manford Ferris, currently associated with the American Institute of Research, Palo Alto, California.

Table E-1

SIGNIFICANCE OF DIFFERENCE IN MEAN DIFFERENCES PRESENTED IN CHAPTER VIII

Pursuit group and scale	$(\bar{X}_1 - \bar{X}_2) - (\bar{Y}_1 - \bar{Y}_2)$	Lower limit	Upper limit	Decision at .05	Lower limit	Upper limit	Decision at .01
College vs. Employed Men (Tables 36, 42)							
Thinking Introversion	0.88	−0.18	1.94	+			
Complexity	3.51	2.29	4.73	*	1.91	5.11	*
Nonauthoritarianism	7.01	5.59	8.43	*	5.15	8.87	*
Social Maturity	4.15	2.99	5.31	*	2.63	5.67	*
College vs. Employed Women (Tables 36, 42)							
Thinking Introversion	4.19	3.18	5.20	*	2.86	5.52	*
Complexity	3.83	2.62	5.04	*	2.23	5.43	*
Nonauthoritarianism	8.40	7.05	9.75	*	6.62	10.18	*
Social Maturity	7.18	6.10	8.26	*	5.76	8.60	*
College vs. Employed Men—High Ability (Tables E-4, E-6)							
Thinking Introversion	0.41	−1.36	2.18	+			
Complexity	3.88	1.84	5.92	*	1.19	6.57	*
Nonauthoritarianism	5.52	3.39	7.65	*	2.72	8.32	*
Social Maturity	4.59	2.69	6.49	*	2.09	7.09	*
College vs. Employed Men—Middle Ability (Tables E-4, E-6)							
Thinking Introversion	0.05	−1.80	1.90	+			
Complexity	3.22	1.09	5.35	*	0.41	6.02	*
Nonauthoritarianism	8.97	6.47	11.47	*	5.67	12.27	*
Social Maturity	5.56	3.50	7.62	*	2.84	8.27	*

+ = Not significant.
* = Significant.

Table E-1 (continued)

SIGNIFICANCE OF DIFFERENCE IN MEAN DIFFERENCES PRESENTED IN CHAPTER VIII

Pursuit group and scale	$(\bar{X}_1 - \bar{X}_2) - (\bar{Y}_1 - \bar{Y}_2)$	Lower limit	Upper limit	Decision at .01	Lower limit	Upper limit	Decision at .01
College vs. Employed Men—Low Ability (Tables E-4, E-6)							
Thinking Introversion	3.48	0.27	6.69	*	−0.76	7.72	+
Complexity	3.00	−0.68	6.68	+	−0.67	6.67	+
Nonauthoritarianism	5.55	0.97	10.13	*	−0.49	11.59	+
Social Maturity	8.57	4.87	12.27	*	3.72	13.48	+
College vs. Employed Women—High Ability (Tables E-4, E-6)							
Thinking Introversion	4.03	2.44	5.62	*	1.93	6.13	*
Complexity	4.14	2.22	6.06	*	1.61	6.67	*
Nonauthoritarianism	7.12	5.02	9.22	*	4.35	9.89	*
Social Maturity	6.53	4.81	8.25	*	4.26	8.80	*
College vs. Employed Women—Middle Ability (Tables E-4, E-6)							
Thinking Introversion	4.30	2.62	5.98	*	2.08	6.52	*
Complexity	3.79	1.71	5.87	*	1.05	6.53	*
Nonauthoritarianism	9.53	7.09	11.97	*	6.31	12.75	*
Social Maturity	7.12	5.30	8.94	*	4.72	9.51	*
College vs. Employed Women—Low Ability (Tables E-4, E-6)							
Thinking Introversion	2.73	−0.30	5.76	+			+
Complexity	0.39	−3.27	4.05	+			+
Nonauthoritarianism	5.41	1.02	9.80	*	−0.39	11.21	+
Social Maturity	6.11	2.03	10.18	*	0.72	11.50	*

+ = Not significant.
* = Significant.

Table E-1 (continued)

SIGNIFICANCE OF DIFFERENCE IN MEAN DIFFERENCES PRESENTED IN CHAPTER VIII

Pursuit group and scale	$(\bar{X}_1 - \bar{X}_2) - (\bar{Y}_1 - \bar{Y}_2)$	Lower limit	Upper limit	Decision at .05	Lower limit	Upper limit	Decision at .01
College vs. Employed Men—High Socioeconomic Status (Tables E-5, E-7)							
Thinking Introversion	0.82	−2.02	3.66	+			+
Complexity	3.43	−0.58	7.44	+			+
Nonauthoritarianism	6.33	2.59	10.07	*	1.40	11.26	*
Social Maturity	4.78	1.34	8.22	*	0.24	9.32	*
College vs. Employed Men—Middle Socioeconomic Status (Tables E-5, E-7)							
Thinking Introversion	0.40	−0.94	1.74	+			+
Complexity	2.74	1.20	4.28	*	0.71	4.77	*
Nonauthoritarianism	6.91	5.10	8.72	*	4.53	9.29	*
Social Maturity	4.58	3.08	6.08	*	2.61	6.55	*
College vs. Employed Men—Low Socioeconomic Status (Tables E-5, E-7)							
Thinking Introversion	3.05	0.06	6.04	*	−0.89	6.99	+
Complexity	4.22	1.12	7.32	*	0.14	8.30	*
Nonauthoritarianism	7.65	3.88	11.41	*	2.68	12.62	*
Social Maturity	7.99	5.15	10.83	*	4.25	11.73	*
College vs. Employed Women—High Socioeconomic Status (Tables E-5, E-7)							
Thinking Introversion	3.28	0.36	6.20	*	−0.58	7.14	+
Complexity	0.05	−3.51	3.61	+			+
Nonauthoritarianism	7.62	2.94	12.30	*	1.44	13.79	*
Social Maturity	3.73	−0.04	7.50	+			+

+ = Not significant.

* = Significant.

Table E-1 (continued)

SIGNIFICANCE OF DIFFERENCE IN MEAN DIFFERENCES PRESENTED IN CHAPTER VIII

Pursuit group and scale	$(\bar{X}_1 - \bar{X}_2) - (\bar{Y}_1 - \bar{Y}_2)$	Lower limit	Upper limit	Decision at .05	Lower limit	Upper limit	Decision at .01
College vs. Employed Women—Middle Socioeconomic Status (Tables E-5, E-7)							
Thinking Introversion	4.23	2.85	5.61	*	2.42	6.04	*
Complexity	4.55	2.92	6.18	*	2.41	6.69	*
Nonauthoritarianism	8.96	7.16	10.76	*	6.59	11.33	*
Social Maturity	7.80	6.38	9.22	*	5.93	9.67	*
College vs. Employed Women—Low Socioeconomic Status (Tables E-5, E-7)							
Thinking Introversion	3.13	0.57	5.69	*	−0.35	6.41	+
Complexity	3.32	−0.21	6.85	+			+
Nonauthoritarianism	9.15	5.04	13.26	*	3.73	14.57	*
Social Maturity	4.79	1.56	8.02	*	0.52	9.06	*
Withdrawals vs. Persisters—Men (Tables 37, 43)							
Thinking Introversion	0.66	−1.16	2.48	+	−0.60	5.00	+
Complexity	2.20	0.08	4.32	*	1.42	6.92	+
Nonauthoritarianism	4.17	2.08	6.26	*	1.42	6.92	*
Social Maturity	4.22	2.52	5.92	*	1.98	6.46	*
Withdrawals vs. Persisters—Women (Tables 37, 43)							
Thinking Introversion	2.84	1.52	4.16	*	1.10	4.58	*
Complexity	4.60	3.06	6.14	*	2.58	6.62	*
Nonauthoritarianism	4.45	2.68	6.22	*	2.12	6.78	*
Social Maturity	4.88	3.46	6.30	*	3.02	6.74	*

+ = Not significant.
* = Significant.

Table E-1 (continued)

SIGNIFICANCE OF DIFFERENCE IN MEAN DIFFERENCES PRESENTED IN CHAPTER VIII

Pursuit group and scale	$(\overline{X}_1 - \overline{X}_2) - (\overline{Y}_1 - \overline{Y}_2)$	Lower limit	Upper limit	Decision at .05	Lower limit	Upper limit	Decision at .01
Employed Women vs. Homemakers (Tables 38, 45)							
Thinking Introversion	1.81	0.45	3.17	*	0.02	3.60	*
Complexity	2.77	1.13	4.41	*	0.61	4.93	*
Nonauthoritarianism	1.10	-0.71	2.91	+			+
Social Maturity	0.21	-1.19	1.61	+			+
Women in Combined Pursuits vs. Homemakers (Tables 38, 45)							
Thinking Introversion	2.15	0.91	3.39	*	0.51	3.79	*
Complexity	1.76	0.31	3.21	*	-0.15	3.67	+
Nonauthoritarianism	2.77	1.16	4.38	*	0.66	4.88	*
Social Maturity	1.33	0.09	2.56	*	-0.29	2.95	+
Women in Combined Pursuits vs. Employed Women (Table 38, 45)							
Thinking Introversion	0.34	-0.53	1.21	+			+
Complexity	1.01	-0.10	2.12	+			+
Nonauthoritarianism	1.03	-0.19	2.25	+			+
Social Maturity	1.12	0.14	2.10	*	-0.17	2.41	+
Public 4-year vs. Private Denominational College Men (Table 44)							
Nonauthoritarianism	0.99	-1.42	3.40	+			+
Social Maturity	0.41	-1.60	2.42	+			+
Public 4-year College vs. Public University Men (Table 44)							
Nonauthoritarianism	0.35	-1.58	2.28	+			+
Social Maturity	-0.12	-1.80	1.56	+			+

+ = Not significant.
* = Significant.

Table E-1 (continued)

SIGNIFICANCE OF DIFFERENCE IN MEAN DIFFERENCES PRESENTED IN CHAPTER VIII

Pursuit group and scale	$(\overline{X}_1 - \overline{X}_2)-(\overline{Y}_1 - \overline{Y}_2)$	Lower limit	Upper limit	Decision at .05	Lower limit	Upper limit	Decision at .01
Private Denominational College vs. Public University Men (Table 44)							
Nonauthoritarianism	−0.64	−2.80	1.52	+			+
Social Maturity	−0.53	−2.37	1.31	+			+
Public 4-year vs. Private Denominational College Women (Table 44)							
Nonauthoritarianism	1.14	−1.23	3.57	+			+
Social Maturity	2.08	0.15	4.01	*	−0.46	4.62	+
Public 4-year College vs. Public University Women (Table 44)							
Nonauthoritarianism	2.21	−0.02	4.44	+			+
Social Maturity	−0.49	−2.24	1.26	+			+
Private Denominational College vs. Public University Women (Table 44)							
Nonauthoritarianism	1.07	−1.36	3.50	+			+
Social Maturity	−2.57	−4.48	−0.66	*	−5.08	−0.06	*

+ = Not significant.
* = Significant.

296

Table E-2

SIGNIFICANCE OF DIFFERENCES IN OMNIBUS PERSONALITY INVENTORY SCORES OF COLLEGE PERSISTERS AND WITHDRAWALS, BY ABILITY AND SOCIOECONOMIC LEVELS [a]

Ability and socioeconomic (SES) levels	N [b] Persisters	Withdrawals	Thinking Introversion $\bar{X}p-\bar{X}w$	Lower limit	Upper limit	Decision	Complexity $\bar{X}p-\bar{X}w$	Lower limit	Upper limit	Decision	Nonauthoritarianism $\bar{X}p-\bar{X}w$	Lower limit	Upper limit	Decision
Men	696	309	3.96	2.70	5.22	.05	−0.16	0	0	n.s.	0.49	0.09	0.89	.05
By ability level														
High	449	145	4.67	2.82	6.53	.05	−0.32	0	0	n.s.	0.67	0.21	1.13	.05
Middle	183	114	analysis of variance				analysis of variance: F = 2.34; p = not significant							
Low	45	36	analysis of variance				analysis of variance: F = 0.79; p = not significant							
By SES level														
High	183	44	3.90	0.90	6.91	.05	−0.27	0	0	n.s.	0.74	0	0	n.s.
Middle	417	187	3.91	2.23	5.59	.05	−0.17	0	0	n.s.	0.23	0	0	n.s.
Low	69	51	3.95	0.85	7.06	.05	−0.28	0	0	n.s.	1.17	0.15	2.19	.05
Women	595	413	2.70	1.57	3.83	.05	−0.12	0	0	n.s.	0.35	0.03	0.67	.05
By ability level														
High	367	185	2.61	0.94	4.28	.05	−0.23	0	0	n.s.	0.41	0	0	n.s.
Middle	185	169	analysis of variance				analysis of variance: F = 1.12; p = not significant							
Low	30	53	analysis of variance				analysis of variance: F = 1.72; p = not significant							
By SES level														
High	184	76	analysis of variance				analysis of variance: F = 1.14; p = not significant							
Middle	324	246	2.61	1.15	4.08	.05	−0.26	0	0	n.s.	0.13	0	0	n.s.
Low	52	64	analysis of variance				analysis of variance: F = 1.45; p = not significant							

[a] The statistical determination of the confidence intervals that follow is explained in Appendix E.
[b] Ability scores and fathers' occupation were not available for some students.

297

3. *Miscellaneous statistical analyses.*

Table E-3

SIGNIFICANCE OF DIFFERENCES BETWEEN MEAN THINKING INTROVERSION
(TI) AND COMPLEXITY (CO) SCORES OBTAINED BY
PURSUIT GROUPS IN 1959 AND 1963

Pursuit group & scale	1959 Critical ratio	1959 Significance level	1959 Higher group	1963 Critical ratio	1963 Significance level	1963 Higher group
College vs. employed men						
TI	12.18	.01	college	13.65	.01	college
Co	.43	n.s.	—	5.42	.01	college
College vs. employed women						
TI	10.76	.01	college	17.52	.01	college
Co	3.79	.01	college	9.98	.01	college
College vs. employed men by ability level						
TI						
High	8.19	.01	college	8.61	.01	college
Middle	5.05	.01	college	5.10	.01	college
Low	2.94	.01	college	4.88	.01	college
Co						
High	.90	n.s.	—	3.02	.01	college
Middle	.45	n.s.	—	2.70	.01	college
Low	1.24	n.s.	—	.44	n.s.	—
College vs. employed women by ability level						
TI						
High	7.34	.01	college	11.45	.01	college
Middle	4.54	.01	college	8.82	.01	college
Low	2.65	.01	college	3.99	.01	college
Co						
High	3.63	.01	college	7.86	.01	college
Middle	.23	n.s.	—	4.01	.01	college
Low	1.10	n.s.	—	1.29	n.s.	—
College vs. employed men by socioeconomic level						
TI						
High	4.10	.01	college	4.49	.01	college
Middle	8.70	.01	college	9.20	.01	college
Low	4.15	.01	college	6.19	.01	college
Co						
High	.36	n.s.	—	1.28	n.s.	—
Middle	.16	n.s.	—	3.63	.01	college
Low	.65	n.s.	—	2.17	.05	college

Table E-3 (continued)

SIGNIFICANCE OF DIFFERENCES BETWEEN MEAN THINKING INTROVERSION
(TI) AND COMPLEXITY (CO) SCORES OBTAINED BY
PURSUIT GROUPS IN 1959 AND 1963

Pursuit group & scale	1959 Critical ratio	1959 Significance level	Higher group	1963 Critical ratio	1963 Significance level	Higher group
College vs. employed women by socioeconomic level						
TI						
High	1.92	n.s.	—	3.53	.01	college
Middle	7.52	.01	college	12.74	.01	college
Low	3.30	.01	college	5.11	.01	college
Co						
High	3.22	.01	college	3.19	.01	college
Middle	1.99	.05	college	7.60	.01	college
Low	.05	n.s.	—	1.97	.05	college
College persisters vs. withdrawals—men						
TI	3.41	.01	persisters	2.78	.01	persisters
Co	1.53	n.s.	—	.59	n.s.	—
College persisters vs. withdrawals—women						
TI	4.61	.01	persisters	4.01	.01	persisters
Co	.49	n.s.	—	5.04	.01	persisters
College persisters vs. employed—women						
TI	10.75	.01	college	17.51	.01	college
Co	3.79	.01	college	9.97	.01	college
College women vs. homemakers						
TI	7.37	.01	college	14.97	.01	college
Co	.99	n.s.	—	7.37	.01	college
College vs. combined pursuits—women						
TI	8.12	.01	college	15.67	.01	college
Co	.08	n.s.	—	9.41	.01	college
Employed women vs. homemakers						
TI	1.02	n.s.	—	1.18	n.s.	—
Co	3.82	.01	homemakers	.44	n.s.	—
Employed vs. combined pursuits—women						
TI	4.60	.01	combined	5.22	.01	combined
Co	4.34	.01	combined	2.51	.05	combined
Homemakers vs. combined pursuits—women						
TI	2.28	.05	combined	5.19	.01	combined
Co	1.00	n.s.	—	1.38	n.s.	—

Table E-3 (continued)

SIGNIFICANCE OF DIFFERENCES BETWEEN MEAN THINKING INTROVERSION
(TI) AND COMPLEXITY (CO) SCORES OBTAINED BY
PURSUIT GROUPS IN 1959 AND 1963

Pursuit group & scale	1959			1963		
	Critical ratio	Significance level	Higher group	Critical ratio	Significance level	Higher group
College vs. employed—men						
Es				10.87	.01	college
College vs. employed—women						
Es				17.09	.01	college
College men vs. women						
Es				13.60	.01	women
Employed men vs. women						
Es				5.32	.01	women

Table E-4

STANDARD MEAN SCORES ON THINKING INTROVERSION AND COMPLEXITY, 1959 AND 1963, OF COLLEGE PERSISTERS AND THE CONSISTENTLY EMPLOYED, BY ABILITY LEVEL

Scales and pursuit groups

Ability and year	(N) College	(N) Employed	Thinking Introversion College	Thinking Introversion Employed	Complexity College	Complexity Employed	Ψ values of college vs. employed TI	Ψ values of college vs. employed Co
Men								
High ability	(469)	(130)						
1959			49.79	41.68	51.34	52.23		
1963			53.03	44.51	51.71	48.72		
Difference			3.24	2.83	0.37	−3.51	.41 +	3.88 **
(t)			(8.76 **)	(3.45 **)	(.92 +)	(3.66 **)		
Middle ability	(190)	(193)						
1959			46.48	41.33	49.63	50.09		
1963			48.80	43.60	50.59	47.83		
Difference			2.32	2.27	0.96	−2.26	.05 +	3.22 **
(t)			(3.63 **)	(3.29 **)	(1.28 +)	(2.90 **)		
Low ability	(45)	(103)						
1959			45.96	40.70	48.76	50.98		
1963			50.61	41.87	49.35	48.57		
Difference			4.65	1.17	0.59	−2.41	3.48 *	3.00 +
(t)			(3.55 **)	(1.19 +)	(.39 +)	(2.15 *)		

+ p = not significant. * p < .05. ** p < .01.

Table E-4 (continued)

STANDARD MEAN SCORES ON THINKING INTROVERSION AND COMPLEXITY, 1959 AND 1963, OF COLLEGE PERSISTERS AND THE CONSISTENTLY EMPLOYED, BY ABILITY LEVEL

Scales and pursuit groups

Ability and year	(N) College	Employed	Thinking Introversion College	Employed	Complexity College	Employed	Ψ values of college vs. employed TI	Co
Women								
High ability	(345)	(150)						
1959			51.87	44.68	49.50	45.94		
1963			55.54	44.32	51.89	44.19		
Difference			3.67	−0.36	2.39	−1.75	4.03 **	4.14 **
(t)			(7.65 **)	(.55 +)	(4.98 **)	(2.06 *)		
Middle ability	(190)	(207)						
1959			47.59	43.03	47.64	47.40		
1963			50.98	42.12	48.89	44.86		
Difference			3.39	−0.91	1.25	−2.54	4.30 **	3.79 **
(t)			(5.30 **)	(1.60 +)	(1.74 +)	(3.26 **)		
Low ability	(31)	(106)						
1959			48.13	42.72	47.29	45.05		
1963			49.55	41.41	46.38	43.75		
Difference			1.42	−1.31	−0.91	−1.30	2.73 +	.39 +
(t)			(1.07 +)	(1.64 +)	(0.57 +)	(1.34 +)		

+ p = not significant.   * p < .05.   ** p < .01.

302

Table E-5

STANDARD MEAN SCORES ON THINKING INTROVERSION AND COMPLEXITY, 1959 AND 1963, OF COLLEGE PERSISTERS AND THE CONSISTENTLY EMPLOYED, BY SOCIOECONOMIC STATUS (SES)

							Ψ values of college vs. employed	
	(N)		Thinking Introversion		Complexity			
SES level and year	College	Employed	College	Employed	College	Employed	TI	Co
Men								
High SES	(199)	(26)						
1959			50.28	41.71	50.89	51.65		
1963			53.45	44.06	51.91	49.24		
Difference			3.17	2.35	1.02	−2.41		
(t)			(5.56**)	(1.74+)	(1.67+)	(1.22+)	.82+	3.43+
Middle SES	(424)	(261)						
1959			48.10	41.23	50.74	50.61		
1963			51.10	43.83	51.11	48.24		
Difference			3.00	2.60	0.37	−2.37		
(t)			(7.69**)	(4.64**)	(.82+)	(3.70**)	.40+	2.74**
Low SES	(73)	(115)						
1959			47.78	41.55	50.07	51.04		
1963			52.06	42.78	50.02	46.77		
Difference			4.28	1.23	−0.05	−4.27		
(t)			(3.63**)	(1.27+)	(.04+)	(3.81**)	3.05*	4.22**

+ p = not significant.   *p < .05.   **p < .01.

Table E-5 (continued)

STANDARD MEAN SCORES ON THINKING INTROVERSION AND COMPLEXITY, 1959 AND 1963, OF COLLEGE PERSISTERS AND THE CONSISTENTLY EMPLOYED, BY SOCIOECONOMIC STATUS (SES)

Scales and pursuit groups

SES level and year	(N) College	Employed	Thinking Introversion College	Employed	Complexity College	Employed	Ψ values of college vs. employed TI	Co
Women								
High SES	(185)	(28)						
1959			51.28	47.39	50.22	43.69		
1963			54.97	47.80	51.17	44.69		
Difference			3.69	0.41	0.95	1.00	3.28 *	.05 +
(t)			(5.86 **)	(.30 +)	(1.53 +)	(.58 +)		
Middle SES	(316)	(291)						
1959			50.04	43.95	48.07	46.46		
1963			53.66	43.34	50.46	44.30		
Difference			3.62	−0.61	2.39	−2.16	4.23 **	4.55 **
(t)			(7.10 **)	(1.27 +)	(4.27 **)	(.54 **)		
Low SES	(46)	(119)						
1959			48.02	42.31	46.79	46.70		
1963			50.52	41.68	48.33	44.92		
Difference			2.50	−0.63	1.54	−1.78	3.13 *	3.32 +
(t)			(2.27 *)	(.89 +)	(1.05 +)	(1.68 +)		

+ p = not significant. * p < .05. ** p < .01.

Table E-6

STANDARD MEAN NONAUTHORITARIANISM AND SOCIAL MATURITY SCORES, 1959 AND 1963, OF COLLEGE PERSISTERS AND THE CONSISTENTLY EMPLOYED, BY ABILITY LEVEL

Scales and pursuit groups

Ability and year	(N) College	Employed	Nonauthoritarianism College	Employed	Social Maturity College	Employed	Ψ values of college vs. employed Na	SM
Men								
High ability	(469)	(130)						
1959			47.40	44.16	54.50	51.22		
1963			53.24	44.48	63.22	55.35		
Difference			5.84	.32	8.72	4.13		
(t)			(12.84**)	(.32+)	(22.52**)	(4.64**)	5.52**	4.59**
Middle ability	(190)	(193)						
1959			44.13	43.49	52.24	49.91		
1963			51.00	41.39	61.85	53.96		
Difference			6.87	−2.10	9.61	4.05		
(t)			(8.34**)	(2.15*)	(14.02**)	(5.08***)	8.97**	5.56**
Low ability	(45)	(103)						
1959			43.17	40.82	46.53	48.64		
1963			48.29	40.39	57.56	51.07		
Difference			5.12	−.43	11.03	2.43		
(t)			(2.66*)	(.32+)	(6.85**)	(2.46*)	5.55*	8.60**

+p = not significant.   *p < .05.   **p < .01.

Table E-6 (continued)

STANDARD MEAN NONAUTHORITARIANISM AND SOCIAL MATURITY SCORES, 1959 AND 1963, OF COLLEGE PERSISTERS AND THE CONSISTENTLY EMPLOYED, BY ABILITY LEVEL

Scales and pursuit groups

Ability and year	(N) College	(N) Employed	Nonauthoritarianism College	Nonauthoritarianism Employed	Social Maturity College	Social Maturity Employed	Ψ values of college vs. employed Na	Ψ values of college vs. employed SM
Women								
High ability	(345)	(150)						
1959			46.12	40.60	54.72	48.96		
1963			54.38	41.74	65.75	53.46		
Difference			8.26	1.14	11.03	4.50		
(t)			(14.98 **)	(1.24 +)	(23.69 **)	(6.03 **)	7.12 **	6.53 **
Middle ability	(190)	(207)						
1959			42.14	41.85	49.82	48.00		
1963			50.25	40.43	60.16	51.22		
Difference			8.11	−1.42	10.34	3.22		
(t)			(9.06 **)	(1.64 +)	(16.80 **)	(4.64 **)	9.53 **	7.12 **
Low ability	(31)	(106)						
1959			40.36	38.65	48.54	45.32		
1963			45.41	38.29	56.38	47.05		
Difference			5.05	−.36	7.84	1.73		
(t)			(2.52 *)	(.35 +)	(4.10 **)	(2.04 *)	5.41 *	6.11 **

+ p = not significant.   * p < .05.   ** p < .01.

306

Table E-7

STANDARD MEAN NONAUTHORITARIANISM AND SOCIAL MATURITY SCORES, 1959 AND 1963, OF COLLEGE PERSISTERS AND THE CONSISTENTLY EMPLOYED, BY SOCIOECONOMIC STATUS (SES)

								Ψ values of college vs. employed	
	(N)		Nonauthoritarianism		Social Maturity				
SES level and year	College	Employed	College	Employed	College	Employed		Na	SM
Men									
High	(199)	(26)							
1959			47.33	44.48	55.01	49.03			
1963			53.38	44.20	65.75	54.99			
Difference			6.05	−.28	10.74	5.96		6.33 **	4.78 **
(t)			(9.41 **)	(.15 +)	(17.86 ***)	(3.56 ***)			
Middle	(424)	(261)							
1959			45.37	43.35	52.82	49.90			
1963			51.60	42.67	61.18	53.68			
Difference			6.23	−.68	8.36	3.78		6.91 **	4.58 **
(t)			(12.76 **)	(.89 +)	(19.55 **)	(5.96 ***)			
Low	(73)	(115)							
1959			47.44	42.63	51.34	50.27			
1963			53.10	40.64	61.89	52.83			
Difference			5.66	−1.99	10.55	2.56		7.65 **	7.99 **
(t)			(3.97 **)	(1.55 +)	(9.92 **)	(2.61 *)			

+ p = not significant.   * p < .05.   ** p < .01.

Table E-7 (continued)

STANDARD MEAN NONAUTHORITARIANISM AND SOCIAL MATURITY SCORES, 1959 AND 1963, OF COLLEGE PERSISTERS AND THE CONSISTENTLY EMPLOYED, BY SOCIOECONOMIC STATUS (SES)

SES level and year	(N) College	Employed	Nonauthoritarianism College	Employed	Social Maturity College	Employed	Ψ values of college vs. employed Na	SM
Women								
High								
1959	(185)	(28)	45.94	40.86	55.14	45.68		
1963			53.06	40.36	65.51	52.32		
Difference			7.12	−.50	10.37	6.64	7.62 **	3.73 +
(t)			(9.87 **)	(.22 +)	(18.19 ***)	(3.57 **)		
Middle								
1959	(316)	(291)	43.84	40.60	51.74	48.03		
1963			52.38	40.18	62.64	51.13		
Difference			8.54	−.42	10.90	3.10	8.96 **	7.80 **
(t)			(13.90 ***)	(.62 +)	(22.14 ***)	(5.84 ***)		
Low								
1959	(46)	(119)	42.06	40.93	50.10	47.75		
1963			51.17	40.89	58.14	51.00		
Difference			9.11	−.04	8.04	3.25	9.15 **	4.79 **
(t)			(4.92 **)	(.04 +)	(5.80 ***)	(3.62 **)		

Scales and pursuit groups

+ p = not significant.   * p < .05.   ** p < .01.

308

Table E-8

ANALYSES OF VARIANCE OF MEAN NONAUTHORITARIANISM AND SOCIAL
MATURITY SCORES OBTAINED IN 1959 AND 1963 AND OF CHANGE
SCORES BETWEEN 1959 AND 1963 AMONG STUDENTS
CLASSIFIED BY TYPE OF COLLEGE ATTENDED

Sex, year, and scale	Source of variation	df	Sum of squares	Mean square	F ratio
Men					
1959					
Nonauthoritarianism	Between means	5	3,147	629	6.29 **
	Within groups	679	67,900	100	
Social Maturity	Between means	5	2,107	421	4.22 **
	Within groups	679	67,900	100	
1963					
Nonauthoritarianism	Between means	5	1,147	229	2.29 *
	Within groups	679	67,900	100	
Social Maturity	Between means	5	2,162	432	4.32 **
	Within groups	679	67,900	100	
Change, 1959 to 1963					
Nonauthoritarianism	Between means	5	1,578	316	3.16 **
	Within groups	679	67,900	100	
Social Maturity	Between means	5	1,470	294	2.94 *
	Within groups	679	67,900	100	
Women					
1959					
Nonauthoritarianism	Between means	5	1,761	352	3.52 **
	Within groups	564	56,400	100	
Social Maturity	Between means	5	3,542	708	7.08 **
	Within groups	564	56,400	100	
1963					
Nonauthoritarianism	Between means	5	1,863	373	3.73 **
	Within groups	564	56,400	100	
Social Maturity	Between means	5	5,940	1,188	11.88 **
	Within groups	564	56,400	100	

* $p < .05.$
** $p < .01.$

Table E-8 (continued)

ANALYSES OF VARIANCE OF MEAN NONAUTHORITARIANISM AND SOCIAL
MATURITY SCORES OBTAINED IN 1959 AND 1963 AND OF CHANGE
SCORES BETWEEN 1959 AND 1963 AMONG STUDENTS
CLASSIFIED BY TYPE OF COLLEGE ATTENDED

Sex, year, and scale	Source of variation	df	Sum of squares	Mean square	F ratio
Women (continued)					
Change, 1959 to 1963					
Nonauthori-	Between means	5	969	194	1.94 +
tarianism	Within groups	564	56,400	100	
Social	Between means	5	594	119	1.19 +
Maturity	Within groups	564	56,400	100	

+ = not significant.
* p < .05.
** p < .01.

Table E-9

STANDARD MEAN RELIGIOUS LIBERALISM SCORES OBTAINED IN
1963 BY THE COLLEGE STUDENTS AND CONSISTENTLY
EMPLOYED, BY ABILITY LEVEL

Sex and ability level	(N)	Pursuit group College	(N)	Employed	Critical ratio: college vs. employed
Men					
High	(495)	49.23	(113)	46.35	2.76 **
Middle	(209)	49.87	(230)	46.99	3.01 **
Low	(52)	47.63	(132)	46.19	0.88 +
Women					
High	(356)	47.95	(162)	41.55	6.75 **
Middle	(207)	46.03	(222)	41.39	4.80 **
Low	(33)	46.03	(122)	41.07	2.53 *
Critical ratio: (men vs. women)					
High ability		1.84 +		3.92 **	
Middle ability		3.92 **		5.95 **	
Low ability		0.72 +		4.08 **	

+ p = not significant.
* p < .05.
** p < .01.

Table E-10

STANDARD MEAN RELIGIOUS LIBERALISM SCORES OBTAINED IN
1963 BY THE COLLEGE STUDENTS AND CONSISTENTLY
EMPLOYED, BY SOCIOECONOMIC LEVEL

SES level	(N)	College	(N)	Employed	Critical ratio: college vs. employed
Men					
High	(199)	52.59	(26)	48.83	1.79 +
Middle	(424)	48.66	(261)	46.72	2.46 *
Low	(73)	47.25	(115)	45.39	1.24 +
Women					
High	(185)	48.69	(28)	39.25	4.72 **
Middle	(316)	46.99	(291)	41.15	7.21 **
Low	(46)	44.03	(119)	41.55	1.42 +
Critical ratio: (men vs. women)					
High SES		3.82 **		3.55 **	
Middle SES		2.23 *		6.55 **	
Low SES		1.71 +		2.93 **	

+ p = not significant.
* p < .05.
** p < .01.

Table E-11

CRITICAL RATIOS OF THE OPI RAW SCORES OF THE
CHANGE GROUPS, 1963, BY SEX

Sex and Scales	Exceptional vs. Average	Exceptional vs. Negative	Average vs. Negative
Men			
Thinking Introversion	6.7 **	8.1 **	2.8 **
Estheticism	3.7 **	5.2 **	2.3 *
Complexity	5.0 **	8.1 **	4.0 **
Autonomy	11.5 **	16.5 **	7.5 **
Nonauthoritarianism	7.8 **	11.5 **	5.4 **
Lack of Anxiety	5.5 **	5.1 **	0.4 +
Impulse Expression	0.2 +	3.0 **	3.1 **
Social Introversion	−3.6 **	−5.0 **	−2.3 *
Women			
Thinking Introversion	7.2 **	10.1 **	4.7 **
Estheticism	7.6 **	9.3 **	3.1 **
Complexity	9.8 **	11.9 **	4.2 **

+ p = not significant.
* p < .05.
** p < .01.

Table E-11 (continued)

CRITICAL RATIOS OF THE OPI RAW SCORES OF THE
CHANGE GROUPS, 1963, BY SEX

Sex and Scales	Exceptional vs. Average	Exceptional vs. Negative	Average vs. Negative
Women (continued)			
Autonomy	15.1 **	21.8 **	10.2 **
Nonauthoritarianism	9.9 **	14.5 **	7.2 **
Lack of Anxiety	3.7 **	6.1 **	3.5 **
Impulse Expression	6.5 **	7.4 **	1.9 +
Social Introversion	—1.9 +	—6.6 **	—6.0 **

+ p = not significant.
* p < .05.
** p < .01.

Table E-12

SIGNIFICANCE OF DIFFERENCES BETWEEN THE SVIB SCORES
OF THE CHANGE GROUPS (INTERVIEW SAMPLE) [a]

SVIB scale and Change groups	Difference in Standard Means	Lower limit	Upper limit	Significance level
Psychologist				
Exceptional vs. Average	3.9	—7.96	—0.04	.05
Exceptional vs. Negative	6.5	—11.58	—1.82	.05
Average vs. Negative	2.6	—7.03	1.63	n.s.
Mathematician		Not significant		
Policeman		Not significant		
Social Worker				
Exceptional vs. Average	4.0	—8.68	0.28	n.s.
Exceptional vs. Negative	5.8	—11.19	—0.81	.05
Average vs. Negative	1.8	—6.38	2.78	n.s.
Accountant				
Exceptional vs. Average	—3.4	—0.95	7.95	n.s.
Exceptional vs. Negative	—5.0	0.17	10.23	.05
Average vs. Negative	—1.5	—2.80	6.20	n.s.
Sales Manager		Not significant		
Author-Journalist		Not significant		
Interest Maturity		Not significant		
Occupational Level				
Exceptional vs. Average	1.5	—3.97	0.97	n.s.
Exceptional vs. Negative	3.1	—5.86	—0.54	.05
Average vs. Negative	1.6	—3.94	0.54	n.s.
Masculinity-Femininity		Not significant		

[a] Exceptional (N = 63); Average (N = 119); Negative (N = 59).

Table E-13

SIGNIFICANCE OF DIFFERENCES BETWEEN SVIB SCORES OF COLLEGE
PERSISTERS AND THE CONSISTENTLY EMPLOYED IN EACH
CHANGE GROUP (INTERVIEW SAMPLE)

Pursuit and SVIB scale	Difference in Standard Means	Lower limit	Upper limit	Significance level
College				
Psychologist	n.s.			
Mathematician	n.s.			
Policeman	n.s.			
Social Worker				
Exceptional vs. Average	6.5	−12.71	−0.69	.05
Exceptional vs. Negative	1.0	−10.66	8.66	n.s.
Average vs. Negative	−5.5	−3.80	15.20	n.s.
Accountant	n.s.			
Sales Manager	n.s.			
Author-Journalist				
Exceptional vs. Average	4.0	−8.92	0.72	n.s.
Exceptional vs. Negative	6.9	−13.79	−0.41	.05
Average vs. Negative	2.9	−9.32	3.32	n.s.
Interest Maturity	n.s.			
Occupational Level	n.s.			
Masculinity-Femininity	n.s.			
Employed				
Psychologist	n.s.			
Mathematician	n.s.			
Policeman	n.s.			
Social Worker	n.s.			
Accountant	n.s.			
Sales Manager	n.s.			
Author-Journalist				
Exceptional vs. Average	−7.1	2.52	12.28	.05
Exceptional vs. Negative	−8.1	1.80	15.00	.05
Average vs. Negative	−1.0	−5.15	7.15	n.s.
Interest Maturity	n.s.			
Occupational Level	n.s.			
Masculinity-Femininity				
Exceptional vs. Average	19.1	−34.62	−4.78	.05
Exceptional vs. Negative	18.0	−34.14	−2.86	.05
Average vs. Negative	−1.1	−9.34	11.74	n.s.

References

ADORNO, T. W., FRENKEL-BRUNSWIK, E., LEVINSON, D., & SANFORD, R. N. *The authoritarian personality.* New York: Harper, 1950.

ALDEN, E. "The creative teacher in the early years." *Educational Comment,* Spring 1963, p. 53.

ALLPORT, G. W., VERNON, P. E., & LINDZEY, G. *Study of values.* (rev. ed.) Cambridge: Houghton Mifflin, 1951.

ATHERTON, K. R. "A comparison of solutions obtained in factor analyses of socioeconomic variables." *Psychological Reports,* 1962, *11* (1), 259–273.

BARRON, F. "Creative vision and expression in writing and painting." In D. W. MacKinnon (Ed.), *Conference on "The creative person."* Berkeley: University of California, University Extension, Liberal Arts Department, 1961.

BARTON, A. H. *Studying the effects of college education: a methodological examination of changing values in college.* New Haven: Edward W. Hazen Foundation, 1959.

BAY, C. "A social theory of higher education." In N. Sanford (Ed.), *The American college.* New York: Wiley, 1962. Pp. 972–1005.

BELL, D. "The bogey of automation." *The New York Review of Books,* Aug. 26, 1965, *5* (2), 23–25.

BELL, G. D. "Processes in the formation of adolescents' aspirations." *Social Forces,* 1963, *42* (2), 179–185.

BERDIE, R. L. *After high school—what?* Minneapolis: University of Minnesota Press, 1954.

BERELSON, B. *Graduate education in the United States.* New York: McGraw-Hill, 1960.

BERELSON, B., & STEINER, G. *Human behavior: an inventory of scientific findings.* New York: Harcourt, Brace, 1964.

BLOOM, B. *Stability and change in human characteristics.* New York: Wiley, 1964.

314

BOHN, M. J., JR. "Vocational maturity and personality." *Vocational Guidance Quarterly,* 1966, *15,* 127–130.

BONE, H. H., & RARNEY, A. *Politics and voters.* New York: McGraw-Hill, 1963.

BORDIN, E. S., & WRENN, C. G. "The counseling function." *Review of Educational Research,* 1954, *24,* 134–146.

BORDUA, D. J. "Educational aspirations and parental stress on college." *Social Forces,* 1960, *38* (3), 262–269.

BRADLEY, W. A., JR. "Correlates of vocational preferences." *Genetic Psychology Monographs,* 1943, *28,* 99–169.

BRITTAIN, C. V. "Adolescent choices and parent-peer cross pressures." *American Sociological Review,* 1963, *28* (3), 385–391.

BRONSON, G. W. "Identity diffusion in late adolescence." *Journal of Abnormal and Social Psychology,* 1959, *59,* 414–417.

BROWN, T. G. "Identifying college dropouts with the Minnesota counseling inventory." *Personnel and Guidance Journal,* 1960, *39,* 280–282.

BROWNE-MAYERS, A. N. "The uses of experience." *Saturday Review,* Dec. 12, 1964, *47,* 24.

BYRNS, R. "Relation of vocational choice to mental ability and occupational opportunity." *School Review,* 1939, *47,* 101–109.

CARKHUFF, R. R. "Counseling research, theory and practice—1965." *Journal of Counseling Psychology,* 1966, *13,* 467–480.

CARMICHAEL, O. C. *Graduate education: a critique and a program.* New York: Harper, 1961.

CARTTER, A. M. *An assessment of quality in graduate education.* Washington: American Council on Education, 1966.

Center for the Study of Higher Education. *A multiple scale inventory for use with college populations.* Berkeley: University of California, Center for the Study of Higher Education, 1960.

Center for the Study of Higher Education. *Omnibus Personality Inventory —research manual.* Berkeley: University of California, Center for the Study of Higher Education, 1962.

CENTERS, R. "Motivational aspects of occupational stratification." *Journal of Social Psychology,* 1948, *28,* 187–217.

CHAMBERS, J. Q., BARGER, B., & TIEBERMAN, L. R. "Need patterns and abilities of college dropouts." *Educational and Psychological Measurement,* 1965, *25,* 509–516.

CHRISTENSEN, A. "Occupational follow-up in a small school." *California Journal of Secondary Education,* 1942, *17,* 16–20.

CHRISTIE, R., HAVEL, J., & SEIDENBERG, B. "Is the F scale irreversible?" *Journal of Abnormal and Social Psychology,* 1960, *60,* 151.

CICOUREL, A. V., & KITSUSE, J. I. *The educational decision-makers.* New York: Bobbs-Merrill, 1963.

CLARK, B. R. "Sociology of education." In E. L. Faris (Ed.), *Handbook of modern sociology.* Chicago: Rand McNally, 1964.

COLEMAN, J. S. *The adolescent society.* New York: Free Press, 1961.

Congressional Quarterly Almanac, 1964, *20,* 214.

COOPER, S. "Employment of June 1959 high school graduates, October 1959." *Monthly Labor Review,* May, 1960, *83,* 501.

COREY, S. M. "Changes in the opinions of female students after one year at a university." *Journal of Social Psychology,* 1940, *11,* 341–351.

CRUTCHFIELD, R. S. "Independent thought in a conformist world." In S. Larber

& R. H. L. Wilson (Eds.), *Conflict and Creativity.* New York: McGraw-Hill, 1963.

CUMMINGS, R. W. "The relationship between authoritarianism and the Strong Vocational Interest Blanks." Unpublished doctoral dissertation, University of California, Berkeley, 1962.

DAHLSTROM, W. G., & WELSH, G. S. *An MMPI handbook.* Minneapolis: University of Minnesota Press, 1960.

DAVIDSON, P. E., & ANDERSON, H. D. *Occupational mobility in an American community.* Stanford, Calif.: Stanford University Press, 1937.

DAVIS, J. A. *Great aspirations.* Vol. 1. *Career decisions and educational plans during college.* Chicago: National Opinion Research Center, 1963.

DAVIS, J. A., & BRADBURN, N. "Great aspirations: the career plans of America's June 1961 college graduates." *Vocational Guidance Quarterly,* 1962, *10,* 137–142.

DEMOS, G. D. "The four year college graduation myth." *Vocational Guidance Quarterly,* 1961, *9,* 220–222.

DENNEY, R. "American youth today: a bigger cast, a wider screen." *Daedalus,* 1962, *91* (1), 124–144.

DIEBOLD, J. "Congressional testimony." In M. Philipson (Ed.), *Automation.* New York: Vintage Books, 1962. Pp. 12–23.

DIXON, J. D., & MASSEY, F. J. *Introduction to statistical analysis.* New York: McGraw-Hill, 1957.

DIXON, J. P. "Mind, spirit, and world." *Antioch notes,* 1963, *40* (8).

DRESSEL, P. L. (Ed.) *Evaluation in the basic college.* New York: Harper, 1958.

DRESSEL, P. L. "Factors involved in changing the values of college students." *Educational Record,* 1965, *46* (2), 104–113.

DRESSEL, P. L., & LEHMANN, I. J. "The impact of higher education on student attitudes, values, and critical thinking abilities." *Educational Record,* 1965, *46* (3), 248–258.

DREWS, E. M. "Counseling for self-actualization in gifted girls and young women." *Journal of Counseling Psychology,* 1965, *12* (2), 167–175.

ECKLAND, B. K. "College dropouts who came back." *Harvard Educational Review,* 1964, *34* (3), 402–420.

EDDY, E. E. *The college influence on student character.* Washington: American Council on Education, 1959.

Editor & Publisher Company. *Editor & publisher 1958 market guide.* New York: Editor & Publisher, 1957.

Educational Policies Commission. *Education of the gifted.* Washington: National Education Association, 1950.

EISENSTADT, S. N. "Archetypal patterns of youth." *Daedalus,* 1962, *91* (1), 28–46.

ERIKSON, E. H. *Childhood and society.* (2nd ed.) New York: Norton, 1963.

Examiner's manual, cooperative school and college ability tests: first manual, 1955. Princeton: Cooperative Test Division, Educational Testing Service, 1955.

FISHMAN, J. A. "Some social-psychological theory for selecting and guiding college students." In N. Sanford (Ed.), *The American college.* New York: Wiley, 1962. Pp. 666–689.

FLANAGAN, J. C., DAVIS, F. B., DAILEY, J. T., SHAYCOFT, M. L., ORR, D. B., GOLDBERG, I., & NEYMAN, C. A., JR. *Project talent: the American high school student.* Pittsburgh: University of Pittsburgh, 1964.

FORD, D. H., & URBAN, H. B. "College dropouts: successes or failures." *Educational Record*, 1965, *46*, 77–92.

FORER, B. R. "Personality factors in occupational choice." *Educational and Psychological Measurement*, 1953, *13*, 361–366.

FRANCOIS, W. *Automation: industrialization comes of age.* New York: Collier Books, 1964.

FREEDMAN, M. B. *Impact of college.* Washington: U. S. Department of Health, Education, and Welfare, Office of Education, 1960.

FREEDMAN, M. B. "Changes in six decades of some attitudes and values held by educated women." *Journal of Social Issues*, 1961, *17* (1), 19–28.

FREEDMAN, M. B. "Personality growth in the college years." *College Board Review*, 1965, *56*, 25–32.

FREEDMAN, M. B. *The college experience.* San Francisco: Jossey-Bass, 1967.

FRICKE, B. G. *Opinion, atttiude, and interest survey.* Ann Arbor, Mich.: OAIS Testing Program, 1963.

FUNKESTEIN, D. H., KING, S. H., & DROLETTE, M. E. *Mastery of stress.* Cambridge: Harvard University Press, 1957.

GALINSKY, M. D., & FAST, I. "Vocational choice as a focus of the identity search." *Journal of Counseling Psychology*, 1966, *13* (1), 89–92.

GARRETT, H. E. *Statistics in psychology and education.* New York: Longmans Green, 1958.

GIBSON, R. L. "Pupil opinions of high school guidance programs." *Personnel and Guidance Journal*, 1962, *40*, 453.

GINZBERG, E. "Toward a theory of occupational choice." *Occupations*, 1952, *30*, 491–494.

GINZBERG, E., GINSBURG, S. W., ALEXRAD, S., & HERMA, J. L. *Occupational choice: an approach to a general theory.* New York: Columbia University Press, 1951.

GORDON, M. *Social class in American sociology.* Durham, N. C.: Duke University Press, 1958.

GOTTLIEB, D. "Social class, achievement, and the college-going experience." *School Review*, 1962, *70*, 273–286.

GOUGH, H. G. "Techniques for identifying the creative research scientist." In D. W. MacKinnon (Ed.), *Conference on "The creative person."* Berkeley: University of California, University Extension, Liberal Arts Department, 1961.

GOUGH, H. G. *Manual for the California Psychological Inventory.* (rev. ed.) Palo Alto, Calif.: Consulting Psychologists Press, 1964.

GREENSTEIN, L. I. *The American party system and the American people.* Englewood Cliffs, N. J.: Prentice-Hall, 1963.

GROPPER, G. L., & FITZPATRICK, R. *Who goes to graduate school?* Pittsburgh: American Institute for Research, 1959.

HATHAWAY, S. R., & MCKINLEY, J. C. *Manual for the Minnesota Multiphasic Personality Inventory.* (rev. ed.) New York: Psychological Corporation, 1951.

HAYS, W. L. *Statistics for psychologists.* New York: Holt, Rinehardt, 1963.

HEATH, R. W., MAIER, M. H., & REMMERS, H. H. "What does youth want from education and jobs?" *Purdue Opinion Panel Report*, 1957, *16* (2).

HECHINGER, L. M. "Antidotes for incompetence." *Saturday Review*, Dec. 12, 1964, *47*, 21.

318

HEILBRUN, A. B., JR. "Prediction of first year college drop-out using ACL need scales." *Journal of Counseling Psychology*, 1962, *9*, 58–63.

HEISS, A. M. "Berkeley doctoral students appraise their academic programs." *Educational Record*, 1967, *48* (1), 33–44.

HEISS, A. M., DAVIS, A., & VOCI, F. *Graduate and professional education.* Berkeley: University of California, Center for Research and Development in Higher Education, 1967.

HEIST, P. "Intellect and commitment: the faces of discontent." In O. A. Knorr & W. J. Minter (Eds.), *Order and freedom on the campus; the rights and responsibilities of faculty and students.* Boulder, Colo.: Western Interstate Commission for Higher Education, 1965. Pp. 61–69.

HEIST, P. "Higher education and human potentialities." In H. A. Otto (Ed.), *Explorations in human potentialities.* Springfield, Ill.: Charles C Thomas, 1966.

HEIST, P. "Creative students: college transients." In P. Heist (Ed.), *The creative college student: an unmet challenge.* San Francisco: Jossey-Bass, 1968.

HELSON, R. "Creativity, sex, and mathematics." In D. W. MacKinnon (Ed.), *Conference on "The creative person."* Berkeley: University of California, University Extension, Liberal Arts Department, 1961.

HILLS, J. R. "Transfer shock: the academic performance of the junior college transfer." *Journal of Experimental Education*, 1965, *33* (3), 210–215.

HOLLAND, J. L. "Major programs of research on vocational behavior." In H. Borow (Ed.), *Man in a world at work.* Boston: Houghton Mifflin, 1964. Pp. 259–284.

HOLMES, D. "An investigation of student attitudes which may be related to leaving college." *Journal of Educational Research*, 1958, *52*, 17–21.

HOWARD, L. P. "Identity conflicts in adolescent girls." *Smith College Studies in Social Work*, 1960, *31*, 1–21.

HOWARD, V., & WARRINGTON, W. "Inventory of beliefs: changes in beliefs and attitudes and academic success prediction." *Personnel and Guidance Journal*, 1958, *37*, 299–302.

IFFERT, R. E. *Retention and withdrawal of college students.* Washington: Department of Health, Education, and Welfare, Office of Education, 1957.

JACOB, P. E. *Changing values in college.* New York: Harper, 1957.

JAFFE, A. J., & ADAMS, W. "College education for United States youth: the attitudes of parents and children." *American Journal of Economics and Sociology*, 1964, *23* (3), 269–283.

JAHODA, M. *Current concepts of mental health.* New York: Basic Books, 1959.

JEX, F. B., & MERRILL, R. M. "A study in persistence: withdrawal and graduation rates at the University of Utah." *Personnel and Guidance Journal*, 1962, *40* (9), 762–768.

KAHL, I. *The American class structure.* New York: Rinehart, 1957.

KARON, B. P. "The stability of equated test scores." *Research Bulletin*, RB-55-21. Princeton, N. J.: Educational Testing Service, 1955.

KNOELL, D. M. "Institutional research on retention and withdrawal." In H. T. Sprague (Ed.), *Research on college students.* Boulder, Colo.: Western Interstate Commission for Higher Education, 1960. Pp 41–65.

KNOELL, D. M., & MEDSKER, L. L. *From junior to senior college: a national study of the transfer student.* Washington: American Council on Education, 1964.

KORN, H. A. "Personality scale changes from the freshman year to the senior year." In J. Katz & Associates, *No time for youth: Growth and constraint in college students.* San Francisco: Jossey-Bass, 1968.

KUDER, G. F. *Manual for Kuder Preference Record—Vocational.* Chicago: Science Research Associates, 1957.

LAYTON, W. L. (Ed.) *The Strong Vocational Interest Blank: research and uses.* Minneapolis: University of Minnesota, 1960.

LEHMANN, I. J., & DRESSEL, P. L. *Critical thinking, attitudes, and values in higher education.* Department of Health, Education, and Welfare, Office of Education, Cooperative Research Project No. 590. East Lansing, Mich.: Michigan State University, 1962.

LEHMANN, I. J., & DRESSEL, P. L. *Changes in critical thinking ability, attitudes, and values associated with college attendance.* Department of Health, Education, and Welfare, Office of Education, Cooperative Research Project No. 1646. East Lansing, Mich.: Michigan State University, 1963.

LEHMANN, I. J., & PAYNE, I. K. "An exploration of attitude and value changes of college freshmen." *Personnel and Guidance Journal,* 1963, *41*, 403–408.

LEVENSON, E. A. "Why do they drop out?" *Teaching & Learning,* 1965, 25–32.

LEVIN, M. M. "Changes in authoritarianism." In J. Katz & Associates, *No time for youth: Growth and constraint in college students.* San Francisco: Jossey-Bass, 1968.

LIPSET, S. M. "Working-class authoritarianism." In B. H. Stoodley (Ed.), *Society and self.* New York: Free Press, 1962. Pp. 527–557.

LIPSET, S. M., BENDIX, R., & MALM, T. F. "Job plans and entry into the labor market." *Social Forces,* 1955, *33* (3), 224–232.

LITTLE, J. K. "The Wisconsin study of high school graduates." *Educational Record,* 1959, *40*, 123–128.

LORD, F. M. "Notes on comparable scales for test scores." *Research Bulletin,* RB-50-48. Princeton, N. J.: Educational Testing Service, 1950.

MCDILL, E. L., & COLEMAN, J. "Family and peer influences in college plans of high school students." *Sociology of Education,* 1965, *38* (2), 112–126.

MACKINNON, D. W. "Creativity in architects." In D. W. MacKinnon (Ed.), *Conference on "The creative person."* Berkeley: University of California, University Extension, Liberal Arts Department, 1961.

MCNEMAR, Q. *Psychological statistics.* New York: Wiley, 1955.

MAGNUM, G. L. "Automation, employment, and human values." *Educational Record,* 1964, *45*, 122–127.

MARCIA, J. E. "Development and validation of ego-identity status." *Journal of Personality and Social Psychology,* 1966, *3* (5), 551–558.

MASLOW, A. H. *Toward a psychology of being.* Princeton, N. J.: Van Nostrand, 1962.

MECHANIC, D. *Students under stress.* New York: Free Press, 1962.

MEDSKER, L. L. *The junior college: progress and prospect.* New York: McGraw-Hill, 1960.

MEDSKER, L. L., & TRENT, J. W. *The influence of different types of public higher institutions on college attendance from varying socioeconomic and ability levels.* Berkeley: University of California, Center for the Study of Higher Education, 1965.

MICHAEL, D. N. *The next generation.* New York: Random House, 1965.

MINER, J. B. *Intelligence in the United States.* New York: Springer, 1957.

MUNGER, P. L. "Factors related to persistence in college of students who were admitted to the University of Toledo from the lower third of their respective high school classes." Unpublished doctoral dissertation, University of Michigan, 1954.

MURRAY, J. B. "The identity image of the college student." *Psychological Reports,* 1964, *14* (1), 267–271.

MYERS, I. B., & BRIGGS, K. C. *Manual for the Myers-Briggs Type Indicator.* Princeton, N. J.: Educational Testing Service, 1962.

NACHMANN, B. "Childhood experience and vocation choice in law, dentistry, and social work." *Journal of Counseling Psychology,* 1960, *7,* 243–250.

NALL, A. W. "The academic success of junior college transfers to the junior level at the University of Colorado." Unpublished doctoral dissertation, University of Colorado, 1958.

NEWCOMB, T. M., & FELDMAN, K. A. *The impacts of colleges upon their students: A report to the Carnegie Foundation,* 1968.

PALMER, G. L. *Labor mobility in six cities: a report on the survey of patterns and factors in labor mobility, 1940–1950.* New York: Committee on Labor Market Research, Social Science Research Council, 1954.

PARSONS, T. "Youth in the context of American society." *Daedalus,* 1962, *91* (1), 97–123.

PETERSON, R. E. *The scope of organized student protest in 1964–1965.* Princeton, N. J.: Educational Testing Service, 1966.

PLANT, W. T. "Changes in ethnocentrism associated with a four-year college education." *Journal of Educational Psychology,* 1958, *49,* 162–165. (a)

PLANT, W. T. "Changes in ethnocentrism associated with a two-year college experience." *Journal of Genetic Psychology,* 1958, *92,* 189–197. (b)

PLANT, W. T. *Personality changes associated with a college education.* San Jose, Calif.: San Jose State College, 1962.

POPENOE, P. (Ed.) Research notes. *Family Life,* 1966, *26* (1), 5.

PREDIGER, D. J. "Prediction of persistence in college." *Journal of Counseling Psychology,* 1965, *12,* 62–67.

ROE, A. *The psychology of occupations.* New York: Wiley, 1956.

ROE, A. "Personality structure and occupational behavior." In H. Borow (Ed.), *Man in a world at work.* Boston: Houghton Mifflin, 1964. Pp. 196–214.

ROGERS, C. R. *Client-centered therapy.* Boston: Houghton Mifflin, 1951.

ROKEACH, M. *The open and closed mind.* New York: Basic Books, 1960.

ROSE, H. A. "Prediction and prevention of freshman attrition." *Journal of Counseling Psychology,* 1965, *12,* 399–403.

ROSE, H. A., & ELTON, C. F. "Another look at the college dropout." *Journal of Counseling Psychology,* 1966, *13,* 242–245.

SANFORD, N. "Developmental status of the entering freshman." In N. Sanford (Ed.), *The American college.* New York: Wiley, 1962. Pp. 253–289. (a)

SANFORD, N. "Higher education as a social problem." In N. Sanford (Ed.), *The American college.* New York: Wiley, 1962. Pp. 10–30. (b)

SANFORD, N. (Ed.) *The American college.* New York: Wiley, 1962. (c)

SANFORD, N. "The freeing and acting out of impulse in late adolescence: evidence from two cases." In R. W. White (Ed.), *The study of lives.* New York: Atherton Press, 1964. Pp. 4–39.

SANFORD, N. *Self and society.* New York: Atherton Press, 1966.

SANFORD, N. *Where colleges fail.* San Francisco: Jossey-Bass, 1967.

SEGAL, S. J. "A psychoanalytic analysis of personality factors in vocational choice." *Journal of Counseling Psychology,* 1961, *8,* 202–210.

SEXTON, V. S. "Factors contributing to attrition in college populations: twenty-five years of research." *Journal of Genetic Psychology,* 1965, *72,* 301–326.

SHILS, E. B. "Must man be idle?" *New York Times Book Review,* November 20, 1966, p. 70.

SHOSTROM, E. L. "An inventory for the measurment of self-actualization." *Educational and Psychological Measurement,* 1964, *24* (2), 207–218.

SILBERMAN, C. E., & the editors of *Fortune. The myths of automation.* New York: Harper, 1966.

SIMPSON, R. L. "Parental influence, anticipation, socialization and social mobility." *American Sociological Review,* 1962, *27* (4), 517–522.

SLOCUM, W. L. "Social factors in academic mortality." *College and University,* 1956, *32,* 53–64.

SMITH, H. A., & PENNY, L. L. "Educational opportunity as a function of socioeconomic status." *School and Society,* 1959, *87,* 342–344.

SOLOMON, D. "Adolescents' choices: a comparison of influence from parents with that from other sources." *Marriage and Family Living,* 1961, *23,* 393–395.

SONTAG, L. W., & KAGEN, J. "The emergence of intellectual achievement motives." *American Journal of Orthopsychiatry,* 1963, *33* (3), 532–535.

STERN, G. G. *The Activities Index: preliminary manual.* Syracuse, N. Y.: Syracuse University Research Institute, 1958.

STERN, G. G. "Environments for learning." In N. Sanford (Ed.), *The American college.* New York: Wiley, 1962. Pp. 690–730.

STRONG, E. K., JR. *Vocational interests of men and women.* Stanford, Calif.: Stanford University Press, 1943.

STRONG, E. K., JR. *Manual for Strong Vocational Interest Blanks for men and women.* Palo Alto, Calif.: Consulting Psychologists Press, 1959.

SUCZEK, R. F., & ALFERT, E. *Personality characteristics of college dropouts.* Berkeley: University of California, Department of Psychiatry, Student Health Service, 1966.

SUMMERSKILL, J. "Dropouts from college." In N. Sanford (Ed.), *The American college.* New York: Wiley, 1962. Pp. 627–657.

SUPER, D. E. "Education and the nature of occupations and careers." *Teachers College Record,* 1957, *58,* 301–309. (a)

SUPER, D. E. *The psychology of careers.* New York: Harper, 1957. (b)

SUPER, D. E., STARISHEVSKY, R., MATLIN, N., & JORDAAN, J. P. *Career development: self-concept theory.* Princeton, N. J.: College Entrance Examination Board, 1963.

TELFORD, C. W., & PLANT, W. T. *The psychological impact of the public two-year college on certain non-intellectual functions.* U. S. Department of Health, Education, and Welfare, Office of Education, Cooperative Research Branch Project SAE 8646. San Jose, Calif.: San Jose State College, 1963.

THEOBALD, R. "Human rights in a cybernated age." *Educational Record,* 1964, *45,* 113–121.

TIEDEMAN, D. V., & O'HARA, R. P. *Career development: choice and adjustment.* Princeton, N. J.: College Entrance Examination Board, 1963.

TIPPET, J. S., & SILBER, E. "Autonomy of self-esteem: an experimental approach." *Archives of General Psychiatry,* 1966, *14* (4), 372–385.

TRENT, J. W. *Catholics in college: religious commitment and the intellectual life.* Chicago: University of Chicago Press, 1967.

TRENT, J. W., ATHEY, I., & CRAISE, J. L. "Technology, education, and human development." *Educational Record,* 1965, *46* (2), 93–103.

TRENT, J. W., & RUYLE, J. "Variations, flow, and patterns of college attendance." *College and University,* 1965, *41* (1), 61–76.

TRENT, J. W., & CRAISE, J. L. "Commitment and conformity in the American college." *Journal of Social Issues,* 1967, *23* (3), 34–51.

TYLER, L. "Research explorations in the realm of choice." *Journal of Consulting Psychology,* 1961, *8,* 195–201.

U. S. Bureau of the Census. *A report of the 17th decennial census of the United States population: 1950.* Vol. 2. Washington: Government Printing Office, 1952.

U. S. Bureau of the Census. *A statistical abstract supplement: county and city data book, 1956.* Washington: Government Printing Office, 1957.

U. S. Bureau of the Census. *Statistical abstract of the United States.* (85th ed.) Washington: Government Printing Office, 1964.

U. S. Bureau of the Census. *Statistical abstract of the United States* (86th ed.) Washington: Government Printing Office, 1965.

U. S. Department of Commerce and Bureau of the Census. *1960 census of population, alphabetical index of occupations and industries.* (rev. ed.) Washington: Government Printing Office, 1960.

U. S. Department of Labor. *Manpower report of the president and a report on manpower requirements, resources, utilization and training.* Washington: Government Printing Office, 1964.

U. S. Department of Labor. *Dictionary of occupational titles.* Washington: Government Printing Office, 1965. 2 vols.

U. S. Department of Health, Education, and Welfare, Office of Education. *Education directory. Part 3. Higher education.* Washington: Government Printing Office, 1963.

WALLER, C. "Research related to college persistence." *College and University,* 1964, *39,* 281–294.

WARNER, W. L., MEEKER, M., & EELS, K. *Social class in America.* Gloucester, Mass.: Peter Smith, 1957.

WEBSTER, H., FREEDMAN, M. B., & HEIST, P. "Personality changes in college students." In N. Sanford (Ed.), *The American college.* New York: Wiley, 1962. Pp. 811–846.

WEISSMAN, M. P. "An approach to the assessment of intellectual disposition among selected high ability students." Unpublished doctoral dissertation, University of California, Berkeley, 1958.

WHITE, R. W. *Lives in progress.* New York: Holt, 1952.

WHITELY, P. L. "The constancy of personal values." *Journal of Abnormal and Social Psychology,* 1938, *33,* 405–408.

WILLIAMS, P. "The relationship between certain scores on the Strong Vocational Interest Blank and intellectual disposition." Unpublished doctoral dissertation, University of California, Berkeley, 1964.

WILLIAMS, V. "Difficulties in identifying relatively permanent characteristics related to persistence in college." *Journal of Counseling Psychology,* 1966, *13,* 108.

WOLFLE, D. *America's resources of specialized talent.* New York: Harper, 1954.

WRENN, C. G. *The counselor in a changing world.* Washington: American Personnel and Guidance Association, 1962.

WRIGHT, C. R. "Success or failure in earning graduate degrees." *Sociology of Education,* 1964, *38* (1), 73–97.

WRIGHT, W. W., & JUNG, C. W. "Why capable high school students do not continue their schooling." *Bulletin of the School of Education,* Indiana University, 1959, *35,* 1–78.

YATES, V. M. "Bert found a niche." *Personnel and Guidance Journal,* 1954, *32,* 548–549.

YOSHINO, I. R. "College dropouts at the end of the freshman year." *Journal of Educational Sociology,* 1958, 32, 42–48.

Index